Rejuvenating the Mature Business

Rejuvenating the Mature Business provides a landmark approach to corporate strategy. In this challenging, newly updated study the authors call into question many of the leading theories in strategic management which emphasize the decline of industries or economic sectors when explaining business success or failure. Instead this book places the individual enterprise itself at centre stage and shows how particular businesses and management teams can achieve spectacular turn-around even in the most hostile environments.

The key message of this book is that organizations *can* rejuvenate and seek industry leadership when they reject standard industry 'recipes' and set out to innovate not just new products and new processes but also, most importantly, new strategies. What has been achieved by innovative managers who avoid the trap of conventional thinking is illustrated by many examples drawn from a wide range of international businesses.

The authors show how progress is possible with limited resources. Achieving the elusive goal of sustainable competitiveness requires building, step by step, an entrepreneurial organization that captures and gains leverage from the values of experimentation, imagination and skill enhancement at all levels.

Charles Baden-Fuller is Chair and Professor of Strategy at City University Business School. He is adviser to many businesses and his publications include *Managing Excess Capacity*. **John Stopford** is Professor of International Business at the London Business School. He is director of the InterMatrix Group and board adviser to Vickers plc, and co-author of the prize-winning book *Rival States, Rival Firms*.

Rejuvenating the Mature Business

The Competitive Challenge

Second Edition

Charles Baden-Fuller and John Stopford

London and New York

First published 1992
by Routledge

Reprinted 1993

Second edition first published in the USA
in 1994 by Harvard Business School Press
and first published in paperback in Great Britain in 1996
by Routledge
11 New Fetter Lane
London EC4P 4EE

Printed and bound in Great Britain by
Redwood Books, Trowbridge

British Library Cataloguing in Publication Data
A catalogue record for this book is available from the British Library

ISBN 0-415-13520-6

To Mary and Sally

Contents

Acknowledgments

This book could not have been written without help from many who contributed to the work and to whom we owe a great debt of thanks. John McGee and Dean Berry, directors of the Centre for Business Strategy, made the work possible at the start. Robert Grant, Sebastian Green, Charles Hampden-Turner, and Gianni Lorenzoni have a special place, for they were colleagues brimming with enthusiasm and ideas, co-authoring papers, and leading parts of the research program. Fillipo Dell'Osso, Steve Downing, Soula Evans, Luigi Forlai, James Lyle, Ronnie McBryde, Phedon Nicholaides, Martin Porter, and David Taylor helped collect and analyze the data and draft papers. Danford Bodrug, Kiran Parmar, and Jim Wilson were Sloan Fellows who wrote two of our cases. We also owe thanks to MBA students at the London Business School whose research reports formed the basis of other cases, notably Philip Airey, David Davis, Amanda Holbrook, and Ashley Mooney. Patrizio Bianchi of the University of Bologna and NOMISMA; Jürgen Mueller of the Deutsches Institut für Wirtschaftsforchung; and Michael Niblock, a French-speaking consultant, all helped us in our Continental research by opening doors and providing valuable insights. John Cubbin, Paul Geroski, John Hunt, Avi Meschulach, and Cyril Tomkins provided encouragement and helpful criticism, as did the editors and anonymous referees of many journals and co-participants in numerous conferences. We also owe thanks to numerous participants in the Executive MBA Program at the University of Bath, to Mary Morgan, who read and commented on drafts of the book, and to Rosemary Nixon of Routledge, who was especially helpful in polishing our European edition.

Nothing could have been done without the cooperation and help of more than a hundred executives who patiently explained how they thought about issues and how their organizations worked. Special thanks are owed to those from organizations we mention: Banc One; Benetton; BOC group and its subsidiary Edwards High Vacuum; William Cook; Courtaulds and its subsidiaries Courtelle; Courtaulds Textiles and its subsidiaries Lyle and Scott, and Wolsey; Electrolux group and its subsidiaries in the United Kingdom and Zanussi in Italy; GEC and its subsidiaries Creda and Hotpoint; Dawson International; McPherson's and its subsidiary Richardson of Sheffield; the Merloni group; Peter Scott; TEM (Thomson Electromenager), formerly part of Thomson SA, now part of Ocean (the Italian Group); and the Weir Group.

We were fortunate to have financial assistance from the Economic and Social Research Council of the United Kingdom, the Gatsby Foundation, and the University of Bath, as well as use of facilities at Bologna University, Duke University, and MIT.

Finally, we owe special thanks to Carol Franco and Natalie Greenberg of the Harvard Business School Press who helped immeasurably to ensure the smooth passage of the U.S. edition, and to five anonymous referees who provided detailed, helpful comments and suggestions for improvement.

Introduction

Must business, like man, go through a life cycle? Must growth inevitably be followed by maturity, decline, or even failure, or can business escape the limits of mortality? We wrote this book because we had studied some remarkable businesses whose managers had—perhaps only for a time—managed to reverse the cycle and found means to rejuvenate their flagging organizations. We believe that others can learn from their experience, not in terms of discovering an elixir of life, but in terms of understanding that there are many rejuvenation possibilities. At a time when so many firms in Europe and North America are facing severe threats from foreign rivals, when unemployment is high, and when politicians, managers, and society at large are all concerned that yesterday's engines of wealth creation may fail, the hope embodied in what we observed assumes a heightened importance.

We started our inquiries in Europe in the mid-1980s, when it was already clear there that resisting the corset of "maturity" had become a central issue in many industries like textiles, shipbuilding, chemicals, where growth was slow or static—a presumed symptom of maturity. The sense of overall stasis masked the fact that many products or segments were growing strongly to offset declines elsewhere. Most striking, however, was the fact that vital and prosperous businesses had existed for years alongside others that were in decline. Because that diversity of experience challenged the widely held ideas that there is one "best way" to compete and that performance is determined by the industry setting, we were spurred to look within firms for explanations of why and how some seem persistently able to resist the enfeeblement of old age. We also searched for and found a few organizations that had peered over the abyss of looming failure and managed not only to pull back in time, but also to find new paths to sustainable growth. From such unpromising positions, some even went on to join the world leaders in their sectors.

These are the true "rejuvenators" whose record is examined closely in this book. They are the exemplars whose stories can provide hope to many other organizations that have yet to find their own path to rejuvenation. They have created many of the attributes of those that so far have managed to avoid allowing their arteries to harden. We believe that they can act as exemplars not only for Europeans, but also for Americans. We are confident that the experience of rejuvenation is not determined by nationality or industry: it is determined by managers for themselves.

We also examined the record of less successful competitors in these "mature" environments to provide the balance needed in our analysis. The contrasts between success and failure in the same line of business helped us identify many salient features of how competition is perceived by different contestants. The managerial processes used by those seeking rejuvenation were tested against alternatives. The detailed evidence in the book bears on several, linked propositions that challenge traditional notions of the possibilities.

As suggested above, we start from the proposition that, in mature industries, managerial choice is more important than the structure of the industry as the prime determinant of profits and growth. Indeed, we consider that maturity is, in effect, a state of mind that can trap managers even in the so-called growth or dynamic industries into believing that yesterday's sources of profits will be tomorrow's. Identifying and removing this stultifying aspect of mature thinking require perception of when the balance of effect really has changed and a willingness to test assumptions, especially relating to competitors' behavior.

Perceptive managers recognize that competition is not exclusively a battle between the large and the small, or the well resourced versus the impoverished, all playing by the same set of "rules." Competition is also a contest among strategies. The power of novel strategies can be harnessed to help firms alter their positions and to expand their scope and profitability. New conceptions of strategy typically require radically different types of investment. These change the capabilities of players, even to the extent of altering the "rules" of the industry.

Innovations in strategy provide the means whereby mature firms can overcome the disadvantages of fewer resources, as conventionally defined. David *can* conquer Goliath, sometimes with only modest capital expenditure. For this to be possible, David has to find a way to build an organization capable of handling and further adapting innovative strategies. Furthermore, innovations that provide more than a fleeting advantage are likely to be developed by finding new ways to combine resources across traditional organizational boundaries. Rather than being trapped in a mentality that says, "We can choose, say, either high quality or low cost"—a conventional dilemma—managers in rejuvenating organizations seek high quality *and* low cost. A capacity to resolve such dilemmas becomes an important attribute of sustainable innovation.

Converting a mature organization into one capable of delivering innovative strategy is a difficult task. Finding effective ways of resolving dilemmas and working across internal boundaries is risky and likely to be resisted; few people naturally welcome the thought that the very foundations of their career success to date is becoming obsolete. Thus, a crucial part of top managers' work in rejuvenating organizations is selling the ideas to others. Successful rejuvenators recognize and balance the competing claims of *all* their stakeholders. The currently fashionable rhetoric of focusing strategic choice on shareholder value seems to us to be misleading and to confuse means with ends. A focus on shareholders to the exclusion of others inside and outside the business misses the point about how to create the wealth that is later to be distributed.

Managers, especially those in the middle who will have to carry the heaviest burden of putting innovative procedures into practice, must be co-opted into the development of a common purpose. There is evidence that large, mature businesses can succeed in this process if they take the time and trouble to build an internal climate receptive to change. The problems of rejuvenation are not solved simply by throwing money at them: experimentation is essential. Instilling the values of corporate entrepreneurship, an essential component of rejuvenation, allows slumbering corporate giants to be woken up and made vital again.

Because mature organizations have only limited abilities to master change, radical change in both strategy and organizational capability can only be accomplished successfully in stages. Dashes for growth, programs of planned top-to-bottom cultural change, or even process reengineering are likely to fail if the foundations of common understanding and the necessary new skills are missing. Sustainable progress is most likely to be achieved by those who build what we call the strategic "staircase of additive capabilities." Timing, judicious pacing, and, again, managers' perceptions of the nature of present and future threats and opportunities are important components of successful step-by-step progress in a consistent direction and with adequate flexibility to adapt to competitors' reactions. Rushing results in failure; moving too slowly yields ground to competitors and increases vulnerability.

To understand how firms have achieved and sustained success, we examined both the economics of competition and the behavioral issues; each affects the other. The academic debate on the merits of strategy as content—emphasizing the economic choices of positioning in markets—as opposed to strategy as process—emphasizing the capabilities of the human organization—seems sterile. Successful rejuvenators strike effective balances between choices of strategy and direction on the one hand and investments in building capability on the other.

In this book we attempt to marry the competing perspectives of economics and the behavioral sciences. In the first part, we build from the outside in and focus on the outcomes of innovative strategy and competitive dynamics. In the second part, we build from the inside out and focus on the means by which change can be fostered and directed. The common ground is the realm of perception—perception of market shifts, combined with perceptions of possibility in creating new advantages. Rejuvenators do not constrain their choices of strategy within the scope of present resources, but are prepared to base their forward direction on the belief they will be able to build capabilities.

We are conscious of unfinished business in our attempt to learn from the success of a few. We cannot, for example, explain why stimuli that provoke some firms to embark on a path to rejuvenation leave others untouched. Why does threat seem a more potent stimulus than opportunity? Is business inherently reactive, or can managers anticipate opportunity and drive themselves and their colleagues to become proactive? We found evidence of both behaviors. Further unfinished business on our agenda includes the issue of leadership and setting standards. Although we are sure of the need for top managers to lead by example at all stages of the recovery process, we are less certain about how high the standards should be set. Is it either realistic or useful to set a goal of global industry leadership when the bailiffs are on the doorstep and the technologies out of date? Again, we found conflicting evidence. We were encouraged, however, to find some CEOs aggressively driving forward the efforts of the teams in their organizations by setting standards of world-class achievement at early stages in the game.

Can the momentum of successful rejuvenation be maintained? Can organizations become indefinitely adaptive or will their arteries harden again, plunging them once more into the painful cycle of reconstruction and recovery? Few enterprises have achieved long-lasting vitality, but more may do so as the winners in our study raise their sights to conquer new peaks.

The reactions of many managers to the first edition of this book give us hope that we may be able to increase the odds for sustainable rejuvenation. Most told us that they recognized the struggles, the dilemmas, the private fears that they might have made wrong decisions; a few, perhaps with the benefit of hindsight, also felt they had done the "obvious." If this book helps make the path to rejuvenation more obvious, we will have contributed something to the industrial revival we all need. But even when the path is clearly defined, it is not easy. Courage, determination, leadership, helped by a little luck, are as necessary and important as ever. The will to win must go together with the plan and the capability to win.

REJUVENATING
THE
MATURE
BUSINESS

Chapter One

Maturity Is a
State of Mind

Mature businesses are those whose managers believe they are imprisoned by their environments and are unable to succeed. At best, they
seem doomed to give poor service to customers and barely adequate
financial returns to shareholders. In contrast, dynamic businesses are
able to sustain above-average performance, introduce new products and
processes, and create new markets. They challenge the conventional
norms and managerial beliefs pervading many mature businesses.

Mature and dynamic businesses exist uneasily side by side in many
traditional, well-established industries. For example, Banc One is
among the United States' most profitable and fastest-growing banks,
with more than $76 billion in assets. Creative and innovative in the
retail market and in the services it offers to other financial institutions,
it is highly successful, while many in the banking industry, led by
Citibank and Chase Manhattan, are racked by falling margins and bad
loans.[1] Benetton, with more than $3 billion in retail sales, is Europe's
first truly multinational textile retailer-producer.[2] Inventive in its approach to young fashion-conscious consumers, it is fast growing and
very profitable in contrast to many of the textile businesses in northern
Europe, which are continuing to struggle against imports from low-
wage areas in southern Europe and less-developed countries.

Can a mature business turn itself into a successful one? It is amazing
that a caterpillar can turn into a butterfly. The caterpillar creeps along
the ground, has limited horizons, and is unable to move quickly. Yet
that small furry larva can become one of nature's most graceful crea-
tures, able to fly and traverse a much wider terrain. Naturally, one
might doubt that a mature firm could become dynamic and entrepreneurial, yet such a metamorphosis is possible.

Most of us know that change is usually painful, slow, and immensely
difficult. Of the many mature businesses that have tried to rejuvenate,

1

some show improved results for a short time before the effects evaporate, and only a few succeed in holding on to improved performance for any length of time.[3] We found and examined many that tried and failed; we studied carefully a group that did succeed, and an even smaller number that went on to become industry leaders.[4] Firms in the last category did more than transform themselves; they transformed their industries and created new competitive rules. Such transformations are rare, but inspirational, and their rich histories suggest many valuable lessons. Our rejuvenation cases are supplemented by the study of other cases, such as Benetton which, with almost no resources, came into hostile textile sectors and built itself a commanding world position, and Banc One, once a small, sleepy bank in Columbus, Ohio, which awoke, grew, and became an industry leader.[5] They serve as role models for rejuvenators, and their actions inspired some of the businesses we surveyed.

Our successful transformations share a common feature: rejuvenation was generated from within, using limited outside resources. Like the caterpillar, they seemed almost self-sufficient in their metamorphoses. They demonstrated that organizations could counter their own history of poor profitability and low growth and operate successfully in the same, often hostile, environment that weighed so heavily on their rivals.

For example, the rejuvenated Edwards High Vacuum, a British-based company, is the world's second largest producer of high-vacuum pumps and arguably the most successful, while its counterparts fight to stay alive. Edwards has had great success in the three major markets of the world—Japan, the United States, and Europe—beating local competition in these tough sectors and overcoming customer preferences to buy local products; yet in the early 1970s, Edwards was broke and near extinction.[6] Edwards is an obvious example of successful rejuvenation, but it may not remain successful forever, as more than sixteen Japanese firms have entered its industry since the mid-1980s.

Another rejuvenator is Hotpoint, the European appliance producer owned by General Electric of the United States and GEC of the United Kingdom, one of Europe's most successful appliance firms and one of the most profitable in the world.[7] It was not always so: in the early 1970s, Hotpoint was almost broke, and Philips was Europe's largest and second most successful producer. Hotpoint has hauled itself from oblivion to become the industry's exemplar, while the European arm of the merged Philips-Whirlpool struggles to succeed. It appears that Hotpoint provides its customers with more reliable, more imaginatively designed products at lower cost. Hotpoint's position is constantly being challenged, but so far it has managed to stay with the leaders in terms of profitability and influence.

2

Butterflies die; so, eventually, do most organizations. We do not claim that our rejuvenators will be different in this respect. Our note of caution is well intended, for if rejuvenators can challenge leaders, they, too, can be challenged. Our focus is not on sustaining success, although we touch on this subject in Chapter 9, but on attaining it. The achievements of our rejuvenators should not be minimized for they required great courage and determination. Showing that there is hope for mature businesses, that rejuvenation is possible on limited resources, we describe a pathway to renewal. In doing this we challenge much conventional wisdom about the capacity of firms to rejuvenate, the management of change, and the determinants of business performance.

PERCEPTIONS

What is a mature business? Is it defined by poor financial performance? It is true that many mature businesses do perform poorly, but this is neither a complete nor a satisfactory definition. Many factors distinguish mature businesses from dynamic or rejuvenated competitors, but the key is perception. Our actions are driven in part by our beliefs, just as our beliefs are informed by our actions and experiences. For a firm to rejuvenate, its managers must learn to act and think differently. Correcting perceptions is a hard task and central to instilling new kinds of behavior; its importance is obvious from contrasting the beliefs of managers in mature and dynamic businesses.

Managers of mature businesses often told us, "Our industry is mature" and "We face many adverse outside pressures" and "Failure is not our fault."[8] They felt imprisoned by their environments. They often said that they experienced poor profitability and low organic growth because demand was growing slowly and the competitive environment was tough. They told us of the impossibility of improving their position significantly or dramatically, and typically rejected the suggestion that their strategy was defective and that they should try something different. "Our industry is not like that," they cried. They seemed to believe that industry and environmental factors determine business performance. They would not accept that stable shares of the market, stable costs, and stable sales—the usual measures of maturity—mask turmoil and change in submarkets, driven by such factors as changing consumer choice and new technology.

In every case we found managers in competing dynamic organizations with quite different views. "We have to ride the waves of the seesaw nature of the environment"; "Outside pressures must be overcome"; and "Failure is always [the managers'] responsibility." These managers thought more positively than their "mature" counterparts; they did not see the environment as a prison or constraint, yet they believed that understanding the detail of their industries was critical. They invested heavily in building specific knowledge of how their technology, customers, and environment work.

The managers in our dynamic firms said that the environment has to be understood, mastered, and subdued. For them, strategies were not fixed in stone but creative and dynamic, to be molded and changed through time. The dynamic firms seemed able to ride their industry's ups and downs. To be sure, recessions and booms affected them, but not in the same way as they did their mature rivals. The evidence we examine at some length in Chapter 2 supports the view taken by the dynamic businesses, namely, that industry factors are rather unimportant in determining business success. In contrast, choosing the right strategy is vital. (See Exhibit 1.1.)

The difficulty faced by mature firms is that their perceptions influence what managers do. One senior executive of a major French appliance firm explained that his firm had undertaken an extensive analysis of the environment, but that the analysis had been limited to firms operating or selling in the French market. This analysis showed that the firm was in a mature and hostile industry, that poor performance was inevitable, and that the business was not out of line with its perceived competitors. Even though customer surveys and profit figures were disappointing, the top team saw no need for radical action. But its analysis had ignored the activities of firms such as Hotpoint, which were neither world scale nor in direct competition. Hotpoint was doing things quite differently; its actions showed that the industry was not

---

EXHIBIT 1.1 THE CHALLENGE OF MATURITY

Mature businesses	Dynamic or entrepreneurial businesses
Managers perceive the industry as stable with slow demand growth and incremental changes in technology.	Managers believe there is potential for change, new ways of operating, and new strategies, many of which have been ignored by mature businesses.
Managers believe that profitability is achieved by giving less value to customers or staff or other stakeholders. Similarly, giving better service means lower profits.	Managers believe that to create better profits a firm must give better service to customers and better value to its staff. Value can be delivered to all stakeholders without trade-offs.

---

mature, that hostile factors could be overcome, and that its performance was remarkably good in comparison with the French firm and its competitors. Because the French managers believed that they could learn nothing from examining noncompeting firms, they had ignored the evidence.

Once this data block had been removed, it became clear that many aspects of the French firm were inefficient and inflexible and that it had misread the trends in customer desires and technological possibilities. The organization was able to rescue itself from its trapped thinking and realize that action was urgently needed to change its performance. It also became clear that its mediocre performance was not the result of "outside forces beyond our control" but internal routines and behaviors "which we can do something about."

In some mature firms, the data have been collected, but then ignored or rejected. Rejection of data was a problem in a mature pump firm competing with Edwards. Its team was shown data on the performance of Edwards and some of the other firms in the sector, which suggested that alternative ways of operating would improve performance. Management rejected the data. It could neither believe the facts nor accept their consequences. It fell into the common trap of refusing to accept that it could do things differently.

We heard many reasons for rejecting data. "We tried that once and it did not work," or "That was X's strategy and look what happened to them, they lost money," or even, "It cannot possibly work, for if it was right we would have done it first!" These responses were nearly always backed up by carefully reasoned arguments that sounded most plausible. "We have had five engineers looking at this one, and they wholly disagree," or "It is well known that that kind of data can be unreliable," or "We are not that kind of organization." The excuses were legion, the consequences always the same: the organization refused to accept its ability to control its own destiny. It is not surprising that this firm took no action to rejuvenate: nothing could shake the managers' enduring belief that they could continue to act as before.

Even when some individuals in such firms find that external signals for change need to be addressed, they may face insuperable obstacles in persuading their colleagues to share their views. It is all too easy to be lulled into continuing inaction by plausible arguments—typically based on past experience—even when the reasoning is superficial and demonstrably false. Resistance can arise from personal unwillingness to face the uncomfortable fact that all one's professional experience might count for little in the future. The prospect of having to relearn how to manage or, worse, of losing relative status can be a powerful obstacle to changing one's mind and perspective. Further, it is often difficult to prove before the event that a deep-seated belief about how to compete has become obsolete. A lone voice on these matters can readily be ignored in a collective determination to uphold the traditional perspectives of the "if it ain't broke, don't fix it" variety.

CREATING VALUE

Not only do perceptions about the environment distinguish mature firms from successful ones: but beliefs about how value is created also differ fundamentally. In mature firms people seem to believe that if one group is doing well, it must be at the expense of another. When management is paid well, workers feel that it is at their expense; when shareholders are doing well, managers feel that they must be exploited, and many firms are suspicious of their suppliers and customers. These beliefs are linked to actions. When shareholders complain that returns are not high enough, managers in mature firms downgrade service to customers, tell staff to work longer hours, and attempt to extract larger discounts from suppliers. They see this as the only way to deliver extra profit. They seem unable to detect a positive connection between doing something differently to give better service to customers, getting staff to work more effectively rather than just longer hours, and integrating suppliers to better effect rather than just looking for the cheapest source.

Managers in dynamic businesses seem quite different. They believe it essential to satisfy all interest groups and treat them fairly and equally. Even in adverse and turbulent environments, successful firms are not only able to give good service and value to customers and a good and fair return to shareholders, but also to improve the lot of their employees and treat their suppliers and distributors properly. Our argument is not the obvious point that the more profitable the firm, the greater the largess it can distribute. Ours concerns the perception of how value is created.

At the time of their crisis in maturity, many of our rejuvenating organizations had poor profits, bad service, poor staff relations, and a bad image with suppliers. The awakening managers saw the way out through rethinking the business, and they typically started with the customer. This building process receives full treatment in Chapters 6, 7, and 8, but it is worth rehearsing some of the points here.

Richardson Sheffield rose from being an almost bankrupt U.K. knife producer to becoming a world leader in profits and market share by its novel approach to customers. It built customer value in stages in an industry whose service was traditionally dreadful. It began by giving speedier service and ensuring that goods always arrived on time. The more accurate service pointed up inefficiencies in the production and operating systems as well as encouraging customers to pay on time and in full. Almost simultaneously, product quality was improved by eliminating errors and reducing rejects. Although this required investment, much of it was modest, especially in the early stages of rejuvenation, and costs were quickly lowered. Rapid innovation and new product introduction came much later, but again the focus was on giving customers more value. Because Richardson became so much better than its rivals, it could produce new and attractive knives with excellent performance at comparable or even lower prices than rivals and still seek better and rising profitability.[9] This customer-slanted approach was central to its purpose and actions; but management did not use it as an excuse to treat other stakeholders badly. On the contrary, building customer value not only improved profitability, but also was consistent with treating the staff better, raising their wages, and giving them better working conditions.[10]

Similarly, Japanese automobile producers captured a large share of both the U.S. and European automobile markets by producing high-quality, reliable cars at low cost. They have not sought to benefit the customer by exploiting the workers, the shareholders, and the suppliers. True, they treat these groups differently from the way we in the West do, but their treatment is considered excellent by local standards.

Managing Stakeholders

Some argue that Western shareholders discourage a long-term horizon by encouraging short-term financial results, making rejuvenation very difficult. Our firms did not find that emphasis on the short term prevented their recovery. Although several complained about the demands for constantly improving financial ratios, they appreciated that their past history had often made shareholders understandably skeptical of their abilities. They all realized that trust had to be created by delivering results and learned how to manage the expectations of their shareholders. They also understood that getting things right for the customers, staff, suppliers, and distributors was the route to financial health. Value must be built as well as extracted.

Initially our rejuvenators had to be content with limited resources. Although some were part of large diversified firms, they did not benefit from generous handouts from their owners. Richardson was typical in that it was allowed to reinvest its profits in the business, but until recently its parent never gave it any other cash. Hotpoint was owned by one of the most frugal financially oriented companies in the United Kingdom, GEC Limited.[11] This parent expected cash and growth. In every case, there was pressure on the top team to deliver good financial results and to justify the usage of cash and capital. They all realized that modern accounting rules prevent their smoothing out some of the earnings fluctuations. All had difficulties, yet they achieved impressive long-run growth in profits and profitability in comparison to that attained elsewhere in the industry. On an absolute standard, they achieved a consistent record of before-tax profits close to 25 percent of capital employed, an enviable distinction even among excellent performers.[12]

Motivating staff to perform differently and better was an essential step in rejuvenation, an issue we explore more fully later. We did not attempt to send questionnaires to employees or to measure wages and benefits accurately, but our interviews always left us with the impression that employees were not forgotten. All our rejuvenators recorded low staff turnover, high morale, and a line of people waiting to join their organizations. Most kept track of employee concerns, using surveys to complement unusual internal information flows. Many spoke of that elusive feature, the ability to work hard and have fun.

Understanding the need to create value among suppliers and distributors was common among our firms.[13] Long before supply partnerships became fashionable, Benetton managed its suppliers and distributors differently. It formed close strategic alliances, involving its partners with many aspects of its business and teaching them the skills they needed. This attitude was quite different from those adopted by many mature firms in the sector.[14] The results were remarkable. A typical Benetton shop is a low-capital, high-turnover operation, and its owner can expect to pay back his or her capital investment in three or four years. Benetton's agents organize distribution, and they average close to $1 million a year per person in remuneration. Benetton also contracts to many firms in northern Italy and around the world. Life for the subcontractors is not a bed of roses, but relative to others in the industry they do well. Since the early 1970s, nearly half the European textile business has disappeared in the face of import competition, yet Benetton has managed to grow its European textile base, allowing many of its subcontractors to prosper.

Many of our rejuvenators took the approach of delivering perceived value to multiple interest groups. This had the effect of growing the overall value created, increasing the size of the "cake" so that all the stakeholders' shares could be larger. They were not concerned merely with profitability for shareholders, for that group was only one of many parties. This approach to business was in marked contrast to that of some firms which did not manage to rejuvenate, which argued about the division of the cake rather than taking care that all the slices of the cake should grow. The cynical may think that creating value among multiple interest groups is impractical idealism for the longer term, especially for mature firms. History is reassuring here, for over the longer time span there is no doubt that Western countries have achieved real wealth creation for all interest groups.

INNOVATION IN STRATEGY

Organizations can challenge maturity and create value for all their interest groups through strategic innovation. This means that they adopt a creative and novel approach to how they compete, where they compete, and with whom they compete. Such creativity does not come easily to mature firms, whose managers are often trapped into thinking that only one set of recipes is appropriate. Typically, they project the past into the future, believing that old approaches which once made leaders rich and enviable are still relevant. Thinking that their industry is stable, they believe that competitive battles are played by a single set of rules and that the winners are those with the greatest resources. They fail to recognize that all industries, especially traditional ones like airlines, automobiles, banking, retailing, and textiles, are capable of flux and that the real competitive battles are fought by those with different approaches. In these battles, the winners are often the less-well-resourced firms, sometimes the entrants, sometimes the rejuvenators, that have chosen to do something different.

Aspiring rejuvenators do well to learn from the past, studying those firms which have changed their industries. Ford was one of the greatest innovators of the century; in the early 1900s it pioneered the cheap production of standardized cars.[15] Henry Ford grew his company from relatively modest resources and soon the Tin Lizzie, or Model T, was in almost every household in the United States and in many in Europe. Industry progress has altered and transcended Ford's paradigm. As is well known, the idea of mass-produced variety was introduced in the 1920s by Alfred Sloan, the founder of General Motors (GM), but in his case variety was limited. For the next half-century, there were many innovations, but since the 1970s the U.S. auto industry has found itself increasingly in trouble, and the firms appear to be stuck in maturity. During the 1980s American automakers invested many billions of dollars in new equipment and training, yet by the beginning of the 1990s they had made little progress in changing their basic cost structure, and their products were similar in many respects. It seems that, despite the investment, they still cling to old beliefs and habits and struggle with old methods of operating. American Motors has disappeared,

9

Chrysler has seen its fortunes seesaw, and although Ford is showing signs of life, even GM seems to be in deep trouble. Both Ford and GM are trying to renew by radically changing the way they operate: both may rise again.[16]

U.S. auto producers' difficulties appear to stem mainly from two quarters: the consumers and the Japanese. Consumers, who have shown an increasing reluctance to value unreliable cars that emphasize gimmicks and the annual model changes so long beloved of the U.S. giants, have turned their attention to reliable compact cars offered first by the Europeans and then by the Japanese. This change in consumer behavior, unanticipated by the major U.S. firms, had profound effects on their fortunes. As important, if not more so, was the power of the Japanese competitors.[17]

In the 1950s, the Japanese automakers, neither well endowed nor well positioned, were saddled with a history of underperformance. On limited resources, they have risen to challenge the mighty U.S. and European giants. The Japanese challenge has been revolutionary: better-quality cars, better appreciation of consumer needs, faster and more creative responses. Even more impressive was that the Japanese made the cars at less cost. They seem to have unlocked the secret of delivering *quality with high productivity,* and they are making good progress on delivering *variety, speed, and flexibility.* They have undermined the economic position of their U.S. rivals by finding innovative and hard-to-copy ways of competing.

Japanese firms have no monopoly on strategically innovative behavior. Bank One, Columbus, Ohio, for example, has developed and refined the idea of service to customers, including consumers, small businesses, and other financial institutions.[18] It was the first U.S. bank to install an automated teller machine; it pioneered the idea of a financial service shopping mall, where a complete range of financial services is offered through retail outlets open, like ordinary shopping malls, seven days a week. Bank One has also been a market leader in developing banks within grocery stores in its region. Its development of services to other financial institutions has been more significant in terms of profits: processing credit card transactions at a greater speed, with greater flexibility and accuracy than most of its competitors. Its systems are sold to other banks around the world. Bank One, a driving force for change, forced many of its competitors to adjust, be taken over, or fail.

Retailing is an industry with all the outward trappings of maturity, for it is competitive, slow growing, and has existed for centuries. Yet it is turbulent in its competitive dynamics. Wal-Mart, one of America's most successful businesses, has effectively beaten Sears, Roebuck and K mart, not by copying their formula but by operating differently. Its locations have traditionally been based in small towns where there is less local competition, it has developed an unusual capability in responding to changes in consumer purchasing patterns, it has a philosophy of delivering high value to customers without raising its costs, and its organization is quick and efficient.[19] In its choice of where, with whom, and how to compete, Wal-Mart is a creative organization.

In Europe, a well-established service firm, British Airways, became one of the most profitable airlines in the world by adopting a new approach to the market. It was ailing and performing badly after years of state ownership and politicization. Under new leadership, it undertook a massive alteration program, changing the destinations it served, cutting out people and routes to focus its activities on a smaller territory. It also changed its procedures. Reassigning 31,000 of its 51,000 people to the newly redesigned marketing organization, it took customer service very seriously. With little real cost, it transformed its ability to deliver quality service and became more flexible and more responsive. The effects on its revenues, market share, and financial performance were dramatic.[20]

Our examples serve to illustrate the great range of possibilities for creating new value by choosing new ways to compete. Thinking about how to compete is the topic in Chapter 3, in which we explore the contrast between dynamic and mature organizations. In mature organizations, such features as greater variety, higher quality, or faster reaction are commonly considered incompatible with one another and with low cost. Dynamic businesses resolve these dilemmas to deliver new combinations: *variety and efficiency; quality and productivity; speed and flexibility, and mass fashion.* These innovations, involve more than product or process change, both of which are vital to progress; they combine many new or better actions to create an alternative approach to providing goods or services. For organizations trying to rejuvenate, parsimony is a necessity. The critical combinations include utilizing fewer resources, e.g., speed at low cost. Low cost is also vital for industry leaders, but, as we explore in Chapter 9, with their greater resources and skills they need to find other combinations as well.

Our rejuvenators followed the same path as the more famous British Airways, Wal-Mart, Japanese automobile producers, and Banc One. Edwards challenged its industry's values with durable pumps delivered quickly to the proper specification. Richardson made knives that were not only inexpensive, but also durable and fun. Courtelle delivered a wide range of multicolor fibers in small lots. While the achievements of each organization were specific to its context, all could be classified as capturing one or more new combinations.

Rejuvenating organizations have to complement their creativity in how they compete with new thinking about where and with whom to compete. In Chapter 4 we explore these issues in depth, explaining that decisions about the scope of a business include selecting location, range of products or services, and channels of supply and distribution. We expound the guiding principles for rejuvenators: selecting a manageable scope and exploiting a market or technological trend ignored by the competition.

Hotpoint's rejuvenation was the result of a combination of factors. Not only did it lower costs and raise quality, but it adopted a creative approach to the scope of its business. It chose to compete in a single country when its rivals were in many countries and becoming Pan-European. Within the United Kingdom, it adopted an even-handed approach to selling through small and chain stores. This policy annoyed the chain stores, which demanded preferential treatment, and surprised competitors, which thought that small stores were an unimportant part of the market. We will explain that by choosing unusual places to compete, Hotpoint was able to exploit ignored consumer trends and competitors' weaknesses.

RETHINKING THE ORGANIZATION

In rejuvenating a business, not only top managers have to change their thinking; everyone in the organization has to act and think differently. The most important and difficult things to change are people and their routines and, as Joseph Schumpeter pointed out, real progress can be achieved only by making people perform differently *inside* the business.[21]

Consider, for example, the change in tasks undertaken at the lower levels in an assembly operation when there is a shift from the old method of homogeneous mass production to the new focus on variety at low cost. The nature of the work changes as do the skills and thinking required. These include ability to create team skills to change tools, alter equipment settings, and reduce the number of substandard items in production. Performance measures change as well. The old order emphasized simple measures of productivity, often of individuals, and focused on maximizing production-run lengths. In the new order, inventory is no longer an efficient buffer and production runs must be adjusted to market needs. Productivity in the single function of, say, production or selling is no longer dominant: the goal of the firm is to maximize responsiveness within the overall constraint of limited resources. Workers and managers alike have to think and act differently, and their performance has to be measured by new standards.

12

A service organization also requires changes in thinking when there is a shift from standardization to a focus on speed and responsiveness. Old systems typically required specialization of tasks by function. The placing of an order for a service might go through several functions. The first checked the creditworthiness of the customer, the second checked the availability of capacity, the third looked for the part, and the fourth scheduled an engineer to do the work in a customer location; finally, the customer was informed of this appointment. It was a slow, cumbersome, and inflexible system. Although the time taken at each station was short, the elapsed time often amounted to days or even weeks because the work waited in lines or piles at each workstation. Worse, the customer was often given short notice of the service call; if it was not convenient, the system found it hard to cope. In some cases it was easier to start again! New systems typically assign one person or a team to take charge of all the work and be responsible for coordination with the customer. Such a process must provide a new way of thinking about data bases (they have to be readily accessible to do the checks), new views about who is allowed to complete schedules (the order taker has to have this power or else the system fails), and new views of authority (the order taker's decisions must not be overruled). Once these systems are running smoothly—usually no easy task—the overall costs fall as much waste and error are eliminated.

Such changes in operating tasks, commonly labeled process reengineering, are not confined merely to production or service operations; they occur in every sphere of the organization. The work of the financial control department alters because the strategic task is different. Many of the reports generated under the old system need to be replaced by reports measuring the new needs. The tasks of the logistics department also change. In both services and manufacturing, orders are no longer processed and dispatched at the convenience of an outdated system but are tailored to customer requirements.[22]

It is not enough to change tasks and processes. Rejuvenating businesses have to rebalance the way their departments interrelate. In many industries, such as cars, steel, fibers, appliances, and cutlery, the old practice was to sell what was produced. That has to change to making what customers order or purchase. The sales department is no longer subservient to production; the two have to work together. The nature and span of the functions also change. In many cases the sales department has to become more active in marketing and new forms of coordination must exist among product development, production, and sales. With an emphasis on speed to market, the traditional isolation of research and development changes, too. Brand-new departments emerge and other functions collapse. As a consequence of the changes within functions, in processes and routines, and in rebalancing the parts, the rejuvenated organization both looks and thinks very differently from its mature former self.

BUILDING STRATEGIC STAIRCASES

Our rejuvenators had to change the mind-sets in their organizations to create value. The change had to be radical and incremental. As discussed in detail in the second half of this book, the change was radical in the sense that beliefs were altered, structures torn down, skills modified, and new technology introduced. Yet it was incremental in the sense that building new competencies, new capabilities, and new resources was not the work of a moment, but was deeply embedded. Starting with relatively modest beginnings, such as lowering the cost of making existing products or improving the quality and reliability of existing services, our organizations moved only a step at a time to more ambitious goals. They built capabilities that permitted them to challenge and resolve dilemmas and achieve sustained renewal. A few of our organizations reached a position of industry leadership in which they set new standards for a whole industry; for them the process from initial steps to achieving global leadership often took as long as a decade. There were no quick fixes.

The experience of our rejuvenators points to a way forward for others. Renewal can come from the process of successive creation of new capabilities we call *building and climbing a strategic staircase.*[23] For our rejuvenators, the labels on the stairs were often similar, but the sequence of steps varied by organization, even within the same industry. Stairs, such as lower cost, quality, speed, flexibility, variety, and so forth, were built as the result of effort and initiatives. (See Exhibit 1.2.)

We talk of staircases, not ladders, to emphasize the need for durability and signal that organizations must work continually at their abilities to maintain their value. Since competitors are always close behind, failure to reinforce the capabilities—or steps—means that their value will diminish and the organizations quickly become sloppy. Building a staircase is difficult because the capabilities have to be kept in balance simultaneously. It is easy to build one step, but the next is harder, and each addition becomes harder still, unless the first are on secure foundations.

Although building takes time, the experience of our firms suggests that mature businesses have to feel a sense of urgency. Tom Peters and Robert Waterman spoke of the bias for action,[24] and our rejuvenators

14

EXHIBIT 1.2   A HYPOTHETICAL STRATEGIC STAIRCASE OF CAPABILITIES

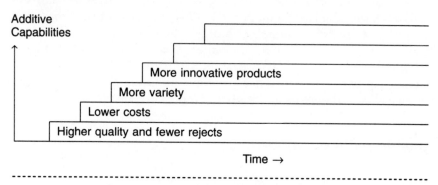

Additive
Capabilities

More innovative products

More variety

Lower costs

Higher quality and fewer rejects

Time →

---

were quick to ensure that things which could be done today were not put off to tomorrow. Things like big projects have to be done in a measured way. Others, like small initiatives in the early stages, can be decided quite quickly. The pace of competition, the impatience of stakeholders, the uncertainties of office, and the politics of organizations mean that there must be a sense of urgency in renewal. As one chief executive of a recently renewed organization put it:

> My life is a series of first hundred days. Like the U.S. president, everyone has a hundred days to put a plan into action and make it work. Each hundred days, I have to have a new and better plan which builds on the last one. When I run out, either I shall be dead or else I shall quit.

Results do not always follow effort simply. Success usually comes in lumps, sometime later. In a new building, work on the foundations produces few noticeable results, but as the walls go up progress looks dramatic; the same applies to rebuilding an organization. This discontinuity of outcomes gives an illusion that rapid results can be achieved quickly, but builders know that walls without foundations do not make a secure house; the same is true in rejuvenated organizations.

Consider, for example, the innovation and production of the Laser knife by Richardson, which is fully described in Chapter 8. This invention was the source of a dramatic increase in the profitability of the firm. The team that worked on the knife produced the inventions in about six months, and the knife was in mass production within a year. This highly successful item, which spawned other innovations, appears to have all the hallmarks of rapid transformational change. But without

15

the laborious effort of building skills in the organization, the invention would not have been produced so quickly. It took more than five years of work to perfect the grinding technology that makes Richardson knives among the best in quality and lowest in cost in the world.

The example of incremental building looking like radical change was common across all our companies. Securing effective change is laborious, and we found many examples of firms that tried to shortcut a change process and failed because they did not alter beliefs or failed to give people the skills and tools to do the task better.

WHO ARE THE REJUVENATORS?

Rejuvenation is not the work of just a few top managers; building a strategic staircase requires effort and creativity from all who work in a business. The task is not impossible, because most mature and poorly performing organizations do have spirited entrepreneurial individuals. The difficulty lies in entrepreneurial behavior being individualistic and unconnected and having little overall effect. In the second half of the book, we show how the process of renewal involves connecting the existing and disjointed individual activities and spreading them through the business.

Renewal is not a final goal; many firms aspire to attain industry leadership. That also requires entrepreneurial behavior which is more extensive, more deeply embedded and connected across the whole organization, including even suppliers and distributors. The fact that industry leaders engage in similar activities, but on a larger scale, to firms which renew lends further support to the notion that rejuvenation has to be built in stages and that transformation of seriously troubled firms cannot happen overnight.

The problem faced by many mature organizations is that renewal and change appear very risky, much more risky than the status quo. This perception has to be altered. The real risks of rejuvenation, especially if it is undertaken in stages, are less than imagined. Clever rejuvenators manage their risks most carefully. They all understand that when one is far behind, only innovative plays will succeed in radically altering their positions. Just as in a sailing race or sports event where the distant follower can catch the leader only if he or she tries a new tactic, so too in industry. The trick in the real world of business is to make creative plays with low risk and with limited resources, something only entrepreneurial organizations can do.

At the start, constrained by their history and their resource limitations, our organizations looked for creative plays that did not expose them unduly. As we explain in Chapter 7, our organizations simplified their businesses so that costs could be reduced and the whole managed better. This could be seen as an attempt to reduce risk. They also encouraged many small investments, each of which could fail without causing serious damage, but each of which, if it succeeded, would further progress. These initiatives were especially aimed to encourage individual and small-team entrepreneurial behavior. We therefore depict the first phases of rejuvenation—*galvanizing and taking many new initiatives*—as of low risk.

As each organization made progress on its strategic staircase, it became more imperative to create new competitive advantages and to take the steps required to secure the renewal. These initiatives were aimed at connecting functions and teams to form a more business-driven entrepreneurial activity. In Chapter 8, we describe this *building* phase and the frame-breaking investments of our organizations. Usually much larger moves than those of the first stage, the risks, although greater, were acceptable because the organization had a more secure foundation and was better resourced. These frame-breaking investments could not have been successfully undertaken earlier; they required a level of skills and capabilities coupled with aspirations and beliefs not previously in evidence.

The few rejuvenators that succeeded in attaining and maintaining industry leadership faced the biggest risk.[25] To get in front, they had to find new patterns of activity that required the whole organization to work together. To stay in front required fending off competitors and, from time to time, undertaking radical reshaping. Teamwork on an organizational scale is risky as well as rewarding. Successful industry leaders have the resources and capabilities to bear these risks, but they too can fail.

Exhibit 1.3 is a diagrammatic attempt to capture these differential risks and spheres of activities and emphasize the staircase of progress from renewal to industry leadership. At the start, many small initiatives (small circles) are undertaken by individuals and small groups throughout the organization, each of which generally involves only small resources. In renewal, the entrepreneurship becomes more prevalent, the smaller initiatives more numerous and supplemented by bigger collective projects (medium-size circles) that cross functional divides. At the third stage, major projects are required which involve all parts of the organization working together entrepreneurially, hence the large circles. These projects supplement other, more numerous individual initiatives and, collectively, permit the business to master its industry.

Those who take risks and succeed know that they have to appreciate the role of fortune, and all our rejuvenators claimed, "We were lucky."

EXHIBIT 1.3   THE LOCUS OF ACTIVITY IN DIFFERENT STAGES OF REJUVENATION

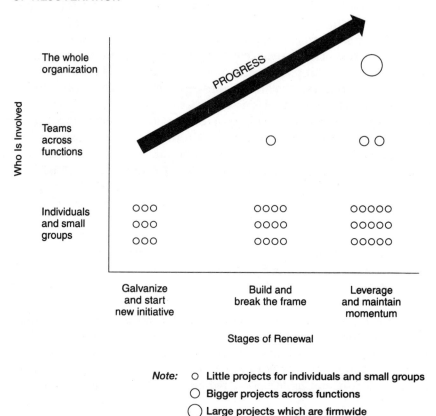

Hotpoint was lucky that its rivals ignored it and that the chain stores eventually fell into line. Edwards was lucky that just as it launched a new pump, designed originally for the chemical industry, the U.S. semiconductor market boomed and created new demand for which this pump was best suited. Richardson was lucky with its remarkable owner who set the challenge of the Laser knife. But luck is exploited best by those who are well prepared. As Arnold Palmer once said of his putting performance, "The more I practice, the luckier I become." Or, as Louis Pasteur, the world-famous French scientist, observed more than a century ago, "Chance favours the prepared mind." So Danny Rosenkranz at Edwards made the luck possible by seeing the boom early and recognizing the potential of the new pump.

REJUVENATORS AIM TO CONTROL THEIR DESTINY

Whereas managers in mature businesses are imprisoned by their beliefs and feel powerless to alter their destiny, rejuvenated firms seek to control their industries and their future. The central theme of our book is that managers need to take control of their destiny; strategy is not a question of fit where the economic environment is uppermost and the firm largely a passive actor. In our view, the firm is a dynamic actor shaping its environment. In this conception, the task of the firm is to read the economic signals and recognize the potential opportunities to shape and harness tastes, technology, and competitor behavior.

Put simply, we suggest that for the dynamic firm the direction of causality is from the organization to the market. It recognizes the role of innovative strategy, choosing territories, building staircases, and using entrepreneurship to shape the environment. In contrast, the mature business sees the causality as the other way around. For such managers, the environment is beyond control, old recipes are best, and value is a subtraction game.

A mechanical analogy may be attractive to some readers, and in Exhibit 1.4 we depict the firm and its market as two large interconnected wheels. The left-hand wheel moves with the changes in the economics of the market, the right-hand wheel moves with the changing organization. A smaller cog represents the top management team, which connects the firms with the market. Top management's position is a difficult one: like the returning Jason with his argosy, management

---

EXHIBIT 1.4   CONNECTING ECONOMIC AND ORGANIZATIONAL CHANGE

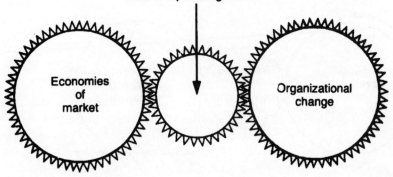

19

is caught between the rock of a potentially intransigent organization and the whirlpool of relentless economic change.

We consider two extreme scenarios—the position of the mature, ossified business and the position of the fully dynamic or rejuvenated organization. In the case of the mature firm (Exhibit 1.5), the left-hand wheel is turned by the relentless force of the market, driven by such factors as competition, changing customer needs, and changing technology. We depict the organizational wheel of the mature business as stationary, which is not quite correct, for change is ever present in all organizations. The change is a projection of the past, which neither responds to current market needs nor creates new rules that others must follow. For example, the U.S. auto producers changed during the 1970s and 1980s, but until recently much of their effort has been devoted to improving their ability to produce cars that consumers find attractive, yet their ability to reduce costs has been less effective than that of their Japanese rivals. The cog representing top management is fissuring, for top management in mature organizations is being slowly crushed as the organization disintegrates under the weight of economic failure. Outside stakeholders always blame top management for the failures of an organization.

Exhibit 1.6 depicts the situation of a truly entrepreneurial organization. Here the right-hand wheel of the organization is moving rapidly, guided and encouraged, but, we suggest, not controlled, by top management. The organization is creating innovations that solve old dilemmas, such as how to deliver *variety at low cost*. The dynamic business is also the driver of some of the change in the economic marketplace, for it creates the new recipes against which others compete. Here the force is from the organization to the market, not the other way around.

EXHIBIT 1.5   THE FORCES FACING THE MATURE ORGANIZATION

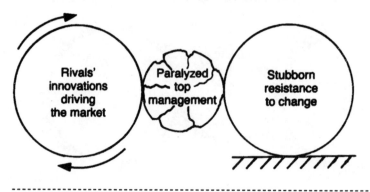

EXHIBIT 1.6   ORGANIZATIONAL CHANGE DRIVING THE DYNAMIC BUSINESS

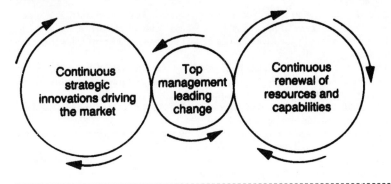

NOTES

[1] Banc One is the holding company for its member Bank One banks. For information on Banc One Corporation and Bank One, Ohio, we are grateful for interviews with executives and numerous articles, including R. Teitelman, "The Magnificent McCoys," *Institutional Investor*, July 1991.

[2] We thank G. Lorenzoni for his research into Benetton, some of which is reported in The Benetton Case, London Business School Case Series, 4, 1988.

[3] It will be clear that we are concerned with business units. It is obvious that a corporation with a portfolio of poorly performing business can improve its statistics by closing some units and purchasing better performers—this of course is not the same as rejuvenating a business. There is a large literature on the turnaround of businesses, much of which is referred to in this book. It is not possible to summarize it here, but note that some of the most valuable studies are of individual organizational transformations, such as R.L. Shook, *Turnaround: The New Ford Motor Company* (New York: Prentice Hall, 1990). Typically these studies look internally. More external studies include P.H. Grinyer, D.G. Mayes, and P. McKiernan, *Sharpbenders: The Secrets of Unleashing Corporate Potential* (Oxford: Basil Blackwell, 1988), which studies both corporate and business sharpbending as well as a few genuine rejuvenations.

[4] For reasons of confidentiality, we cannot list the many who tried to rejuvenate but failed. They came from the sectors of appliances, chemicals, cutlery, fibers, pumps, steel, and textiles. Those which renewed include vibrant organizations such as Wolsey of Courtaulds Textiles, Merloni Electrodomestici, TEM of Thomson (now Ocean). Those which renewed and achieved industry leadership include Edwards High Vacuum (part of BOC, the large industrial gases group), Hotpoint (part of GE-GEC), Cook (the Sheffield casting firm), Richardson (once independent and now part of McPherson's), and Weir pumps (part of the Weir Group).

[5] We also studied Courtelle, a division of Courtaulds, which was becoming mature and managed to rejuvenate.

[6] Much of the evidence on Edwards High Vacuum is reported in J.M. Stopford, *Edwards High Vacuum International*, London Business School, 1989.

[7] Some of the data on the European appliance industry are reported in C.W.F. Baden-Fuller and J.M. Stopford, "Globalisation Frustrated," *Strategic Management Journal* 12, no. 7, 1991: 493–507. For the early Hotpoint account, see M.R.S. Green, *The Hotpoint Story: A Study in Excellence*, London Business School, 1987.

[8] An exploration of such statements in the context of appliances appeared in M.R.S. Green, "Beliefs, Actions and Strategic Change: A Study of Paradigms in UK Domestic Appliances Industry," in *Papers and Proceedings of Academy of Management Conference,* New Orleans, August 1987.

[9] Much of the information about Richardson is reported in R.M. Grant and C.W.F. Baden-Fuller, *The Richardson Sheffield Story,* London Business School Case Series, 2, 1987. The company has been acquired by the Australian group McPherson's, which now holds 15 percent of the world market.

[10] The staff, of course, had to change their work practices and style of operating. Not all were able to adjust, but those who did found the changes were rewarded. Richardson claims that it pays above the average for its local market.

[11] See M. Goold and A. Campbell, *Strategies and Styles: The Role of the Centre in Managing Diversified Corporations* (Oxford: Basil Blackwell, 1987).

[12] Where possible, we used internal accounting records for the relevant business unit, cross-checked with public accounts.

[13] R. Lamming, *Beyond Partnership: Strategies for Innovation and Lean Supply* (Hemel Hempstead: Prentice Hall, 1993), provides an up-to-date review of these issues.

[14] An exception is Marks and Spencer, the U.K. retailer, which for decades has followed a policy of close links with its suppliers. But until more recently, Marks and Spencer did not involve its suppliers in its strategic thinking.

[15] Explored more fully in Chapter 3; see also D. Hounshell, *From the American System to Mass Production* (Baltimore: Johns Hopkins University Press, 1984).

[16] Shook, *Turnaround,* describes some of Ford's progress. J.P. Womak, D.T. Jones, and D. Roos, *The Machine That Changed the World* (New York: Rawson Associates, 1990), confirms the slow emergence of the results.

[17] There is an extensive literature on the causes of the demise of the U.S. automobile companies. Of particular note are Womak, Jones, and Roos, *The Machine That Changed the World,* and Shook, *Turnaround.*

[18] Bank One is a subsidiary of Banc One Corporation.

[19] We have borrowed this analysis from P. Ghemawhat, *Commitment: The Dynamic of Strategy* (New York: Free Press, 1991).

[20] We are grateful to Nick Georgiardis, former director of British Airways, for the background information on its transformation. Many of the details have appeared elsewhere.

[21] In highlighting the importance of innovations we owe our intellectual debt to J.A. Schumpeter, whose *Theory of Economic Development,* which first appeared in German in 1912, is better known in the 1934 English version. Schumpeter emphasized the role of innovation in the dynamics of competition and, in particular, in the way in which successful firms emerge. It was here that he coined the famous phrase, "the perennial gale of creative destruction."

[22] All our rejuvenators reengineered their business processes. The nature of such changes is documented in several books, including T.H. Davenport, *Process Innovation* (Boston: Harvard Business School Press, 1993); H.J. Johansson, P. McHugh, A.J. Pendlebury, and W.A. Wheeler, *Business Process Reengineering* (New York and Chichester: Wiley, 1993).

[23] The need to create multiple advantages is an old idea, and the concept of this being a staircase is neatly captured by our colleagues P. Williamson and M. Hay in "Strategic Staircases," *Long Range Planning* 24, no. 4, 1991: 36–43.

[24] T.J. Peters and R.H. Waterman, Jr., *In Search of Excellence* (New York: Harper & Row, 1982).

[25] This point is also made persuasively by R.T. Pascale, *Managing on the Edge* (New York: Touchstone, Simon & Schuster, 1990).

Chapter Two

The Firm Matters More Than the Industry

To rejuvenate, managers of mature businesses must reject many of their preconceived notions of what determines business success and of how value is created. Unless they jettison their baggage, they will waste time and resources following the wrong strategies, putting their organizations at risk. On the other hand, if they understand the basic economics of how value is created, they have put their foot on the first step of the staircase for rejuvenation. The Banc One story is a good place to start, for it shows that a firm can be successful in a hostile environment, that the value Banc One created came before it grew into a large bank, and that it achieved much with limited resources.

In the late 1980s and early 1990s, the U.S. banking industry became depressed partly because of excess capacity. Retail banking became less profitable, as overborrowed consumers defaulted on their debt and savings and loan institutions were hit by scandals and incompetence. The commercial sector fared little better. Giants such as Chase Manhattan, Chemical Bank, and Citibank suffered catastrophic losses from debt to third world countries, overleveraged corporations, and loans to the property sector. Shareholders suffered as did customers who often complained that their needs were not being addressed. Nor were the troubles confined to the shores of the United States: banks based in London and Tokyo were also reeling from write-offs, slower growth, and falling margins.

At first sight, the banking industry had all the features of a hostile environment where it would be hard to grow and be consistently profitable. Yet some banks have achieved success by occupying profitable niches; others have succeeded by performing the basics better or differently. Banc One is an example of the latter. Focusing on the relatively prosaic markets of retail and small commercial customers, it has maintained its highly successful record of value creation and growth in the depressed U.S. banking market. While competitors have seen their capital bases eroded, Banc One has powered ahead. It achieved for its shareholders, a return on assets of 1.3 percent, considered excellent in this industry, which translates into a 14 percent post-tax return on equity for its shareholders.[1] It regularly tops the charts of bank analyst surveys; *Euromoney* rated it the best bank in the United States and the third most successful worldwide. Banc One's constituent banks have created value for customers, too; surveys show that the organization gives good service and is creative and responsive.

Banc One's success has not been based on the usual factors emphasized in textbooks. It has not sought an industry characterized by rapid growth and high profits. It did not create value by first buying market share and then exploiting its position, but rather the other way around. From humble beginnings as a small bank (third in size) in Columbus, Ohio, it has transformed itself, first building its competitive advantage on a relatively small share of the market, then capitalizing on its abilities with organic growth and growth by merger. Initially, Banc One was not well endowed. It did not have the plentiful resources of many of its bigger competitors, but it still managed to transform itself.

The success of Banc One resulted from a combination of the many factors that make up its strategy. Some have noted Banc One's focus on a few market segments—retail banking and the middle commercial market—yet these markets are not usually associated with success. Many banks serving these markets have done badly. Some have noted Banc One's emphasis on technology, yet many competitors have invested in technology and failed. Of course, careful focus and apt use of technology are part of the strategy, but both are subservient to a vital key factor: the commitment to finding ways of conducting business that differ from those of erstwhile leaders.

Banc One began by emphasizing operational efficiency, creating a capability to undertake data processing actively. After these achievements, it took on work for other banks and financial institutions as a data processor, using its great volumes and market share to exploit and further secure its competitive advantages. Banc One also emphasized service, particularly to retail and commercial customers, contrasting with the approach of many other banks, which sought to compete solely on price or failed to appreciate what customers really wanted. Again, it established an excellent reputation in the local market before its rapid growth by merger and organic expansion.

Banc One correctly sees itself as an innovator, and it has shown its forward thinking in all parts of the business by emphasizing aspects its competitors neglect. As John B. McCoy, the chairman, put it: "One of the personalities associated with the company is John Fisher. The sense of innovation he created is pervasive. . . . One of the reasons we are so successful is that we are willing to try. . . . I can't believe the number of experiments going on inside the company."[2]

Banc One claims that its emphasis on innovation dates back many years; the story goes that the bank was the first to install proper drive-in banking facilities in the 1950s. When John G. McCoy, father of the current chairman, took charge in 1959, he formalized the commitment to innovation by allocating 3 percent of annual profits to research and development. Many innovations have emerged since then, many small but important, some rather more noticeable. For instance, in 1966 it was the first bank outside California to link up with Bank Americard, now Visa; in 1971 it installed the first automated teller machine in the United States. More recently it innovated new methods of processing, and in 1988 initiated a number of successful designs in branch layout. Banc One's emphasis on innovation illustrates an important theme: the fallacy of simplistic, generic strategic recipes such as "Choose a profitable industry," "Go for market share," and "Amass resources."

THREE THEMES

Managers of mature businesses need to reject many of the preconceived ideas about creating value that get in the way of the rejuvenation of their firms. Some of the ideas are held close to the heart and based on a misunderstanding of the laws of economics. For example, there is no economic law which says that some industries have to be less profitable than others, or that winning market share is the route to creating value.[3] The activities of successful rejuvenators show that success is possible against seemingly difficult conditions. Cook, Richardson, and Hotpoint, three rejuvenators whose stories are introduced in this chapter, illustrate three themes that we wish to address.

First, a business can be successful in an industry that seems unpromising. Our rejuvenators were successful in industries where others were doing badly. In each case, these businesses created value for their many stakeholders despite the existence of excess capacity, stable or falling overall demand, and strong competition from rivals, often those in other countries. Opportunities for progress are not measured by the *average* performance of all competitors.

Second, our firms showed that building market share is not the route to success. They showed that market share should be seen as the reward for creating added value, and that the real value in market share is in exploiting and spreading hard-won advantages. Build your competitive advantage first, then go for share.

Third and closely related is the realization that rejuvenating firms (or entrants) can succeed even though they are initially endowed with limited resources. Our rejuvenators became leaders by combining their resources in new ways and building new competencies from within. This method of competing has proved successful even for those vying in international markets where rivals appear to be better resourced and supported by their local governments. (See Exhibit 2.1.)

The essence of competition in mature industries is the creation of new rules of the game, and the rejection of simplistic ideas that success is predetermined by mechanistic formulas. These themes, touched on in the Banc One story, are dealt with at greater length in this chapter.

THE INDUSTRY IS NOT TO BLAME

Our first and central theme is that its industry is not to blame for any shortcomings in the performance of a business. Managers in mature firms often claim that the environment is the cause of their failure. They point to powerful buyers that force down prices, foreign competitors that steal customers, powerful labor unions or skill shortages that

----

EXHIBIT 2.1 CRITICAL FACTORS INFLUENCING AN INDUSTRY'S ECONOMICS

The views of mature managers	The views of dynamic managers
External economic forces determine the ability to add value. In mature sectors, it is difficult for a business to achieve high profits because the firm's performance is predetermined by the industry.	The firm determines the industry's profits, not vice versa. Profitable industries are typically inhabited by a large number of imaginative firms, unprofitable industries by many uncreative ones. Such unprofitable industries offer great opportunities for success.
Market dominance is vital to achieve success: to become more profitable, first win a large market share, then exploit the dominant position.	Market share should be seen as the reward for creating value and the lever to exploit advantage. Mature firms should not see market share as a way of creating advantage.
Leaders are immune from the competition of small followers: in international markets, only firms with large resources can win.	The important contests are those between different strategic approaches to the market. In these contests, small firms with limited resources can challenge the leaders.

----

drive up labor costs, excess capacity, government legislation, and so forth. The list is long and varied. Without doubt, these factors can be troublesome and have to be managed. But the business does not have to succumb to them.

Managers in mature firms pointed out to us the texts of many strategy writers who claimed that environmental factors influence firm performance. Some even cited Michael Porter, an acknowledged authority on the subject, who said:

> The state of competition in an industry depends on five basic competitive forces . . . The strength of these forces determines the ultimate profit potential in the industry, where profit is measured in terms of long-run return on invested capital. . . . the forces range from intense in industries like tires, paper, and steel, where no firm earns spectacular returns, to relatively mild like oil-field equipment and services, cosmetics and toiletries— where high returns are quite common.[4]

While Porter adds that the forces affecting profitability can be modified, and that firms can influence them, many have taken these words to mean (incorrectly) that choice of industry matters. When it is pointed out to managers in mature firms that one or two competitors are doing well, the response is usually "They are lucky," "It's not really true," or "Their success is temporary." These managers do not seem to appreciate that looking for profitable sectors is usually a waste of time and that choosing good strategies is far more important.

For a business to rejuvenate, it must learn to ride the waves of industry misfortunes, not be sunk by them. Managers in dynamic business understand that industry forces are important to comprehend, but that the negative ones can be overcome by appropriate strategies. Managers in mature businesses feel imprisoned and powerless. The issue is not merely one of perception; it is also a question of economic reality.

The naive notion of there being "better" or "worse" environments received its first major body blow in the late 1980s and early 1990s, when firms were forced to reassess their diversification moves of the 1970s and early 1980s. Many firms that had failed in one industry had diversified into another sector on the basis of industry attractiveness without proper regard to the match of their capabilities with the challenges posed by the new sectors. They ingenuously thought that mastery of a new sector would be simple. Such views were even more remarkable when it was obvious that the firms' managers had not mastered their previous environment. The consequences were often disastrous; successful entry proved much harder than originally imagined. Now we are seeing much unbundling of these early "mistakes."

In contrast, managers of dynamic firms realize the difficulties of diversification. They realize that mastery of one sector may help a move into another, but that success is not guaranteed. The new sector may have different economics, require new skills and capabilities and new understanding. They certainly appreciate that notions of "attractive" and "unattractive" industries are not the basis for creating value and strategy formulation.

The statistical evidence clearly shows that the firm is critical and the industry hardly matters at all. Many economists have looked at the data on business unit performance, their samples ranging from small ad hoc surveys to big data bases. A brief survey of some of this work appears in Exhibit 2.2. One of the best data bases, that developed by the U.S. Federal Trade Commission, is comprehensive and carefully constructed. Richard Rumelt analyzed these data, and his results are as instructive as they are simple. He assessed the relative importance of four factors: the importance of industry or sector choice; the importance of firm factors—strategy; the role of ownership; and the role of unexplained factors, including luck.

Rumelt's findings, reported in Table 2.1, may startle the reader.[5] He found little support for the notion that the choice of industry is important. Only 8.3 percent of the differences in profitability between one business unit and another can be related to the choice of industry. By implication, more than 90 percent of profitability variations are not explained by the choice of industry, and at least half appear to be attributable to the choice of strategy. Put simply, the correct choice of strategy appears to be at least five times more important than the correct choice of industry.

Readers may be skeptical of the relevance of the statistical data, which are an average over many businesses in many sectors. While willing to accept that, in general, industry factors may be unimportant,

Table 2.1 Percentage of business units' profitability explained by industry and strategy factors

Choice of industry	8.3%
Choice of strategy	46.4%
Parent company	0.8%
Not explained—random	44.5%

Source: Abstracted from Richard Rumelt, "How Much Does Industry Matter?" Strategic Management Journal 12, March 1991: 167–186.

EXHIBIT 2.2   THE ROLE OF INDUSTRY FACTORS DETERMINING FIRM PERFORMANCE

In 1951, Joe Bain argued that some industries had features that made them inherently more profitable than others. An economist by background, and one of the founders of the field of industrial organization, he statistically correlated the profitability of firms with their kind of industry. He found that some industries, characterized by high concentration, that is, few important players, were more profitable than others, which had low concentration. Bain's results, first published in the *Quarterly Journal of Economics* in August 1951, sparked a mountain of further work and debate.

The debate has had two parts: over whether there is an industry effect and what its implications are. After years of extensive research by more than a hundred economists, it has become clear that there was at best a small statistical relationship between profits of a business unit and its industry. Some early work had indicated that industry effects could be as large as 20 percent; that is, one-fifth of the difference between the performance of business in one industry versus another could be ascribed to choice of industry. More recently, better-quality data and better statistical work have shown that the size of the effect was smaller. Lately, there have been two important studies on U.S. data, representing the culmination of much previous work. One was that undertaken by Richard Schmalensee and published in the *American Economic Review* in 1975. Using data collected by the U.S. Federal Trade Commission, he argued that choice of industry contributed some 14 percent to the performance of the business. His results were based on studying data from a single year across a wide number of U.S. industries. Richard Rumelt expanded Schmalensee's data to include other years. In his article "How Much Does Industry Matter?" (*Strategic Management Journal,* March 1991), he showed that the choice of industry explained at best 8.3 percent of a business unit's profitability. His results seem more compelling, for Rumelt looked at effects over time, albeit a rather short period of four years. Across the water in the United Kingdom, John Cubbin ("Is It Better to Be a Weak Firm in a Strong Industry, or a Strong Firm in a Weak Industry?" Centre for Business Strategy, London Business School, no. 49.) was also concerned with examining industry effects over time. In contrast to Rumelt, he used thirty years to examine industry effects. He found that over this longer period there were no persistent industry effects.

The fact that there are profitable and unprofitable industries does not necessarily mean that it is choice of industry which yields high profits. On the contrary, the Austrian and Chicago schools of economists, including Nobel Prize winner Milton Friedman, have asserted that the causality goes the other way. They suggest that some industries seem more profitable than others because profitable firms are unevenly distributed across industries. What makes firms profitable is not the industries they chose to be in, but the strategies they follow. Those industries which are apparently unprofitable are populated by large numbers of firms that are not efficient or innovative. If some industries seem to be more profitable than others, it is because more of their firms are creative, innovative, and successful.

----

they wish to believe that in their own industry the situation may be "different." We examine further arguments to support our point.

MATURE INDUSTRIES OFFER GOOD PROSPECTS FOR SUCCESS

We think that managers of mature businesses need to rethink. Low-growth "mature" markets or troubled industries may offer greater chances of rewards than ones that appear to be glamorous and profitable. Our reasoning is simple. In general, more profitable industries are those which are populated by more imaginative and more creative businesses. These businesses create an environment that attracts custom, grows the industry revenues, and makes the industry attractive. But creative and innovative businesses are also more fiercely competitive. To win in such environments may be difficult, as the pace of change may be rapid and the minimum standards high. In contrast, many less profitable industries are populated by sleepy, uncreative businesses that fail to innovate. In such environments, the potential for success by a creative newcomer may be greater. The demands of competition may be less exacting, and the potential for attracting customers better. (See Exhibit 2.3.)

Managers in mature firms must realize that businesses do not have to follow products in their life cycle. We all know that products mature and decline; the horse and buggy, although enjoying a minor revival, does not have the popularity that it did a century ago. But products do not define a business; a business can enjoy a long life by adjusting.

For most organizations, decline in demand is the signal of lost competitiveness. In the automobile industry, the sales of European and American producers have been declining in recent years because of locally changing conditions and better, stronger foreign competition,

----

EXHIBIT 2.3   THE INDUSTRY-PROFIT RELATIONSHIP

Managers of mature firms believe that the causal direction of influences on profits is as follows:

> Factors affecting the industry
> $\rightarrow$ the level of firm profits

Managers of dynamic firms believe that:

> Innovation by firms
> $\rightarrow$ firm profits
> $\rightarrow$ industry profits

----

not because of a decline in the product. The global market for cars is booming, with rapid expansion in developing and former communist countries. Automobile producers in Western Europe have discovered that such growing segments of demand as those in eastern and southern Europe can be profitably served if firms adapt.

Declining demand for a product is rare and forces businesses to create new competencies to serve related markets. This is not disastrous. Many horse-and-buggy carriage builders have evolved into highly successful service stations and farm equipment dealers.[6]

Most mature markets can be revived with better products and services. Before Xerox, the copying industry was stable and based on photography or thermal processes. The industry must have seemed to some to be mature. After xerography was developed, the market boomed. When the market appeared to mature again, the entry of Canon with small photocopiers also increased the size of the market as unexploited segments were developed. Sales of large mainframe computers have declined in recent years because of the surge in sales of powerful desktop personal computers, and smart firms have extended their capabilities from making one type of product to making another. Laptop computers have given a new boost to the computer industry. Similarly, Walkman boosted the tape recorder industry—and also transformed it. Until the entrance of Honda the motorcycle market was in steady decline. With Honda's innovations—new bicycles with attractive features sold at reasonable prices—the market revived.

Managers of mature firms must realize that businesses can be transformed with new products, new processes, new service delivery systems, and new strategies. We suggest that the growth rate of an industry is a reflection of the kinds of businesses in it, not the intrinsic nature of the environment. We do not wish to overstate our case, but rather force the reader to focus attention away from the mentality of labeling and prejudging opportunities based only on historic industry performance.

FIRMS CAN SUCCEED IN HOSTILE ENVIRONMENTS

William Cook is an old, established firm that makes steel castings. Its story reinforces the point that organizations can be successful in even the most hostile environments. It also sheds light on the relationship between industry conditions, firm action, and value creation. After a number of boom years that ended in 1978, most British steel casting businesses were operating at a loss. Industry sales were declining, there was excess capacity, rationalization schemes had been tried and had

31

failed and foreign competition was emerging with great intensity. At this time Cook's resources were extremely limited. In less than ten years, Cook moved from being a barely profitable business, with only a 2 percent share of its industry, to a highly profitable business, earning an excellent rate of return, delivering high-quality service to its customers, and having more than a 30 percent share of its industry. Its actions stimulated new competitors to enter the industry to copy and rival Cook. Partly on account of all the activities of these organizations, sales stopped declining, excess capacity disappeared, and the industry looks more attractive. But, as we explain below, the sequence of events was from firm action to industry improvement, not the other way around.

In 1981, Andrew Cook took over the management of William Cook. The situation did not look good: the firm was only a small player in a big-company industry. Four rivals—F.H. Lloyd, the Weir Group, the Davy Corporation, and British Steel (then state owned)—controlled 60 percent of industry output. There were other, medium-size firms and many small firms like William Cook. The outlook was appalling. The industry had always been cyclical, but between 1975 and 1983, orders and output fell, in an unprecedented fashion, by more than 60 percent, from 268,000 metric tons to 115,000 metric tons. The average industry margin had dropped from a healthy 9 percent of sales to zero, with many large and small firms showing losses. Excess capacity was everywhere evident, for many firms had expanded at the height of the previous boom (see Table 2.2).

In the view of Andrew Cook, most firms in the industry had only themselves to blame for their problems. At the time he said, "In the 1970s, the industry was grossly overmanned; costs were rising and only world demand sustained it. . . . The slump was good for the foundry industry. Many companies were not fit to survive."

In 1983, at a time when capacity was more than double the level of industry sales, and its rivals were either cutting back investment or

Table 2.2 Output, capacity utilization, productivity, and profitability in steel castings

	1975	1977	1979	1981	1983	1985	1987
Output	268	246	192	155	115	118	122
Capacity utilization	100%	93%	76%	66%	58%	61%	72%
Productivity	12.6	12.1	11.5	12.3	13.4	15.7	20.3
Profitability	9.0	7.5	−2.0	−1.0	0.0	−2.7	n/a

Note: Output is thousands of metric tons, productivity is output in tons per person, and profitability is profit before tax as a percentage of sales.

closing, Cook embarked on an investment program to increase efficiency, quality, and capacity. Its stated objective was to challenge the conventional norms of the industry, especially those held by the industry leaders. Rivals thought that Cook was unwise and predicted disaster. Its plans seemed especially dangerous because its resources were limited. Although it had a stock market quotation, its shares had performed so badly that there was little opportunity to raise cash by this route and it was in a poor position to raise its debt level. Raising prices would have been impossible; its record on quality was not good, and it certainly did not have the image of a Mercedes-Benz or an IBM among its customers. Neither was it a leader technologically; it had no secret processes that would grant it an everlasting stream of income. Its ambition and resolution to win was high, a factor which, we argue in later chapters, was important.

Conventional thinking would have suggested that Cook either milk the business or go for a high-value differentiated niche. In the castings industry, the traditional measure of differentiation was the value per ton of output, and convention suggested that there were three segments: high-value steel alloys, basic alloys, and the casting of unalloyed or basic steel. Many firms participate in the higher-valued segments. In 1981, at the beginning of its path of rejuvenation, Cook focused on the lowest-valued segment of the market. (Out of a sample of twenty-five foundries comprising more than 70 percent of the industry, Cook's value per metric ton was £931, at the bottom.)

Cook's decision to remain in the lowest price segment of the business was coupled with the decision to invest to improve company capability and quality at that low end of the market. Cook emphasized service to its customers and ensuring the right quality. These two dimensions, now commonly recognized, were not self-evident in the early 1980s. Its modest investment program aimed at improving quality and customer service yielded results very quickly. In 1984 Cook's profits rose to 10 percent of sales, while the rest of the industry recorded losses averaging 1.6 percent of sales and continued to suffer from excess capacity.

Cook did not stop there: it continued to invest in quality and service improvement. In 1985 it was the first business in the industry to win the U.K. government's quality award BS5750, and it had put its own operations onto a secure footing. In 1986 Cook's management felt able to expand and made a bid for the Hyde foundries, about the same size as Cook, which failed. Cook then bid for Weir's foundries, the largest in the industry. Industry members were amazed at the audacity of such a small player's seeking to take over the largest operator: most thought that Cook was mad to buy further into the troubled industry. Cook's bid succeeded, and the management set about rationalizing the Weir business, closing some parts and investing heavily in others. In 1988 Cook again bid for Hyde and this time secured the prize. By the end of 1988, Cook was the largest business in the industry, recording even better profits.

The Cook story provides an excellent illustration of how businesses can become successful in a hostile environment. Before Cook transformed itself, the castings industry was unprofitable. It is arguable that much of the lack of profitability was owing to the existing businesses' inability to compete. Because the companies could not satisfy customer requirements at a low price, orders shrank as customers were forced to buy abroad or use substitute products. Cook's improvement of quality and service levels saved the customers money and so increased the demand for the product. Like Banc One, Cook understood that features such as quality, reliability, and service could also reduce its own costs. Thus Cook generated a double advantage—higher value and lower cost. When others in the industry finally realized what Cook had done, they changed, too. They sought to catch up to Cook and invoked intense battles. The fortunes of the industry are being transformed, customers are buying, and demand has stopped declining. The causes of the transformation were principally the actions of the firms.[7]

LARGE MARKET SHARE IS THE REWARD, NOT THE CAUSE OF SUCCESS

We believe that many managers are mistaken in the value they ascribe to market share. Enlarging market share should be seen as beneficial for a dynamic firm that wishes to leverage advantages it has won, but increasing market share is not the route to rejuvenating a mature firm. Banc One and Cook achieved significant positions in their industries after they had built new capabilities and new routines.

Cook's successful domination of the U.K. industry was the consequence, not the cause of its rejuvenation. In the early 1980s, Cook's business, like that of its rivals, was in bad shape. The sequence was that management first changed its own organization, seeking to improve quality and efficiency, simultaneously reducing cost. It was content to operate with a small share of the highly competitive "low-price" segment of the market. Only when the new philosophy was ingrained, new capabilities built, new resources won, value created, and profitability established did it set about growing rapidly. Mergers were an important part of Cook's growth, and in each merger Cook set about changing the acquired business, importing Cook's best practice to leverage the benefits it had achieved.

Banc One is well known for its aggressive attitude toward growth and mergers, but this attitude came only after the organization had established its superiority. Banc One's philosophy was to first develop its capabilities, then to grow them. When Banc One undertook a merger, it was clear that the merged organizations had to change to fit the philosophy of their dynamic parent. This has been relatively easy, as the partners recognized that Banc One has many superior routines. Banc One also has a program for ensuring that the skills of its newly merged partners are learned and integrated into the rest of the Banc One network and that the cycle of improvement does not stop. It recognizes that advantages must constantly be augmented. As with all the rejuvenated firms we studied, growth is seen as a way of exploiting advantages in the virtuous cycle of improvement illustrated in Exhibit 2.4.

The essence of the policies of our rejuvenators was different from

----

EXHIBIT 2.4   THE ATTITUDE OF DYNAMIC AND MATURE FIRMS TOWARD GROWTH AND COMPETITIVENESS

For creative organizations we see an upward spiral.

Dynamic and rejuvenating business

→   Internal change and value-added

→   Merger and internal growth

→   More change

→   Greater value-added

→   Number one position

For organizations that are not creative, we see a downward path.

Mature business

→   Growth by merger and internal expansion

→   Reinforce old ways of thinking

→   Declining competitiveness

→   Lost position

----

those adopted by the mature businesses we studied. Some of the latter had sought a way out of their troubles by merging with other mature firms rather than tackling the root causes of their problems. The consequence was to create a bigger, still mature organization with greater difficulties. Generally, these firms found that they were on a path of decline. Their growth preceded rejuvenation and had the effect of making the necessary change harder. (See Exhibit 2.4).

Our views on the role of market share run counter to much of the literature on strategy and what is believed in many corporate boardrooms (see Exhibit 2.5). It is commonly but incorrectly held that being number one or number two in an industry gives a business unique advantages, which are greatest in industries characterized by slow growth. With a large market share, it is often argued, a business can achieve lower costs and charge higher prices than its rivals. In slow-growth markets, it is said, this may prove to be a decisive factor. Such thinking ignores the importance of innovation.

EXHIBIT 2.5   MARKET SHARE AND PROFITABILITY

There is a lively debate on the role of market share in strategy. The first question is, Does the evidence really show that high-market-share firms are better at creating added value? And the second asks, Is high market share the consequence of increased added value, or the cause or both?

The early debates on market share reach back a long way. Alfred Marshall noted that some processes, such as power generation and communication networks, had the property that a single operation could often serve a local market.[1] This when coupled with other factors such as government licenses could lead to a single firm's monopolizing the market, to the detriment of consumers.

Barry Hedley and The Boston Consulting Group are generally credited with first writing about the scale effects that may exist in all industries which could affect the choice of strategy.[2] In their work they examined the role of the experience curve, suggesting that firms which had the largest cumulative output (usually but not always the largest-market-share player) would in general find it easier to exploit the experience curve.[3]

Robert Buzzell and Bradley Gale are generally credited with popularizing the value of market share in strategy, although it too has many earlier antecedents.[4] They note that large market share can have a beneficial influence on profitability through many triggers. It can reduce costs owing to scale or experience effects in production, service delivery, logistics, and marketing. It may allow a firm to charge higher prices, because the service or product may seem intrinsically less risky to consumers, and entrants may be discouraged.

In trying to identify the size of the effects of market share, the work of Robert Buzzell and Bradley Gale is most accessible. Using the PIMS data base drawn from a large sample of business units across a range of industries, they asserted the existence of a strong relationship between relative market share and profitability. Their figures, cited below, suggest that a firm which has first rank in an industry is more than twice as profitable as one of fourth rank.

36

Industry rank (by market share)	1	2	3	4	5 or below
Pre-tax profits/sales (index: Rank 1 = 100)	100	72	56	43	35

Source: Adapted from Robert D. Buzzell and Bradley T. Gale, *The PIMS Principles: Linking Strategy to Performance.* Copyright © 1987 by the Free Press, a Division of MacMillan, Inc. Reprinted with permission of the publisher.

As mentioned in the text, the relationship is not statistically robust. The evidence suggests that only a small amount of the variability of profits (the usual way economists try to capture value-added) is explained by market share. The bigger problem lies in interpreting the meaning of the relationship. Is it successful firms which grow or is it that large share firms become more successful? This question cannot be answered by simple statistical relationships.[5] Intuition tells us that dynamic firms experience rising market share and value creation. They simultaneously grow their capabilities and their market share as a consequence of their superiority. Our evidence suggests that mature firms would do well to consider improving their capability before improving their market share.

Notes:
1. Alfred Marshall, *Industry and Trade: A Study of Industrial Techniques and Business Organizations and of Their Influences on the Conditions of Various Classes and Nations,* and *Principles of Economics* (London: Macmillan, 1961).
2. The Boston Consulting Group, *Perspectives on Experience* (Boston: The Boston Consulting Group, 1968).
3. The dynamics of entry and profitability under various scenarios to do with learning and experience effects has received much attention, including modeling by writers such as Spence (see, for instance, A.M. Spence, "Entry Capacity, Investment and Oligopolistic Pricing," *Bell Journal of Economics* 8, 1977: 534–544).
4. Robert D. Buzzell and Bradley T. Gale, *The PIMS Principles: Linking Strategy to Performance* (New York: Free Press, 1987). See, for instance, F.M. Scherer, *Industrial Market Structure and Economic Performance* (Skokie, Ill.: Rand McNally, 1973), for a review.
5. The work of Rumelt and Wensley is most suggestive, for they find that changes in market share are positively associated with changes in profits. R. Rumelt and R. Wensley, *In Search of the Market Share Effect,* Proceedings of the Academy of Management, August 1981, pp. 1–5.

These widespread false beliefs appear in many guises. At one extreme are chief executives who say, "We are only interested in industries where we hold a number one or number two position." Such statements, if unaccompanied by an emphasis on innovation, give the wrong signal that high share leads to success. At a more mundane level, managers are encouraged to write in their plans, "We should dominate the industry and seek success by capturing a number one position." Again, such statements are dangerous when the writer and reader believe that share is the source, not the measure of success.

Those who advocate that large market share leads to greater profits point to the importance of several causal factors. First, large market share gives rise to the need to deliver large volumes of the service or product. Increased volume in turn gives rise to opportunities for cost savings by exploiting scale economies in production, service delivery, logistics, and marketing. Second, large market share permits a firm to benefit from experience or learning effects, which also lower costs. Third, large market share may allow a firm to charge higher prices. A product or service with a large share may seem intrinsically less risky to consumers. Finally, with a large market share, new entrants may be discouraged because they perceive the incumbent to have a substantial commitment to their industry through perceived or actual sunk costs.

From the view of mature firms, it is important to point out that these supposed benefits of large share are overrated. As we explain in the next chapter, the way out of maturity is in innovation, and innovators realize that new ways of competing can achieve their advantages by new approaches that do not necessarily need large market share. However, those with new approaches may win market share, in which case large share is a reward for success. This Darwinian view of the market suggests that the competitive process is one in which success goes to the firm that successfully innovates.

Statistical evidence supports our view: in a large proportion of the industries studied, the firm with largest rank is *not* the most profitable. Often the picture is quite different; indeed according to the statistics published in Robert Buzzell and Bradley Gale—two of the strongest advocates of the value of market share—only 4 percent of the differences in profitability of one business unit versus another could be explained by differences in market share.[8] Richard Schmalensee, in his extensive study of more than 400 U.S. manufacturing firms, found that less than 2 percent of the variations in profitability between one business and another could be explained by differences in market share.[9] Market share effects appear to be relatively unimportant across a wide sample of industries.

Growing market share is not a panacea for an organization's ills, even in mature slow-growing markets. The belief that gaining market share leads to greater profitability comes from confusing cause and effect. Many successful business have a large market share, but the causality is usually from success to share, not the other way around. Successful businesses often, but not always, grow because they have discovered an overwhelming source of competitive advantage, such as quality at low cost. Such advantages can be used to displace even the most entrenched incumbents.

SMALL-SHARE FIRMS CAN CHALLENGE INTERNATIONAL PLAYERS

While growing market share may be unwise before rejuvenation, should mature firms try to hang on to their market share because it has some value? The stories of Banc One and Cook show that firms with small market share can grow advantages and win. The story of Hotpoint, a moderate-size player with less than 5 percent of the European appliance market, shows how a firm can even diminish its market share and still rejuvenate in the face of intense international competition. This is a theme to which we return at length in the latter part of the book.

In the early 1960s, the appliance industry of Europe was dominated by the Italians and the Germans. Five Italian entrepreneurial firms—Zanussi, Zoppas, Ignis, Indesit, and Candy—had grown in two decades to capture more than 40 percent of all European production and sales. These Italian firms were highly profitable for many years; some, such as Ignis (acquired by Philips), Zanussi, and Indesit, had established commanding brand positions with substantial European market shares. The other major players in this period were the German firms AEG, Bauknecht, and Bosch-Siemens. Others in Europe had either established niche positions or else, like Hotpoint, were doing badly; with poor products and poor cost control, they were suffering from severe competitive pressures.

The 1980s saw a new era, and the once successful leading firms found themselves in some difficulty. The profits of Indesit and Zanussi plunged (see Table 2.3), and several leading German firms, especially AEG and Bauknecht, were near bankruptcy. The problems extended to the United Kingdom, where Hoover, the largest firm, also found itself in trouble.

The managers of many of the poorly-performing organizations blamed "industry forces" for their malaise. They commissioned studies to examine the industry's economic circumstances and encouraged government departments to do the same. The main thrust of their findings was typical of many similar reports for other businesses doing badly in other industries. According to experts, the appliance industry suffered from excess capacity, barriers to exit for losing businesses, poor demand prospects, too many competitors, import competition, and subsidies.

The experts were right in what they saw: the excess capacity in the appliance industry in the 1980s was severe, demand forecasts had been too optimistic, and projected demand growth had not materialized. To make matters worse, many competitors had increased capacity to take account of the forecasted growth, so supply had grown even faster than expected demand. None of this would have been a problem if the excess

Table 2.3 Europe's largest troubled appliance firms

	Profitability		
Name	1974–1979	1980–1984	Subsequent events
Zanussi (includes Zoppas)	9.6	0.5	Bought by Electrolux in 1984
Philips (includes Ignis)	4.2	3.6	Bought by Whirlpool in 1989
Indesit	8.4	−5.2	Bought by Merloni in 1987
AEG	profits	losses	Electrolux bought 10 percent in 1992 and control in 1993
Hoover	6.2	1.3	Bought by Chicago Pacific[1]
Bauknecht	profits	losses	Bought by Philips in 1982

Note: Profitability is profit before tax and interest as a percentage of sales.
[1]Bought by Maytag (United States) in 1989.
Source: C.W.F. Baden-Fuller and J.M. Stopford, "Globalisation Frustrated," *Strategic Management Journal* 12, no. 7 (1991).

supply had exited from the market, but it had not. The barriers to exit were clear: loss-making organizations owned plant that had little resale value and saw no reason to quit. Moreover, quitting involved write-offs and payments to workers who lost their jobs. Only rich organizations could afford these expenses; most of those showing losses did not have the resources to quit. The natural barriers to exit were compounded by government policy. Since the cost of unemployment is a local or state rather than EC-level issue, each country wished to export the competitive problem or hide it by subsidizing local producers in the hope that other firms would quit.

Although the excess capacity provoked price-cutting and low margins, the prices were not low enough to keep out imports from outside the European market area. Spanish and East bloc firms continued to expand their efforts to sell in the EC market. The reports typically claimed that Spain benefited from low wages, while the East bloc countries had the benefits of both low wages and low capital costs. By any account, the reports made grim reading, and managers of most businesses used them to justify their poor profits. There were exceptions.

Chaim Schreiber at Hotpoint refused to accept the verdict that it was "someone else's fault that we are doing badly." He saw the problems of the industry as rooted in managerial failures, failure to build a product consumers wanted, failure to produce efficiently and distribute efficiently. Schreiber came to Hotpoint in 1974, just as the industry was going through its lowest point. He and his team rejected such previous beliefs of the industry as the importance of capturing a large sales volume. The top management team decided to cut out all sales to Continental Europe and focus effort exclusively on the United Kingdom. This reduced the sales and share of the firm in the European market—the measure used by key competitors such as Philips. In the United Kingdom, Hotpoint did not retreat to a high-price or specialist niche but concentrated its energies in selling to the mass market in competition with the other major British firm, Hoover, and the leading Continental firms from Italy and Scandinavia. This was no easy market, for prices were low and margins keen.[10]

Hotpoint's rejuvenation was initially based on reducing costs and increasing quality and flexibility. As is later documented in detail, there was first only modest investment; in time the investment grew. Ultimately, Hotpoint was able to prove that even with a small share of the European market, it could achieve lower costs, better flexibility, and better service to the customer than the strongest competitor. Hotpoint showed that adding extra value could be achieved without first increasing market share.

Under Schreiber's leadership, Hotpoint proved that all the doom-and-gloom assertions made in the public commentaries were wrong. The firm showed that the excess capacity was really "outdated capacity" and that the low-cost imports were a signal of the inefficiency of existing producers unwilling to change. The price wars were the consequence of businesses continuing to sell models that were designed ten years earlier and had not kept pace with consumer wants. The subsidies merely propped up the inefficient; they did not threaten those which did their job properly.

Schreiber's leadership at Hotpoint was like fresh air to a stale and smoke-filled room. Hotpoint was one of the first European appliance firms to set itself the task of transformation. Like Cook in steel castings, Hotpoint did things differently, investing where others were cutting, building novel production lines and new distribution systems, and launching new products. Also like Cook, Hotpoint did not create its success in a small niche, for it was competing directly with Hoover, Indesit, and Zanussi in the mass markets of the United Kingdom. Hotpoint's transformation of profits was dramatic, as Table 2.4 indicates.

Hotpoint triggered change throughout the appliance industry. In every case, organizations went through major upheavals. By the end of the 1980s, the industry had been transformed. Old management had been removed and new managers had arrived. The structure of ownership had also altered. The resulting combinations had forced new

41

Table 2.4 Hotpoint's performance

	1975–1979	1980–1984	1985–1991
Profit/sales (percent)	2.3	8.9	9.8

Note: Profit is before tax and interest.

groups: Electrolux (including Zanussi, Thorn DA, White), Whirlpool (including Philips and Bauknecht), Bosch-Siemens, Thomson, Merloni (including Scholes and Indesit), and last but not least, GEC-GE (including Hotpoint, GE Europe, Creda, and the British appliance firm, Cannon).

BUILDING RESOURCES AND COMPETITIVE ADVANTAGE

Just as small-share firms can win, so can firms with modest resources, even when battling against international competition. In understanding the role of resources, skills, and competencies in a competitive battle, it is important to distinguish between the quantity of resources and their appropriateness. The "resource school" of strategic thinking rightly points out that mobilizing the resource base is a critical element in an organization's success (see Exhibit 2.6). Building and learning to deploy that base properly are elusive skills, particularly for a mature firm.

Lucky mature firms, such as Walt Disney in the 1980s, have been endowed with magnificent resources left by previous excellent management. The task for these firms is to build competencies to exploit the resources. Such a task requires a new approach to the market with the building of complementary skills and capabilities so that brands are fully exploited, intangible assets are utilized, and the people are motivated and directed to work more effectively. Managers in these firms can move along a path of rejuvenation with innovative approaches, confident that absence of resources will not inhibit their program of action.

Having substantial resources is no guarantee of success. General Motors and Ford had large financial reserves, outstanding brand reputations, excellent dealer networks, and impressive research and development laboratories. For all their resources, they are still unable to master the challenge posed by their Japanese competitors, which until recently were less well endowed. They have found it hard to discard the past and build new skills. Even the relatively poorly resourced Korean producers

----

EXHIBIT 2.6   RESOURCE-BASED THEORIES OF THE FIRM

The resource-based theories of competitive advantage, such as that of David Teece, Gary Pisano, and Amy Schuen,[1] stress the role of resources, skills, and capabilities in determining a firm's long-run health. Basic resources include access to finance, the existence of machines, skilled, intelligent employees, knowledge of products, processes, and systems, and reputation. In the battles between organizations in markets, those with superior resources appear to be at an advantage.

However, having more resources is neither necessary nor sufficient for success. Robert Grant, in "The Resource-based Theory of Competitive Advantage," points out that many well-endowed firms find it difficult to exploit their resource bases.[2] For years the hidden assets of Walt Disney went unexploited; only when new management arrived and set about building on the resource base in the mid-1980s did the company's declining fortunes revive. IBM is clearly better resourced than many of its rivals, but this has not guaranteed it value creation. It struggles to deploy its resources effectively.[3]

Combining resources is what leads to value creation. This ability lies in the skill base of the employees, the hidden routines, the systems, and the "culture" of the business. Its effect can be powerful. As C.K. Prahalad and Gary Hamel point out, competencies such as Sony's ability to miniaturize electronics or Canon's capabilities in optics, imaging, and microprocessor controls are key to those firms' success.[4]

The ability to compete does not require large resources, but rather effective combinations and capacity to create from within. Thus it was that Microsoft rose to become one of the world's largest computer firms, Wal-Mart one of the most successful retailers, and Banc One one of the most successful bank holding companies.

Notes:
1. David Teece, Gary Pisano, and Amy Schuen, "Dynamic Capabilities and Strategic Management," Working Paper, University of California at Berkeley, 1992.
2. Robert Grant, "The Resource-based Theory of Competitive Advantage," *California Management Review* 33, no. 3, 1991: 114–134.
3. A point also made by G. Stalk, P. Evans, and L.E. Schulman in "Competing on Capabilities: The New Rules of Corporate Strategy," *Harvard Business Review*, March–April 1992: 57–69.
4. C.K. Prahalad and Gary Hamel, "The Core Competence of the Corporation," *Harvard Business Review*, May–June 1993: 79–91.

----

have done better than some Western producers, making the point clear that resources alone are not sufficient for success.

More commonly, mature businesses find that their brands and reputations are of dubious value because of past poor product quality. Their intangible assets of skills and capabilities are appropriate for a bygone age, better suited to a museum than the competitive world, and their other assets have, like the family silver, long since been sold to pay debts or satisfy the needs of other stakeholders. For these organizations, we say there is hope. Renewal is possible.

Richardson is an exemplar of an organization able to grow and deploy its own resources.[11] In the late 1960s, Richardson was a small cutlery firm in Sheffield, England. It was not profitable, had neither famous brand name nor financial resources, and while its share of the U.K. market was small, its share of the world market was insignificant. In a little more than two decades, it has reached the number one world position in kitchen knives against competition from the Far East. Its resource base is formidable, and most of its resources were developed in-house. It has demonstrated a capacity to renew and reconstruct from within.

The background to the story, later discussed in more detail, is as follows.[12] In the late nineteenth century, the Sheffield cutlery industry was the best and strongest in the world. A large exporter of knives and forks to all parts of the world, it had an enviable reputation for quality. In the twentieth century the situation changed, and by the early 1970s, Sheffield's position had declined greatly. The industry represented only a marginal producer on a world stage dominated by Japan, Germany, the United States, and Far Eastern manufacturers in Japan, Hong Kong, and Korea.

U.K. producers blamed some of their problems on unfair competition. Steel, the principal ingredient in the production of knives, cost more in the European Community (EC) than elsewhere. Because the EC cartel supported the steel producers, the 1978 price of chrome steel in the United Kingdom was £807 a metric ton, whereas similar steel was available in South Korea for £487 a metric ton. In this period, steel represented about 40 percent of the producers' sale price. At one time, the landed price for cutlery in the United Kingdom was lower per ton than the cost of buying raw unprocessed steel.

Richardson was clearly in a disadvantageous position to lead the battle against foreign competition. Although its workers were loyal, their skills were in outdated technologies and methods of operation; the managerial systems creaked badly or were nonexistent; the knowledge base of the market and the horizon of new technologies was sadly lacking. The plants were old and the customers dissatisfied. Richardson could not even rely on the local infrastructure because its immediate environment contained many hopeless businesses that were losing money and international competitive edge. By all normal accounts, the situation seemed hopeless. Many of Richardson's U.K. competitors had subcontracted production from low-cost overseas sources to become marketing specialists, while others retreated to craft niches, selling low volumes at high prices. Neither strategy of appeasement seemed durable.

Richardson took a different approach. Its managers did not believe that the demise of the U.K. industry was inevitable. Despite the twin handicaps of high input prices and no established brand name, they chose to fight back. They noted that between 20 and 30 percent of imported knives came from Japan, about 10 percent from France, 10 percent from Switzerland, and more than 5 percent from Germany. These countries had neither a wage rate advantage nor always a raw material price advantage. Most continental suppliers, however, enjoyed strong consumer brand names, built up over many years of expensive advertising. Richardson's most severe competition came from Hong Kong and South Korea, which had advantages of both low wages and low steel prices.

Bryan Upton, Richardson's managing director, and his managers believed that the importers' advantages were not overwhelming and that the British businesses failed to invest in the right technologies and to make a decent product, sell it right, or present it better, and crucially failed to innovate. "They did not deserve to survive," Upton said.

Richardson rose like a phoenix from the ruins of the U.K. industry by doing what the other organizations should have done. It invested in human and physical capital to improve first the process by which the product was made. The small initial investments—the resources were limited—were directed at both reducing costs and improving customer service. Remarkable progress was made quite quickly, and the better profits were reinvested in the business. The approach had to be nontraditional because of capital shortage. The managers combined optical, electronic, and mechanical technologies simply and cheaply. They also reorganized the flow of the work, especially in support services and between the traditional functions. In the course of time, Richardson developed better ways of making cheaper knives and became one of the world's lower-cost producers of blank knives. Simultaneous investments in customer service through speed and flexibility served to cement the competitive advantage over its British and foreign competitors. It chose to compete in the "rapid response sector," where distance placed Far Eastern suppliers at a disadvantage. This, however, was not enough. Richardson went on to innovate products, including the famous Laser knife, and new marketing techniques. By the early 1990s, it had captured 15 percent of the world's knife market to be among the world's leaders. It is hard to summarize all the multiplicity of skills and resources that the organization built over a comparatively short period, but Exhibit 2.7 gives a flavor.

COMPETING RECIPES

Organizations looking to rejuvenate should realize that the winners of today's battles have often been able to overcome their disadvantages

---

EXHIBIT 2.7 THE RESOURCES AND CAPABILITIES CREATED BY RICHARDSON

Resources	Capabilities
Specialized machinery	Ability to design and build machines in-house
Multiskilled labor force	Ability to adapt generalized machines
Reputation for quality	Ability to make high-quality products at extremely low
Strong brand identity	unit costs
Distribution network	Ability to respond rapidly to customer orders
Overseas factories	Ability to create and lead fashion
	Ability to create and cope with variety
	Ability to understand and then sell into diverse world markets

---

by deploying new combinations of skills and competencies. They can become innovators and develop approaches to resolving their problems. In a competition among different approaches, the best-endowed organizations do not always win. Just as large armies can be defeated by small ones, and as David slew Goliath, so in the corporate sphere we see battles between giants and upstarts sometimes resulting in victory for organizations with modest resources.[13] Even in so-called mature industries, where incumbent strategies have evolved and been honed over long periods, new ideas displace existing leaders.

Mature firms harbor prevailing beliefs about the sources of competitive advantages. These beliefs often come from a recognition of what has worked well in the past. When firms reach maturity, the beliefs can become folklore, or even a religion. Notions that some industries are intrinsically more profitable, that share is the source of added value, or that the scale of resources, not their deployment, is the way to win, have already been attacked.

Managers in mature firms believe that their sector allows them only a few fundamental choices, or generic strategies. These are typically described as being between a low-cost strategy or a differentiated strategy. The low-cost strategy involves the sacrifice of something—speed, variety, fashion, or even quality—in order to keep costs low, the lowest in the industry. In contrast, the high-cost, differentiated strategy involves focusing on the very factors ignored by the others. Advocates of generic strategy make an implicit or explicit assertion: that opposites cannot be reconciled. According to the generic strategists, it is not possible to have both low cost and high quality, or to be low cost and fashionable, or low cost and speedy. Trying to reconcile the opposites means being stuck in the middle. This, it is suggested, is the worst of both worlds.

For a mature firm, generic strategies are a misleading way to think about the strategic future. Rejuvenating and dynamic organizations are always striving to reconcile opposites. Banc One established its premier position by rejecting orthodoxy and emphasizing aspects hitherto neglected by industry leaders. Cook won in the steel casting industry by emphasizing quality and service to customers. Hotpoint emphasized variety and quality in its approach to both its retailers the final consumers. Richardson built a world position from nothing by combining quality, speed, variety, and fashion. As Chapter 3 makes clear, no single approach works well in all industries; rather, a multiple set of approaches is necessary. The real competitive battles are fought between firms with a diversity of approaches to the market.

NOTES

[1] Data as of the end of 1991.

[2] R. Teitelman, "The Magnificent McCoys," *Institutional Investor*, July 1991.

[3] There is a long tradition of economists, called variously the Austrian school or the Chicago school, which have held out these views against those of other universities. In strategy, this theme was first stressed with careful evidence by W.K. Hall in "Survival Strategies in a Hostile Environment," *Harvard Business Review*, September–October 1980: 75–85:

> Even a cursory analysis of the leading companies in the eight basic industries leads to an important observation: survival and prosperity are possible even when the business environment turns hostile and industry trends change from favorable to unfavorable. In this regard, the casual advice frequently offered to competitors in basic industries—that is, diversify, dissolve, or be prepared for below average returns—seems oversimplified and even erroneous.

[4] M.E. Porter, *Competitive Strategy* (New York: Free Press, 1980), pp. 3–4.

[5] R. Rumelt, "How Much Does Industry Matter?" *Strategic Management Journal* 12, March 1991: 167–186. Rumelt's article, like that of R. Schmalensee, "Do Markets Differ Much?," *American Economic Review* 75, 1985: 341–351, discusses business and industry effects. Business unit effects are the consequence of either intended or unintended strategy.

[6] P. Ghemawat, B. Nalebuff, and others have written on the correct strategies for declining products, examining the optimal timing for abandonment of plant, e.g., C.W.F. Baden-Fuller, ed., *Managing Excess Capacity* (Oxford: Basil Blackwell, 1990); P. Ghemawat and B. Nalebuff, "Exit," *Rand Journal of Economics* 16, no. 1, 1985: 184–194. Abandonment of product capacity does not mean death for the business unit. Some intriguing strategies for truly declining products are explored in K. Harrigan, *Strategies for Declining Business* (Lexington, Mass.: Lexington Books, 1980).

[7] Cook unwisely expanded into the United States, but found itself lacking capability and overstretched. While profitable, it has recently lost some momentum.

[8] R.D. Buzzell and B.T. Gale, *The Pims Principles* (New York: Free Press, 1987).

[9] Schmalensee, "Do Markets Differ Much?."

[10] For evidence on prices in the United Kingdom versus Europe, see C.W.F. Baden-Fuller

and J.M. Stopford, "Globalisation Frustrated," *Strategic Management Journal* 12, no. 7, 1991: 494–507.

[11] The story of Richardson was jointly researched with Robert Grant, and many details appear in R.M. Grant and C.W.F. Baden-Fuller, *The Richardson Sheffield Story*, London Business School Case Series, 2, 1987.

[12] I am grateful to Robert Grant for this information. See R.M. Grant and S. Downing, "The UK Cutlery Industry 1974–1982: A Study of Structural Adjustment, Business Strategies and Firm Performance," Working Paper, Centre for Business Strategy, London Business School, 1985.

[13] This point has been advanced by many authors, starting with Alfred Marshall and then Joseph Schumpeter, in the economics literature. In the strategy literature, there is a long tradition of emphasizing the power of new approaches. Gary Hamel and C.K. Prahalad have received much attention for their timely reminder of this fact.

Chapter Three

Strategic Innovation

The ability to create new strategies that alter the competitive rules of the game in its industry is the hallmark of a successful organization.[1] McDonald's did not invent the American hamburger or the french fry. It did not invent the idea of takeout service, but it did bring these together with many other small and large inventions to achieve the principle of mass merchandizing hamburgers. The inventions were numerous: new equipment designs, new standards for quality, new standards for training, new standards for building, new innovations in distribution, and franchising on a large scale. As a result, it provided consumers with a reputation for consistency and quality unmatched by its competitors. McDonald's not only delivered value to its customers, it also gave value to its workers. It gave new meaning to labor relations in an industry with a reputation for exploiting workers. Training was given to everyone, including casual and part-time labor. Clear guidelines were established to tell employees what was expected. Assessment procedures were rigorously applied. High standards were also set for franchisee and supplier relationships. All together, these procedures allowed McDonald's to develop the concept of fast food and introduce a new method of competing. McDonald's was to fast food what Henry Ford was to the car industry: it perfected a method of delivering standardized food at low cost.

Benetton, one of the new wave of innovators whose success in Europe has been emulated elsewhere in the world, began in 1965 as a small producer of knitwear in Veneto in northern Italy. It was a family-run business of three brothers and one sister. Luciano was the head, Giuliana the designer, Gilberto in charge of finance, and Carlo in charge of production. In 1968 they opened their first two shops to sell the brightly colored knitwear designed by Giuliana. By 1975 they had launched more than 300 shops in Italy, all of which bore the now well-developed distinctive features of the organization; in particular, the outlets were small and of simple design, offering a limited range of garments. The original product range was confined to brightly colored ladies' knitwear, but it was soon extended to include jeans, then shirts, jackets, trousers, and other accessories and later, children's wear as well.

Within fifteen years of opening its first shop, Benetton had created a worldwide organization that integrated the activities of a chain of production and distribution. The 1982 value of Benetton sales was more than $400 million; by 1991 it was greater than $2 billion (see Table 3.1). The achievement was even more remarkable considering that Benetton, the central firm, in 1991 employed fewer than 4,000 people and its profits per employee were more than $60,000 in a low-wage industry.

Fashion is notoriously fickle, and most fashion producers believe that they face high costs. The problems arise from short life cycles coupled with highly uncertain demand. Fashion producers would like to forecast their sales volume accurately, but this is a nearly impossible feat. If the forecast is too low, sale and profit-margin opportunities are lost. If the forecast is too high, inventories have to be sold at a loss.

Benetton avoided these difficulties by two simple expedients. It designed an information system that enabled fast communication between the retailers and production, and a production system that could respond quickly. The information system ensured that everyone in the organization, from retailers and agents to subcontractors, knew what had been sold and could easily determine what was needed to replace stocks. Initially a manual system that relied on the telephone, it is now electronically based. Because Benetton relies on small shops dedicated to the sale of its items in minimal inventories, there are only

Table 3.1 Some key statistics of Benetton

	1976	1978	1980*	1982	1984	1986	1988	1991
Sales (lire billions)	40	66	196	400	714	1,090	1,475	2,304
Percentage of sales outside Italy	0	2	44	44	47	62	61	66
Number of shops, incl. franchisees	n.a.	n.a.	n.a.	1,917	2,644	4,102	5,483	6,457
Profits before tax (lire billions)	1.2	1.3	13	24	37	113	130	165

Note: Sales are recorded at wholesale prices; retail sales value is about 50 percent greater.
    In 1992, 1 billion lire equaled approximately $900,000.
*1980 figures are estimates from one 18-month fiscal year.

short time lags between production and the final consumer. By integrating sales and design into the production process, Benetton could supply merchandise within days, and introduce new products cheaply and quickly. This required careful integration of traditionally separate functions like stock and dyeing systems. At the same time, Benetton pioneered technical innovations such as late-dyeing techniques to ensure that low costs could be maintained.

It should be noted that Benetton has been on the leading edge in many technical areas. It was among the first to late-dye in large quantities, link point of sale to the factories, and develop the late rush design system it called called *pronto moda.* Equally significant were its new methods of organization, which facilitated pulling together its diverse empire. It developed the concept of the strategic center, where retailers, agents, designers, purchasing, and factories were linked not by formal long-term contracts but by information sharing and a sense of common purpose. The strategic center achieved common goals without bureaucracy, a combination many other organizations had sought and failed to achieve.

Like McDonald's, Benetton's success has been built on developing multiple capabilities to achieve multiple advantages. The original and fundamental idea was to provide fashion at a price and quality accessible to young people—a mass-fashion market, which went against prevailing conventional wisdom. Fashion, it was always assumed, had to be expensive, while most of what was accessible to the young at low prices was staid, tatty, or out of date and boring. To achieve its goal, Benetton had to employ techniques that reduced the costs of the garments it sold while producing clothes which appealed to young people. Exhibit 3.1 outlines Benetton's challenge.

Overtime, Benetton developed other ideas new to its sector, many of which were closely related to its original concept. One was the ability to act quickly and at low cost, which is essential in a fashion-oriented business. Another was the ability to manage variety at low cost. Variety to Benetton is evident not in its range of goods but in the markets it serves. Benetton was the first textile producer-retailer to become truly international, with a large network of retailers catering to young people in different parts of the world.

Benetton's achievements form a strategic staircase, where each step can be visualized as one of a set of closely linked capabilities (see Exhibit 3.2). The bottom step is mass fashion for youth, for this was the initial concept. It meant specially designed clothes that could be made cheaply yet look good. Closely related was speedy response, in particular the ability to respond to competitors' new ideas with "specials." The scale of Benetton's operations greatly exceeds that which

----

EXHIBIT 3.1   FASHION: HIGH-COST OR LOW-COST?

Traditional Alternatives

Seasonal changes in design	Few changes
Fashion for rich people	Unchanging designs
Short runs	Long runs
Variety and color	Little variety
High cost	Low cost
Small niche markets	Mass markets

Benetton's challenge

Mass fashion especially for youth
Seasonal changes in color
Specials
Mass markets
Low cost

EXHIBIT 3.2   BENETTON'S STRATEGIC STAIRCASE

Additive
Capabilities

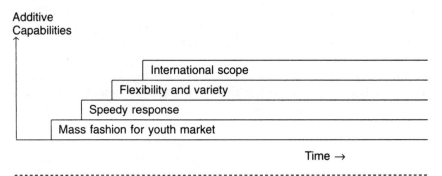

Time →

----

is normally attempted by firms selling fashion items; it is shared by only a few organizations, for example, Swatch. As the scale increased, it was necessary for the organization to become flexible to cope with the differing needs of diverse outlets. Flexibility was also a prerequisite to becoming international, but an international empire demands more than production flexibility; the whole organization has to be sensitive to various market opportunities and able to redesign its systems and transfer its capabilities across national borders.

The labels of the steps on Benetton's strategic staircase for adding capabilities are those which we have imposed. They indicate that a whole series of initiatives was needed to build and broaden the capabilities of the organization. The horizontal axis indicates that as each new capability was added, such as the international scope, the organization had to adjust and ensure that the other capabilities were still secure. Even today, Benetton continues to strive for progress in each of these dimensions, simultaneously seeking to add more steps.

STRATEGIC INNOVATION: CREATING NEW OPTIONS

While competition takes many forms, one of the most powerful is strategic innovation, namely, the creation of combinations of actions hitherto deemed impossible. Benetton and McDonald's were strategic innovators. Benetton's ability to create mass fashion at low cost gave the organization a significant advantage over its competitors. For the target audience—young people—it provided unrivaled value for money, which allowed it to gain a significant share of a world market. Benetton was the first truly global textile organization. McDonald's ability to deliver high-quality hamburgers at low cost also took it to a world position. Both firms changed the rules of the game in their respective industries and forced their competitors to compete on a new basis, and both started from a position of limited resources.

Managers of mature firms should realize that innovations in strategy are not confined to new entrants. They can play an important role in the rejuvenation of mature organizations, especially those with limited resources. Because they are often able to change the rules of the game in their industries, innovators can reverse seemingly hopeless positions to ones of great strength. At the same time, by changing the rules of the game, they upset the current positions of many of the other players. We suggest that businesses which try to innovate strategically create possibilities and opportunities for themselves for a sustained period of success. Richardson, Cook, and Hotpoint used strategic innovations to haul themselves from near oblivion to challenge the leaders. Courtelle, whose story we present in this chapter, was another example, as was Toyota.

Strategic innovations may provide a more lasting benefit to an organization, and they tend to complement rather than substitute for new products and services. Unless protected by patents, new products or services can often be copied by rivals with relative ease. In contrast, strategic innovations require new combinations of actions and functions. Understanding how to make strategic innovations work requires significant investments and a change in the mental models held by managers. Typically, a strategic innovation achieves the supposedly impossible. For this reason, copying by rivals often takes a long time, and perfect duplication may not always be achieved.

In this chapter we explore some of the strategic innovations that are currently changing the dynamics of competition in manufacturing and service industries, including

- mass fashion
- quality and productivity
- variety and efficiency
- speed at low cost
- strategic networking

We also point out that organizations do not seek to create just one new combination: they also look for multiple advantages. Meeting the challenge of strategic innovation requires a sustained effort through many initiatives. At the end of the chapter, we chart some of the ideas relating to the strategic staircase. We begin, however, with the classic case of Ford and the strategic innovation of mass production.

MASS PRODUCTION: HENRY FORD AS A STRATEGIC INNOVATOR

Many current innovations, such as those of McDonald's and Benetton, are extensions and improvements on mass-production methods.[2] Mass production was itself a strategic innovation. Henry Ford is generally credited with the development of the highly productive moving-assembly-line system. However, this innovation could not have been achieved without the prior achievement of producing standardized parts to high levels of *accuracy and at low cost.*

Before Ford, producing automobiles involved craft labor. Each part for each car was made to a basic shape, but fitting the parts together required special skills, as the finish of the parts was crude. Even screws had to be individually filed to fit nuts. There were production methods available to turn out standardized, more finished parts, but they were expensive. Most relied on production to a technical standard using the old craft method. The concept of a mechanized process, producing standardized high-quality parts that could easily be assembled was not well developed, and those organizations which practiced standardization usually incurred even higher costs than the craft-based system.

As with many modern strategic innovations, the evolution of the modern mass-production system required two kinds of developments.

One was the deepening of understanding of technical expertise in traditional functions. Thus, machinery design had to achieve levels of perfection not previously thought possible; similarly, raw materials had to be made or purchased to much higher quality standards. The other was that the functions had to work together in new ways. The flow of production had to be carefully designed and the position of machines carefully coordinated; historically, these matters were not considered important. Sales had to be more closely coordinated with production targets so that volume could be achieved at low cost. Exhibit 3.3 gives a short synopsis of the history behind this innovation.

The failure of American automobile firms to hold on to world leadership is one of the clearest examples of the dangers of believing that past strategic approaches can endure. The Japanese did not seek to replicate the conventional wisdom that emphasized the importance of large-scale factories and large cars. Instead, they displaced the

---

EXHIBIT 3.3   HENRY FORD AND THE MASS-PRODUCTION SYSTEM

During the late nineteenth and early twentieth century, firms such as Wheeler and Willcox, Singer, Pope, and the Ford Motor Company pioneered a new wave of thinking and acting. Their system, mass production, combined two other systems, the high-quality but nonstandardized production system and the low-quality standardized system. The high-quality system was the craft method of production. In cars assembled by the craft method, the parts were machine made to a crude standard and each component was individually shaped during assembly to fit with other components. Such fitting, filing, and shaping was essential because the components were not made to high tolerance. Without the shaping and fitting, they could not be assembled. Craft assembly methods were expensive in labor time, and the final good was of high quality. But despite the quality, parts were not interchangeable between different units of the same good, which made repairs also a skilled job.

In contrast, customers like the American military had demanded, from the early nineteenth century, that the goods they ordered, principally guns, be made to such standards that their parts became interchangeable. If that were possible, soldiers in the field could undertake repairs without costly or specialized tools. Interchangeability required standardized production methods antithetic to the craft mentality. Parts would no longer be shaped to fit but made to an exacting standard. Substantial R&D costs were borne by the U.S. government, yet the cost of introducing such standardization was high, for special machines had to be built to shape and produce the individual parts of the guns. But the subsequent costs of producing more units were very low, and repairs were also inexpensive. It is important to note, however, that although these guns were made to sufficiently exact standards so that their parts were interchangeable and the guns worked, the quality, for example, in accuracy, of the guns in other respects was lower than in those made by craft methods. That is, the standards of exactness, while sufficient for the task, were not very good.

EXHIBIT 3.3 Continued

In the mid-nineteenth century, most believed that producing high-quality products with standardized machine methods was impossible. In modern parlance, high quality and standardization were opposing generic strategies. They were wrong, but there was no simple solution. For example, Singer sewing machines were originally created by combining modern machine-made parts and craftsmen who fitted and assembled the finished product. This was because the level of accuracy of the machine-made parts was not sufficient to allow the delicate mechanisms required for a sewing machine to work smoothly without individual fitting. It took Singer twenty years or so of incremental changes to solve this problem, with the final change achieved only through a management decision to forbid the taking of files and other fitting tools to the assembly room!

Singer, Pope (the bicycle manufacturer), and others perfected the large-scale production of interchangeable parts at low cost. Their achievement was to merge the systems of mechanized production, which were generally able to make interchangeable parts cheaply, with the smaller-scale systems that made high-quality goods expensively.

Ford, employing processes pioneered by others, perfected the combination strategy by using a large number of innovations, some well known at the time and some new. His culminating innovation was the moving-assembly-line production system of 1913–1914. (This was probably modeled on moving "disassembly" lines used in the processing of agricultural products such as canned meat.) With a moving line, no "fitting" was possible, so the parts had to be of sufficient quality to fit closely and exactly the first time. At the same time, the organization of the work flow reduced the "assembly" time drastically by the application of division of labor solutions to the assembly problem.

Along with his moving assembly line, Ford developed a completely vertically integrated plant to produce his Model T at very low cost. He also invented a distribution channel to sell the Model T motor. Few of his rivals in the auto industry survived the onslaught of these innovations. Those which did were firms like General Motors, which borrowed Ford's ideas.

Ford's success is legendary. So is Ford's failure, for by the end of the 1920s, Henry Ford was in serious trouble because he did not appreciate the need to modify his initial strategy. His production system was efficient but monolithic: too rigid to cope with model changes. General Motors developed a more flexible system and was able to capture the high ground. The Ford story shows the power of strategic innovation and the fact that it occurs continuously.

Source: David A. Hounshell, *From the American System to Mass Production* (Baltimore: Johns Hopkins University Press, 1984).

American and European firms as leaders because their new ways of thinking about manufacturing and marketing rendered traditional Western techniques obsolete. Borrowing from rejected Americans such as W. Edwards Deming, they pioneered the idea of zero defects, just-in-time production, total quality control, and flexibility in all stages of production. These new approaches to competition are examples of what we call strategic innovation. They required new methods of operating in each and every part of the organization, and they altered the traditional relationships between functions. As a result, the Japanese have shown that they can produce better cars at lower cost than almost everyone else in the world.

The greater efficiency of the Japanese automobile firms is not limited to production methods; much is also gained through innovations in the supply chain, which ensure that bought-in components cost less. Equally important is their attention to the process of new product design and new product introduction. Here the differences are even more remarkable: new models cost less to develop in Japan than they do in Western countries and can be introduced more quickly.

Appreciating the success of the Japanese automobile and other innovative firms is made easier by considering strategic innovations one by one. We begin with quality and productivity, on which the Japanese auto firms' success was founded.

QUALITY AND PRODUCTIVITY: TOYOTA AND DEMING

Although the early pioneers of mass production set high standards for quality, these were not high enough for the discerning twentieth-century consumer. Higher standards were usually achieved by testing and rejecting substandard products. Testing machinery and quality added to the cost of the process and created extra steps. Rejected parts or products were either discarded, at great cost, or recycled for further processing. Service firms often undertook checks between the production and delivery to the customer.

There has been a movement challenging this orthodoxy; organizations have discovered a new way to achieve higher quality that is consistent with raised productivity of people and capital.[3] The thrust of the initiatives is to eliminate the causes of quality defects by examining and rectifying a process rather than by massive capital investment in new machines or expensive testing procedures. These challenges have carried banners like total quality control, quality circles, and the like. In Exhibit 3.4 we suggest the ways of mature firms and the challenge posed by dynamic organizations. The goal moves all the time, for even the best organizations recognize that they can improve.

W. Edwards Deming, the famous American statistician who has advised the Japanese since the 1950s, explains why low cost and high quality are not opposites. *Doing it right the first time,* Deming says, means *less rework* and *not so much waste.*[4] He points out that an organization which achieves near-perfect quality can eliminate a great deal of expense. He lists many sources of cost associated with errors,

---

EXHIBIT 3.4   QUALITY AND PRODUCTIVITY: THE CHALLENGE TO MATURE PRACTICES

High

Mature habits   **The Goal: Quality and**
High quality   **Productivity**
Testing, rejecting, and reworking   Make it right the first time.
    to eliminate errors   Standard quality is high quality.
Low productivity   High productivity

Quality

                                                              Mature habits
                                                              Standard low quality
                                                              Errors passed on to user
Low   High productivity

Low   *Productivity*   High

---

including the costs of inspection, rectifying mistakes, loss of capacity, and delays. In addition, near-perfect quality means more satisfied customers, because they need not have quality checks, rejects, delays, and lost capacity on account of errors.

Deming's philosophy has had a profound effect on many Japanese—and now American—companies. Deming's approach has underpinned the strategies of many Japanese automobile producers in their quest for world domination. The magnitude of their progress can be measured by statistics comparing plant-level productivity and defects in car assembly of a Japanese firm with those of a U.S. firm: Toyota, an exemplar, at its plant in Takaoka, Toyota City, built in the mid-1960s, with General Motors (GM), at its plant in Framingham, Massachusetts, now shut down.[5] Although Toyota did not achieve perfect quality, its rate of defects was about one-third that of GM, and its costs—hours to assemble and inventories required—were considerably lower. There appears to be little difference between the two in extent of automation—in which Toyota has not invested heavily—but less downtime and much smaller inventories in the Japanese plant led to better utilization of assets. Table 3.2 is testimony that quality improvement and low cost are compatible.

Toyota's technical achievements were not trivial, as U.S. and European car manufacturers have discovered. Reducing defects and simultaneously improving productivity requires new approaches to managing, to gathering information, and to exercising control. All in turn depend on many differences in methods and procedures and new ways of thinking and acting.

Achieving high standards requires a multitude of steps. Some are

Table 3.2 Comparisons of productivity and quality between GM and Toyota, 1986

	GM	Toyota	Ratio
Gross assembly time per car	40.7 hours	18.0 hours	2.3
Defects (per 100 cars)	130	45	2.9
Assembly space (per car)	8.1 square feet	4.8 square feet	1.7
Parts inventories (average)	2 weeks	2 hours	168

Source: Adapted from James P. Womak, Daniel T. Jones, and Daniel Roos, *The Machine That Changed the World* (New York: Rawson Associates, 1990), Table 4.1, based on original data from IMVP World Assembly Plant Survey.

aimed at altering the perceptions of managers and workers to make them understand that errors cost money and that correcting errors is the responsibility of everyone in the organization. To make this shift in responsibility work, all personnel have to be trained to see how they can affect the system. Understanding how to measure failures and eliminate them are two parts of this training process.

Eliminating failures also requires greater understanding and new competence *within* each function. The importance of correct design of work flow and procedures in the factory, in the sales department, in the purchasing department, and elsewhere all contribute to fewer mistakes. Measurement and correction of errors also require higher standards in systems design, product design, and maintenance. Individual initiatives within functions are not enough; some of the biggest gains need the functions to be pulled together.

The Toyota story is most apposite for managers in mature organizations. In the 1950s Toyota was a mature organization, finding it difficult to compete in a world of giants. The American producers were more profitable and better resourced. Toyota has managed to displace these leaders, establish itself in their place, and show that it is possible to rejuvenate.

Hotpoint's rejuvenation also incorporated the ideas of quality and productivity. Hotpoint, the first European appliance producer seriously to adopt the idea of fault-free products at low cost, found that organizational changes were necessary, as important was changing the mutual perceptions of workers and managers. To facilitate this and other changes, Chaim Schreiber, Hotpoint's managing director, abolished the infamous prescribed breaks and permitted workers to take them when they wished. He also upgraded the standing of shop-floor workers in the eyes of management by making the company dining room a single-status facility where all employees ate together.

This brings us to the second change for the organization: in the way functions operate. In the case of Hotpoint and fault-free products, the most obvious change occurred in the after-sales service department. No longer was it a profit center (and the major profit-producing area of the business): it had to become a cost center. Previously, a production error meant more money for the after-sales staff, so the feedback loops were poor. Schreiber made after-sales service part of production, arguing that this would provide a tight feedback loop to production should any fault occur with a product.[6]

It is not surprising that exponents of total quality control also point to new forms of organization within a firm and between the firm and its suppliers and customers. For example, many product defects are caused by failure of bought-in components or by suppliers misreading the buyer's design instructions. Eliminating errors requires functions to coordinate their efforts effectively, not only within the firm but also across firm boundaries. We have already mentioned Benetton's development of the strategic network. Japanese automobile producers developed similar network relationships with their suppliers.

Near-perfect quality is not an exclusive preserve of Japanese producers. Organizations such as Richardson have also achieved near-perfect quality at lower costs. For instance, over a ten-year period Richardson achieved a sevenfold increase in labor productivity, a fivefold increase in machine utilization, and reduced rejects from 5 percent to less than 0.1 percent. Like those of the Japanese car producers, Richardson's achievements required radical alterations in skill and understanding within the functions. Engineers were no longer expected to be versed in purely mechanical skills; added optical and electronic skills allowed new standards to be realized. In addition, relationships between the functions altered. Maintenance, design, and manufacturing had to work together closely to achieve the new objectives.

Better quality with better productivity can also be attained in services. Florida Power and Light, a seemingly unlikely example for instituting total quality control procedures, instituted a quest for quality of service in 1985. It focused on a variety of aspects of the business, for example, billing and dealing with customer complaints. However, one of the most taxing and intransigent problems was the interruption of service owing to errors in generation and transmission. Over a period of four years, the company made significant improvements, and the costs of almost all the changes paid for themselves quickly. The magnitude of the savings was sometimes startling. For example, according to Andrea Gabor, a small change in pipe-laying procedures costing some $260 saved the company $5,500 in one year.[7] Overall, the estimated costs of the company's quality control procedures in the first half of 1988 were about $2.5 million, while the savings from recently instituted improvements were nearly $13.5 million.

VARIETY AND EFFICIENCY

Just as quality and productivity were once believed to be opposites, so too with variety. Managers in mature firms typically believed that *efficiency* and *variety* were incompatible: they could improve one or the other but not both.[8] Efficiency was believed to be synonymous with standardized items, little variety, and almost no flexibility to change on short notice. In contrast, flexibility was the ability to produce short runs, but only at a large cost penalty. Dynamic organizations such as the successful rejuvenators we studied achieved the seemingly impossible task of combining these opposites. We show in Exhibit 3.5 the two strategies as opposites; we picture *variety with efficiency* as reconciling these two opposites. Again, our dynamic firms recognized that they could make yet further progress.

Mature organizations oriented toward volume production of goods or services have trouble coping with variety. They usually divide the overall task into subtasks, link them together inflexibly. For example, the factories of one mature firm we visited had central departments with special skills to adjust the settings on the machines when a change of product was required. With greater variety, the demands on this department grew and production line workers were idled while waiting for the fitters to arrive and do their specialist work. Similarly in service organizations, different services typically required different systems and different coordination patterns, which in turn required alterations in the work flow and crossing of boundaries. More variety meant more work and a clogging of the systems.

EXHIBIT 3.5   VARIETY WITH EFFICIENCY: THE CHALLENGE TO MATURE WAYS

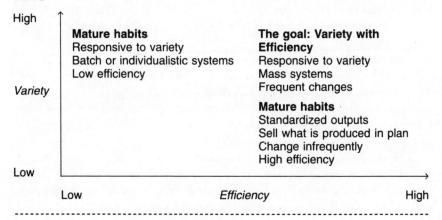

High

Mature habits
Responsive to variety
Batch or individualistic systems
Low efficiency

The goal: Variety with Efficiency
Responsive to variety
Mass systems
Frequent changes

Variety

Mature habits
Standardized outputs
Sell what is produced in plan
Change infrequently
High efficiency

Low

Low   Efficiency   High

In manufacturing, the technical issues in producing variety at low cost include reducing machine changeover times and eliminating associated costly trial runs. Such changes place new demands on machine tolerances and on the workers who operate the machines. No longer are they merely operators, but skilled mechanics, sometimes with greater knowledge than the engineers whose tasks they perform. The efficient production of variety requires changes in other functions of the organization. Sales, once geared to selling what was produced, has to change its orientation to gathering orders on what is required. This, too, requires new skills, new knowledge, and new investment in systems and procedures. Marketing also demands a new approach to understanding customer needs and new skills in identifying customer wants. The demands on design are greater as well. In addition, accounting and control systems have to be changed, for many of them are geared to dealing with long runs and infrequent changeovers.

The efficient delivery of variety requires not only changes within but also in the relationship between functions. As with the achievement of quality at low cost, the various functions of the organization have had to work together in new ways to solve the challenges. Design has to work closely with both marketing and production to meet the needs of the consumer and the demands by production that changes be made simply and quickly. Purchasing has to work closely with both sales and production so that the necessary inputs are ready when product changes are made. Personnel has a new role too, for workers have to be trained to cope with new demands. Information systems, which may or may not involve the use of computers, have a new role in coordinating flows between stages of a process.

Just as quality at low cost presents technical and organization challenges, so does variety at low cost. While some of the issues are similar, many are different. Variety at low cost requires a high level of quality, but continually improving quality levels is quite different from demanding that an organization cope with ever greater variety.

The Courtelle Story

Courtauld's actions in the man-made fiber industry provide a vivid story of the power of variety at low cost in changing the rules of the game to a company's advantage.[9] To appreciate the scale and effect of Courtelle's actions we must first tell a little of the story of Courtelle's industry.

Through most of the 1970s, the major man-made fiber companies in Europe and the United States followed the large-scale, low-cost strategy. The managers of these companies built ever larger and more complex plants to exploit scale economies, producing a standardized output that could be varied only with difficulty and at great cost. Their overall strategy was to lower costs with fixed routines, and they were forced to use price as a weapon to gain market share. The strategies were originally very successful: costs fell rapidly, more rapidly than prices. World markets grew and the firms gained in size with rising margins and volume and hence profitability.

By the late 1970s, the value of the old strategies was diminishing fast. First, as more and more firms followed the same strategy, the increases in plant size brought excess capacity to the industry, so prices fell rapidly—more rapidly than costs. Margins and volumes fell, pushing the producers into unprofitability. Slow growth in demand and competitive pressures made matters worse, as each firm tried to recapture lost volume by cutting its prices further. The situation was made even more difficult by the actions of governments, which sought to stop the least efficient firms from quitting, exacerbating excess capacity.

Some firms responded to the problems of excess capacity by shifting production to new locations where input costs were less. No longer were these the United States, which for many years enjoyed below world market oil prices, or Western Europe, which hid behind the nontariff and tariff walls, but the less-developed and Middle Eastern countries whose governments were eager to add value to their exports and willing to give favorable treatment to investors. Those located in these newly industrializing countries had a sustainable cost advantage over the more traditional Western firms, which did not receive such favorable treatment.

Courtelle, a division of Courtaulds, was one of the major producers following the old low-cost volume strategy. It also produced colored fiber for specialist downstream users. Colored fiber was considered to be a niche but highly profitable subsegment of the main business. Originally, colored fiber cost more to produce because of the demands of flexible production. However, customers complained that the minimum order sizes were too large and delivery delays too long for the service to be of real value. Initially, Courtelle's response was that *nothing could be done: it was inherent in the process.*

Courtaulds slowly realized (almost by accident) that if colored fiber could be produced on a large scale but flexibly (in small lots) *without sacrificing efficiency,* it could make much more money. This was because it could charge a substantial premium for dyed fiber. Dyed fiber uses less dyestuff than other means of dyeing, and the quality of the color is better because it is integral to the fiber.

After several internal working parties and conferences, the organization decided to take action. Over a period of time it managed to reconfigure its plant and internal organization to tackle the difficulties. Efficient order sizes for a color were reduced from fifty tons to five tons, then to half a ton, and then even smaller lots. In reducing the minimum order size, the company also increased the range of colors it offered in small lots from about fifty to more than several hundred and finally several thousand. Customers appreciated the speedier response to their needs. Because users perceived a real advantage to its products, Courtelle gained a triple benefit—low costs, flexibility, and high margins—and made handsome profits where others were losing money.

In addition to being able to raise prices, the firm developed a flexible capability and achieved a tangible, overall cost reduction. Initially, production costs rose as the greater flexibility meant investments in new machines, new training, and higher levels of employment. Moreover customers demanded greater levels of service in order processing, delivery, and technical assistance. Though such demands for improved responsiveness added further costs, they were offset as inventories, with their associated costs of finance and storage were reduced. Further gains were made as the organization learned how to produce ever more precise quantities of on-specification fiber, thus lessening the costs of waste. The early cost increases were replaced by later falls in unit costs, measured on a systemwide basis, showing that the organization had achieved its goal of producing *variety at low cost.*

Exhibit 3.6 lists some of the changes that took place at Courtelle. Just as we suggested in the opening paragraphs of this section, Courtelle found functional change very important, as important as the technical production changes. For example, marketing, accustomed to selling what was produced, had to develop close and different links with production so that customers could get what they needed rather than what was available. There were corresponding changes in the other functions, particularly accounting and research and development. As far as accounting was concerned, the old systems were geared to measuring costs, not contribution. Moreover, the systems were not flexible enough

---

EXHIBIT 3.6   THE CHANGES AT COURTELLE

Before	After
Inflexible systems	Flexible systems
Make to stock	Make to order
Changeover takes hours	Line never stops
Minimum run half a day	Minimum run less than an hour
Short runs cost more	Long and short runs cost less

Source: Discussions with Courtelle's managers.

---

to give profit data either by customer or by product line. The focus was on total volume and total labor content. The system was almost useless for the new business in which value contribution (margins), not volume, was the key to success. New accounting systems had to be designed and introduced.

Similar changes took place in the research department at Courtelle. Hitherto, the emphasis of research was on cost reduction, 90 percent of the budget being devoted to such activities. The department had to shift its emphasis to quality improvement and enhancing flexibility. This radical change had to be introduced carefully, as the research department technically reported to a different part of the Courtaulds empire.

The Courtelle story is mirrored elsewhere; the efficient production of variety has also appeared at the consumer end of the textile market. Scottish knitwear companies have for many years been famous the world over for their cashmere sweaters and high-quality products sold under such brand names as Pringle, Barrie, and Peter Scott. Until recently, the organizations producing these garments offered little variety. However, as their markets became more international and their customers more concerned with fashion and more discerning as to features such as fit, it became apparent that the companies would have to offer greater variety than that in the traditional range of sizes and colors. Order sizes were reduced from dozens to singles as the number of possibilities rose from a few hundred to thousands. The Scottish firms had to learn to make small lots of a dozen or less to high-quality standards within a mass-production system, which taxed their ingenuity. Their ability to cope with variety far outclassed the achievements of most textile organizations, including Benetton.

Variety also forced functional changes in the Scottish knitwear industry. Here the changes took place in a department that lay on the boundaries of the organization. Most of the companies did not have large marketing or sales departments; they relied on a highly international and extensive group of agents to promote their products. The agents had formerly played a passive role in gathering orders from their retail customers, responding to what was being manufactured. The advent of fashion into this industry changed the relationship of retail agents to producers. First, the agents were pressured by their customers to encourage the producers to offer merchandise to beat the competition, and second, the agents had to be more closely linked to the organization to become active in the design and marketing of the merchandise. This required holistic change in the agent relationship.[10]

Delivering variety efficiently is not only a phenomenon exclusive to manufacturing, but also a new wave sweeping service organizations.

For many years, banks, restaurants, and the like have segmented their markets into two broad categories: those in which they offer standardized services and those in which services are tailor made—at higher prices. Such distinctions are being broken down. Customers of financial firms can expect *mass customizing* of many services that are standard in origin but tailored to individual needs. To achieve variety at low cost in a service firm, as with manufacturing, there must be changes within the organization. Traditionally, many service firms have achieved low cost only by standardization. Variety interferes with the systems. Again, the necessary changes require not only that each function change, but also that the relations between them change.

Variety and efficiency need not refer exclusively to the range and types of products or services offered. Organizations such as Benetton and Edwards, which operate in world markets, face complexities because of the span of their geographic operations. Procedures that are perfectly acceptable for managing one operation in one corner of the world need significant modification elsewhere. Thus Benetton, famed for its dislike of legal contracts, has to modify its position when undertaking business in the United States, where legal documents and lawyers are part of the culture. These organizations have learned to deal with this dimension of variety by deepening their understanding of the workings of their own organization and their knowledge of other countries' operations. Agents often help them in this process, but ultimately the whole organization has to learn to adjust and adapt to a new flexibility of approach.

SPEED AT LOW COST

A new phrase circulating among consultants and businesses—"time-based competition"—captures the essence of what has been known to many, namely, that speed and low cost are not necessarily opposites but a single reconcilable course of action.[11] Speed, or rapid response, has some affinities with, and may occur along with, variety, but the two are not the same. The contrast between the old and new ways is shown in Exhibit 3.7. In the old way, low cost is associated with a fixed pace and order determined by the organization. To achieve anything more quickly, special procedures involving higher cost are required. In the new way opposites are more closely reconciled, and although many have made great progress, there is often some way to go.

The first and most obvious manifestation of speed is the ability to respond quickly to fluctuations in the demand for an *existing* range of

---

EXHIBIT 3.7 SPEED AND COSTS: THE CHALLENGE TO MATURITY

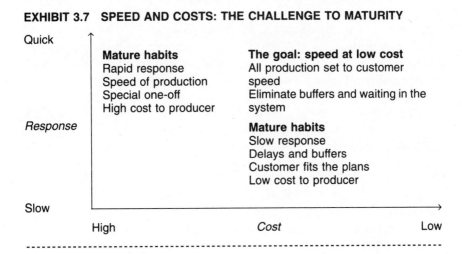

Quick

Mature habits
Rapid response
Speed of production
Special one-off
High cost to producer

The goal: speed at low cost
All production set to customer
speed
Eliminate buffers and waiting in the
system

Response

Mature habits
Slow response
Delays and buffers
Customer fits the plans
Low cost to producer

Slow

High   *Cost*   Low

---

products or services. This capability is of course different from the skills needed to produce variety at low cost, which implies an expansion of the range. The ability to respond quickly can bring enormous benefits to customers. In the case of physical products, the customer does not need to carry stocks if speed can be guaranteed. In services, it eliminates the need for lines and customer downtime.

The second way speed is manifested is in the ability to *introduce* new products or services quickly. Generally there are long cycles between design and bringing to market, and when these can be reduced, an innovative organization may steal a march on its competitors.

Hotpoint, the British appliance producer, realized the importance of being able to respond rapidly to fluctuations in both the level of demand and the mix of products. Although its markets were mature in the sense that most demand was for replacement, the levels of demand for individual items tended to be volatile, dependent on fashion, whim, the weather, and economic factors. Making factories flexible to create variable levels of output in quick response to demand has allowed Hotpoint to ride the waves of industry fluctuations. For example, when it introduced the washer-drier, sales were forecast at only 10 percent of factory output. Actual demand outstripped the forecasts, and production was quickly adjusted so that 50 percent of output was of this new product. Again, during the 1989–1991 downturn in industry demand, when most other organizations were struggling to break even, Hotpoint was able to adjust quickly to new levels of sales and cut back production without building large inventories and showing a loss.[12]

At Richardson, Bryan Upton realized that if knives could be delivered quickly at no extra cost, his organization could capture a significant share of the knife market. More than a decade ago he summarized his firm's philosophy: "Answer every telephone in seconds; answer every telex in minutes; send every sample within forty-eight hours." This message, in later years adjusted with more demanding targets, focused the minds of the whole work force on working at the speed the customer wanted, not the speed most convenient to the organization.

Knives are hardly complex items, yet many customers found that they received poor service in the sense that products were not delivered quickly enough. This cost customers money. Speed and reliability meant that customers need hold only small inventories. It also meant that seasonal and rush needs could be catered to. In such markets, promotion ideas are often inspired at short notice, and responsiveness at low cost is vital. Perhaps most significant, speed at low cost allowed Richardson to extend its reach into new markets profitably. One example was the market for corporate gifts. A measure of the intense service demands of this segment is the performance required for one Italian order. Richardson had to deliver within a few weeks of receipt of the original order of 1.5 million knives, each in a custom-designed gift package and each costing less than a dollar. The product was a "special," that is, not a standard item in the range. Yet the order was normal in this segment and could be met only by those suppliers that had invested in the needed capabilities.

For Richardson, achieving speed at low cost did not require major capital investment but rather a new approach to organizing the work flow. Some of the most notable improvements came in order processing, the service side of the business. As in most of its rival firms, orders spent more time waiting to be processed than in the actual processing. For example, booking an order into production takes only a few minutes, yet that order might wait several weeks for the next processing cycle. Eliminating such "work in progress" inventories shortened cycle times. By reorganizing its work flow, Richardson was able to speed up deliveries and set new standards for competitors.

Being able to deliver quickly reduced costs for both Richardson and its customers. Rapid response eliminated the need to hold large stocks of finished products, eliminating financing and storage costs and the possibilities of waste. Similarly, customers had advantages: their inventories were also reduced and they were able to order more fashion items, knowing that when their goods were delivered, their market would still be there.

Speeding up their process has also helped automobile companies reduce their costs. In this industry, the lag between a company's registering and delivering an order was months. Most organizations have made efforts to reduce this time, but as usual, the Japanese were in the vanguard. Now response times are commonly a matter of days between a showroom sale and the factory turning out the car for delivery or replacement to stock.

Edwards High Vacuum, had similar concerns over time delays between order placement and final delivery. With customers all over the world being served from a few factories located in the south of England, delays in processing were magnified by shipping delays. After many years of effort involving intensive work between the functions and investments in new systems, Edwards achieved a major breakthrough. Its cycle time for many products from order to delivery has been lowered from three months to two weeks. The result is much happier customers and an astonishing reduction in inventory, which has more than paid for all the investment costs.

Just as speed or rapid response in existing product lines brings major benefits, so are there major benefits for speed at low cost in the product development cycle. Time to market of new products or services is a key factor influencing competitive position. For example, in textiles the typical cycle has been four or five months between design and final delivery. Customers that required a shorter cycle have traditionally paid large premiums. Benetton has developed systems for fashion flashes— *pronto moda*—that permit new lines to be introduced at short notice without interrupting current flows. Benetton has also cut the traditional cycle time for new product development from six months to a few weeks. Thus Benetton has solved the double conundrum of responding quickly to order changes in the current range and introducing new lines without disruption.

Japanese car producers have also achieved significant superiority over U.S. organizations in their ability to introduce new models quickly. Toyota, the leading Japanese automaker, has shown considerable progress in this area in the face of the huge complexities of launching new automobile products. To give a flavor of their progress, we report the following figures. In the 1980s American automobile producers took, on average, five years to develop a new car, employing nearly 900 people for 3.1 million hours. In contrast, Japanese firms had reduced the time to just under four years, employing just under 500 people for 1.7 million hours.[13]

Whether by reducing response times to existing order ranges or introducing new products and services more quickly, achieving speed at low cost requires an organization to reexamine its method of operations within and between functions. Existing functional arrangements are often imperfect, with queuing systems for work waiting to be done. Organizations tend to operate linear systems of dealing with orders or new product introduction, in which each department waits for the previous one to finish before starting its part of the process.

Achieving faster cycle times requires two sets of initiatives. One is speeding up activities within departments, for speed at low cost requires a close link of one step with the preceding one, with fewer buffers and delays. The second is introducing ideas of parallel activities, which change the relationships between departments. Instead of bunching work before sending it on, departments must learn to work on a product or new way of making it while other departments are completing their work. Breaking the linearities of work flows may not only save time, but is also likely to create greater cooperation, to the advantage of the design and production processes of the new product.

In every sector, firms are faced with dilemmas of seemingly irreconcilable opposites. Thus far we have dealt with four—fashion, quality, variety, and speed—but there are others, some general and others specific. For example, the Japanese are among the leaders in *low-cost miniaturization*, particularly in the camera and hi-fi fields. The Sony Walkman personifies the major steps here. The hi-fi industry traditionally believed that, apart from transistor radios, portability meant either inferior quality or high costs. Sony developed the portable hi-fi system at a low cost. In the course of development, its personnel realized that miniaturization could result in savings on materials. In seeking to reduce size, they were forced to simplify, which meant that they could focus on a few high-quality features, enabling them to lower costs without reducing performance quality. Thus they achieved the double benefit of consumer satisfaction and low cost. Not surprisingly, the Sony Walkman and its associated products gained a great initial advantage over the other products in the marketplace. The computer industry also discovered the benefits of low-cost miniaturization. Early portable computers were inferior to desktops and unattractive. Consistent investment and innovation by Compaq and Toshiba, followed by that of other firms, have produced a stream of cost-competitive products that are more attractive than their larger desk counterparts.

BUILDING MULTIPLE ADVANTAGES AND CONTINUOUS INNOVATION

Whether a business is an entrant, a rejuvenator, or even an established leader, it may be helpful for its managers to think of the innovative challenge as building and climbing a strategic staircase. The steps are the capabilities and mounting them allows a business to win its competitive battles, creating value for stakeholders. Each stair is created and strengthened as a result of initiatives undertaken inside the organization. The concept of the staircase can be used visually to reinforce the organization's past achievements and point to future challenges.

Although a single strategic innovation helps the organization, rejuvenation requires more, for only with multiple advantages can organizations hope to beat their many rivals. The visual image of a staircase reinforces the importance of creating multiple advantages and continuously adding to the stock over time. For example, it is futile for an organization to invest in achieving superior quality and productivity, but fail to respond when competitive shifts demand that it also supply variety. The staircase is, in effect, never ending.

The stretch and strain that continuous additions of new capabilities impose on an organization are severe. A capability, once acquired, needs constant effort and attention if it is to retain its utility. Neglect can mean that initial standards slip as people become forgetful or bored. More serious, neglect can also deny the organization the possibility of improving standards. Rivals can catch up and turn what was once an advantage into the minimum needed to stay in the game. Adding new initiatives can make it harder to sustain the attention and effort needed for existing capabilities, for fresh urgencies and excitement invariably deflect attention and alter top managers' priorities. It is hard for a team to remain enthusiastic about its own achievements when another team leading the latest initiative is in the limelight. To combat such difficulties and help retain consistency in building old capabilities as well as new ones, the initiatives can be designed to be mutually reinforcing. Each team can draw strength from others around it in the search for continuous improvement. The steps on the staircase are thus overlapping.

In Exhibit 3.8 we draw a simplified strategic staircase for Toyota. In its first postwar years, Toyota, with the help of its advisers, tackled the twin objectives of quality and low cost. In the early days, quality meant reliability or no fault, features that U.S. auto producers valued. The twin steps were not always easy to build, as some moves to improve quality brought rising costs. Achieving these two capabilities was the basis of Toyota's renewal and sustained attack on the U.S. automobile market. These qualities made an impact on American consumers who appreciated a car that seldom needed repairing.

Toyota's staircase was different from that built by U.S. firms, emphasizing that the competitive battle between the Japanese and U.S. giants revolved around differing approaches. U.S. firms had invested in developing and sustaining a high level of dealer service through their networks. This capability was once essential, given the failure rate of

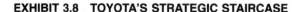

EXHIBIT 3.8   TOYOTA'S STRATEGIC STAIRCASE

Additive
Capabilities

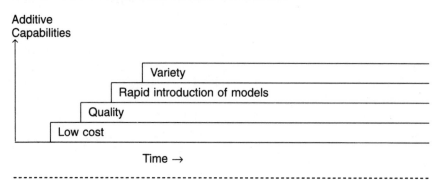

Time →

U.S.-produced automobiles in the early 1980s. However, the Japanese approach did not require such an extensive network. Their customers did not have to return their cars for repair so often. Moreover, the Japanese tailored their designs, with many features included as standards, to fit a more modest network. The U.S. firms also had delusions about their cost position, nurtured partly by their mind-set and partly by outdated systems, which failed to consider overall costs and focused only on parts of the enterprise, not the linkages.

By the 1990s the U.S. automakers had caught up with the Japanese firms in quality, in the sense of reliability. That step on Toyota's staircase is now less valuable than it was. But new steps have been built. Toyota and its Japanese rivals have moved on to emphasize other innovations while continuing to work on improving quality. They paid attention to reducing the time it takes to introduce new models, and they have made significant inroads into achieving variety at low cost. With a new approach to producing short runs of high-performance cars, the Japanese are invading the highly profitable niches of Mercedes-Benz and BMW.

Courtelle also built a strategic staircase; we give a simple rendering of it in Exhibit 3.9. Courtelle always had a reputation for high-quality fibers, but the value of this capability was being diminished by the activities of its competitors. Before it changed its strategy, it believed it was a low-cost producer. However, its measures of cost gave false signals. Management was looking at the high-volume lines, but productivity improvements made there were not matched by an overall cost reduction owing to the costs of producing ever greater numbers of short runs. Trying to cut out short runs was not possible because of customer

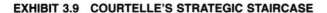

EXHIBIT 3.9   COURTELLE'S STRATEGIC STAIRCASE

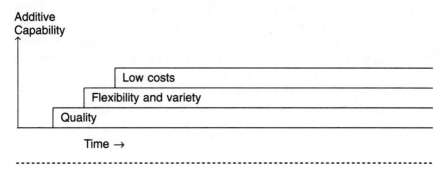

Additive
Capability

| Low costs |
| Flexibility and variety |
| Quality |

Time →

demands. After the changes, total costs fell, overall productivity increased, and capability to produce variety rose.

Richardson, the U.K. knife producer, initially searched for speed of response, low cost, and quality in its early moves to restore its competitive edge; we depict its staircase in Exhibit 3.10. It is clear that at times the objectives were in conflict. Rapid response sometimes brought overtime and waste. Improving quality meant costly investment in machines and in more expensive skills. But with each cycle, the organization searched to maintain its new levels of achievement and reduce costs. Sometimes this was easily done, as the new routines proved to be better and more efficient; sometimes it was not and the organization had to think again.

After building the first three steps, Richardson's management moved

EXHIBIT 3.10   THE STRATEGIC STAIRCASE OF RICHARDSON'S SUCCESS

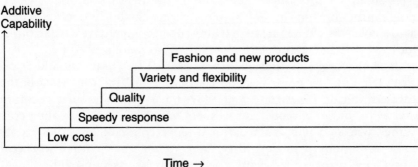

Additive
Capability

| Fashion and new products |
| Variety and flexibility |
| Quality |
| Speedy response |
| Low cost |

Time →

the emphasis to product innovation, which led to the Laser knife. This opened new vistas, and the company moved quite quickly to seek a fashion-led organization, and to produce many new products. Variety became a more serious challenge and urgent need, and this capability was better developed. At one time it threatened to get out of hand, and the organization had to pull back. The emphasis on variety and fashion has been undertaken with some compromise on speed of response, showing that building new advantages can diminish old ones. However, speed of new product introduction has assumed an important place, especially as it has moved from producing one or two new designs a year to fifty.

SEQUENCING ADVANTAGES

Is there an order that firms should follow in their quest for multiple advantages? Is it true, as some have suggested, that quality or speed are the points of initial departure? Or is it best for organizations to advance on multiple fronts simultaneously? These obvious questions need addressing.

Our research suggests that there is no universal rule as to which advantage to build first. Quality was an important feature of early battles in cars, appliances, and cutlery; it is also important in winning battles in many other industries, but by no means all. For example, in both textiles and fibers there were several instances where building for higher quality did not provide the initial break. Like most of its rivals, Courtelle was well aware of the importance of quality to its customers. Poor quality fibers cause machine breakdowns among downstream users. All leading European producers used quality as a weapon against imports, but the differences in quality among the leading organizations were small. Quality improvement did not provide a solution to Courtelle's difficulties in the 1970s. In contrast, the ability to offer variety at low cost was a major move that altered the competitive battleground, for it was a move competitors found hard to match.

It is also arguable that quality, measured by durability and error-free garments, has never been a major issue for Benetton. Most of the garment industry is used to dealing with natural fibers such as cotton and wool, in which consumers expect variations. To the young consumer, who may not wear a garment long, feel, look, and color are far more important than durability. By contrast, the Scottish knitwear firms have managed to secure a valuable business in providing high-quality garments. They have specialized in the use of expensive combinations such as cashmere, mohair, and wool, and emphasize durability and perfection—qualities their customers value highly.

The sequencing of steps in building multiple advantages is specific to the organization and its customers. For example, Richardson built speed of response, quality, and low cost at the same time; coping with fashion and variety appeared much later. Benetton did not have to hone its capability to deal with variety until it moved out of Italy. The Japanese automobile producers emphasized quality before they added new advantages.

It is rare for an organization to be able to reach perfection in any dimension, so adding new advantages has to go hand in hand with making progress on other fronts. The Japanese automakers have not solved the problem of producing the perfect car, and as more variety is introduced, the problem becomes more difficult. Similarly at Richardson, new product introduction and new fashions have forced the firm to downgrade the importance of some kinds of rapid response to customer requests, which at one time was high on the agenda.

Identifying the potential for a strategic innovation requires the organization to know and study its customers. Courtelle realized the potential of variety at low cost after its managers did some research. A study revealed that customers would be willing to pay a 20 percent price premium if Courtelle could supply small lots of fiber in a wide range of colors, in contrast with its policy of supplying only large lots in a limited range. This encouraged management to reorganize the operations, with the initial goal of increasing variety without allowing costs to rise by more than 20 percent. The possibility that increasing variety might decrease costs was not fully appreciated until sometime after the first steps were taken. Richardson realized its initial priorities of quality and speedy response by informal discussions with its customers. Its research served the company well. Subsequent moves required more sophisticated market research, which revealed that there were new challenges and possibilities for trading off some of the existing advantages for new ones.

STRATEGIC NETWORKING: AN INNOVATION IN ORGANIZATION

It is not enough to generate strategic innovations inside a business; they must also be transmitted through a chain. Organizations that try to deliver high quality productively know that it is necessary to enlist the help of suppliers and distributors. If component goods or service are below standard, adding high quality at the intermediate stage is frustrated. Speed at low cost has little value to customers if the rapid response of the organization is sabotaged by delays in distribution. The problems are even more pressing in international markets. Advantages realized in domestic production and service delivery systems evaporate as a source of advantage in foreign markets if the local sales force and delivery systems are not also tied in. The mature organization trying to become innovative faces such problems in a particularly pressing manner. How can outside relationships be transformed to match the changes that are only beginning to take place inside? If suppliers and distributors are to innovate, they too must find new ways of working, new skills, new systems, and above all, work with the host organization in new ways. We suggest that mature organizations can learn from the innovations practiced by *central firms* and their *strategic networks*.[14]

Nintendo, the Japanese computer game supplier, is a central firm that operates a web of strategically aligned partners. It employs more than 30 principal hardware subcontractors and 150 software developers. Through this web, Nintendo generates nearly $4 billion in sales with fewer than 900 people, which translates into sales per employee of more than $4 million and profits per employee of more than $1 million.[15] Nintendo generates exceptional added value for its partners, too. Benetton, as mentioned, is another central firm that employs a web of strategic partners in supply and distribution. It is highly successful with more than $500,000 in sales and $60,000 in profits per employee.[16] Both firms approach the management of the value chain in a particularly creative manner, using retailers and suppliers as providers of ideas and testers of market trends. Corning Glass, McDonald's, McKesson, Nike, and Sun are similar in that they all operate webs of strategically allied partners and, at least at present, are recognized as exceptional creators of value.

The value creation of these central firms is associated with innovation, which comes from the partners as well as the central firm. Nintendo's partners design and make its games; Sun's suppliers design new workstations; Benetton's retailers and suppliers give it new ideas for its products; and McDonald's franchisees deliver new ideas like the Egg McMuffin.

These central firms create real value by combining in many subtle and special ways the opposing forms of organization: market and hierarchy. Traditionally, market contracting was seen as having its greatest value in allowing each party to be free to experiment and innovate with only minimal reference to its partners. Under market bidding arrangements, supply or distribution contracts would be sought—by tender, request, or other, perhaps informal, approaches—with desired targets specified. The system anticipates that partners will respond, delivering what is requested or better (see Exhibit 3.11).

EXHIBIT 3.11 ORGANIZATIONAL INNOVATION TO COMBINE
ADAPTABILITY WITH CONTROL

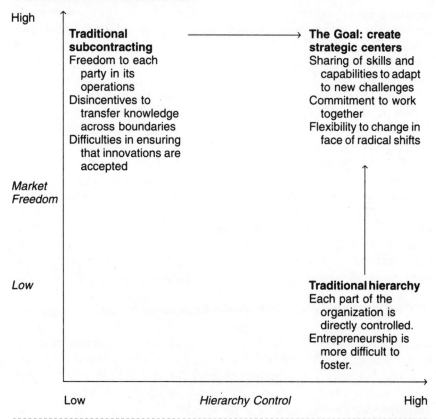

Market mechanisms are prone to certain kinds of failure. Typically, the skills associated with new ideas are transmitted slowly between organizations as each sees itself in potential competition with its rivals. Moreover, when a host organization wants to break the rules of its industry, it will likely have to induce its suppliers to operate differently as well. This is something they may be unwilling, or even unable, to do. We say "unable" advisedly, because change for partner organizations is no easier than it is for the mature host firm. Partners also have mind-sets that resist change. Their prior investments in routines and skills to support particular, perhaps outdated, methods of operation are not readily abandoned.

Market failure is illustrated by the events that took place when the Japanese automobile assemblers set up their first plants in Europe and the United States. They had to cope with a great disadvantage when they discovered that the local suppliers lacked the skills and capabilities to deliver parts and services to the high standards they set. The ability to deliver total quality, speed, and reliability seemed not to exist. More serious, the Japanese found that Western suppliers did not appreciate the importance of these requirements. The suppliers apparently did not have the right mind-set; many were "mature" in their thinking.

The Japanese invaders moved a significant step beyond the traditional market-style contract to resolve these difficulties. Using the approach of the strategic network to relationships, common in the Toyota system in Japan, they taught their suppliers the skills they needed, helped them in their systems, coached them in the use of the equipment, and provided high-quality technical support. These investments have apparently paid off for the Japanese firms.

Many managers of mature organizations see such sharing of ideas and skills as risky. They fear that such loose alliances can go wrong, and that when it has gained the insights, knowledge, and skills given it by the host firm the collaborating party will exploit these benefits for private gain.[17] For these reasons, mature firms often wish to extend the degree of control, perhaps to the extent of owning the supplier chain.

Ownership, or formal long-term contracts, while eliminating opportunistic behavior, can lead to great problems, especially for a mature organization. Increased scope creates bureaucracy and moves away from "lean concepts" stressed in the earlier part of this chapter. Mature firms discover that it becomes even more difficult to be speedy, flexible, high quality, all at low cost, if the scope of the firm is extended and the organization made more complex. More important, in dynamic, fast-changing environments, where the future is uncertain, the integrated organization is committed to activities, systems, individuals, and assets which, because of their size and scope, may make future change even harder.

The notion of *strategic centers* and *webs of partners* challenges conventional thinking, for it finds a path between "hierarchy" and "market." Although most of the successful experimenters of such ways of operating are new organizations like Benetton, Sun, Nike, and Nintendo, their activities can be exemplary for the mature organization. A full appreciation of what these organizations do is beyond the scope of this book, and we refer the reader particularly to the work of Gianni Lorenzoni and Charles Baden-Fuller.[18] Here we merely present a taste of the ideas.

Strategic networking has its origins in franchising, an old idea dating back to the nineteenth century. Since the 1960s, franchising has been developed to a fine art in food and hotel services. In the franchise arrangement, the franchisee accepts many of the disciplines imposed by the franchisor regarding the format of the enterprise, the levels of quality, and the standards of the offering. The disciplines may extend further into various other aspects of the work. However, some areas are left to the franchisee, for example, the details of its internal organization and the levels of reward the franchisee gives to its employees. In its turn the franchisor has a number of duties, including monitoring quality throughout the system, central marketing and promotion, choosing franchisees, and implementing change in response to competition. The contract between the franchisor and the franchisee is both formal and informal. Ordinarily a legal contract spells out minimum necessities on both sides. In addition, the franchisor and franchisee are expected to work together in many areas not specified in the contract. Franchising systems are clearly beneficial in cases where there is a need for local delivery flexibility within a standardized format.

McDonald's did not invent franchises, but it showed how a huge worldwide empire of fast-food restaurants could be set up quickly and run efficiently from a relatively small corporate center. It also showed how much of the rigidity of the bureaucratic system could be overcome without sacrificing tight controls. But McDonald's has moved beyond the traditional franchise to a strategic network; its franchisees contribute to the innovations of the whole group; the Egg McMuffin cited earlier is an excellent example.

Business format franchising is generally a system high in operational control. It is less suitable for value chains where creativity is vital and parts of the value chain must work together dynamically and interactively. In fields such as textiles, where design and flair are important, designers prefer to work for small flexible units, yet the benefits of their work are greatest if they can be spread across a large number of units quickly. The strategic network tries to combine the benefits of small market-based organizations with those of great size in a different and new way. Although outwardly the strategic network is similar to franchising, there are important differences.

In a strategic network, organizations are bound together by an information system and a common purpose to achieve the necessary outcomes. Organizations in the network agree to share their operational details, but they do not share their revenues and profits as divisions in a large organization would. Nor, surprisingly, are they linked by complex operational contracts as in franchising. They thus eliminate many of the costly features of the market without losing the benefits *and* they gain many features of an integrated organization without many of its costs. People who work in the strategic network feel that they have a great deal of independence and freedom to act without constraints. Yet they are tied to a common standard and achieve a common sense of purpose with the help of their information sharing.

The Benetton organization involves strategic networking.[19] Benetton prefers to call its distribution arrangements a "branded store system" rather than a franchise network. In part, this preference seems to reflect the fact that outside North America the central organization does not enter into any formal contracts with the "franchisees," even though they handle more than 80 percent of the business. The same lack of formal contract marks Benetton's relationships with its suppliers. How does it manage to run the system without disputes? There are, to be sure, some conflicts, but they are minimized by the long-term evolution of an information system that permits all parts of the strategic network to behave as though they were in a unified enterprise. The sophistication of the system has grown to the point where all parts work closely with one another, sharing data and information necessary for every aspect of the operations. Thus producers in the system know how much was sold, where it was sold, and what was sold, allowing them to forecast their needs in anticipation of orders. There is sharing in the design and formulation stages, too. By concentrating on integrating what is necessary to make the business go forward, the organization has bound together its disparate parts to make an integrated whole. It has done so without bureaucracy, yet with the requisite disciplines.

When contrasting the strategic network with the franchise, we see some essential differences. In the franchise system tight controls on operations are symbolized by clear-cut manuals and formal legal contracts. Franchisees are not involved in the strategic thinking or in new products. In contrast, the strategic network often has quite loose controls on operating procedures, encouraging much local flexibility; yet all the participants are expected to contribute in some way to new product design and the generation of new ideas. The lessons from strategic networking are slowly being learned in other contexts, where organizations are seeing joint ventures not as independent, parochial activities but as part of a sequence of actions to achieve a more effective purpose in the wider market.

NOTES

[1] We are grateful to Charles Hampden-Turner for his stimulating contributions to the ideas behind this chapter. See in particular Hampden-Turner and C.W.F. Baden-Fuller, "Strategic Choice and the Management of Dilemma: Lessons from the Domestic Appliance Industry," Centre for Business Strategy Working Paper, no. 51, London Business School, 1988; and Hampden-Turner, *Charting the Corporate Mind* (New York: Free Press, 1990). The notion that different rule playing is vital if one wants to catch up from behind is admirably explained in Pankaj

Ghemawat, *Commitment: The Dynamic of Strategy* (New York: Free Press, 1991); and A.K. Dixit and B.J. Nalebuff, *Thinking Strategically* (New York: Norton, 1991). W.J. Abernathy and R.H. Hayes, "Managing Our Way to Economic Decline," *Harvard Business Review,* July–August 1980: 67–77, suggest new rules of the game. Robert Grant, "The Resource-Based Theory of Competitive Advantage," *California Management Review* 33, no. 3, 1991: 114–134, also notes the powerful role of innovation in mature industries. We also owe a debt to M. Piore and C. Sabel, *The Second Industrial Divide: Possibilities for Prosperity* (New York: Basic Books, 1984). However, in our view, only Joseph Schumpeter places strategic innovation, playing by new rules, as the central point of the strategy process for firms in traditional industries. We feel this point has been consistently overlooked.

[2] Many writers have emphasized Ford's innovative role. For historical detail we rely on David A. Hounshell, *From the American System to Mass Production* (Baltimore: Johns Hopkins University Press, 1984).

[3] Many books on this theme have appeared. Almost all owe a debt to the pioneers, Joseph Juran and W. Edwards Deming.

[4] See, for instance, W. Edwards Deming, *Out of the Crisis* (Cambridge, Mass.: MIT Press, 1982).

[5] These data are drawn from the study by the MIT team of James P. Womak, Daniel T. Jones, and Daniel Roos in *The Machine That Changed the World* (New York: Rawson Associates, 1990).

[6] The department, also had important responsibilities for customer care and marketing.

[7] This example is drawn from Andrea Gabor, *The Man Who Discovered Quality* (New York: Times Books, 1990).

[8] Many aspects of producing variety efficiently are touched on in total quality management books. B. Joseph Pine II, *Mass Customization* (Boston: Harvard Business School Press, 1993), deals with the subject explicitly.

[9] Details of this case can be found in J.M. Stopford and C.W.F. Baden-Fuller, *Note on the European Man-Made Fibre Industry,* London Business School, mimeo, 1982. Further data can be obtained in Joseph L. Bower, *When Markets Quake* (Boston: Harvard Business School Press, 1986).

[10] For more details, see D. Bodrug and J. Wilson, *Wolsey Knitwear,* London Business School, 1988, and J.M. Stopford and C.W.F. Baden-Fuller, "Flexible Strategies—The Key to Success in Knitwear," *Long Range Planning* 23, no. 6, December 1990: 56–62.

[11] Much valuable work on this subject has been documented by George Stalk, Jr., and Thomas M. Hout, *Competing Against Time* (New York: Free Press, 1990).

[12] Hotpoint's management claimed that demand for some products fell by 30 percent. Even though its margins have fallen, Hotpoint is much more profitable than Electrolux and Philips, its largest rivals.

[13] See Womak, Jones, and Roos, *The Machine That Changed the World,* p. 118.

[14] We are indebted to Gianni Lorenzoni for the ideas in this section. A full and better exposition is available in Lorenzoni and Charles Banden-Fuller, *Creating a Strategic Centre to Manage a Web of Partners,* discussion paper, University of Bath, 1993.

[15] 1991 data.

[16] Ibid.

[17] See for instance: R.B. Reich and E.D. Mankin, "Joint Ventures with Japan Give Away Our Future," *Harvard Business Review,* March–April 1986: 78–86; J. Bleeke and D. Ernst, "The Way to Win in Cross Border Alliances," *Harvard Business Review,* November–December 1991; 127–135, and G. Hamel, "Learning in International Alliances," *Strategic Management Journal* 12, special summer issue, 1991: 83–103.

[18] Lorenzoni and Baden-Fuller, *Creating a Strategic Centre.*

[19] In the United States, Benetton has had considerable difficulties because it dislikes legal contracts and its style of operations was alien to Americans, but its attitude is changing.

Chapter Four

Creative Scope

The creative aspect of strategy is not limited to how a firm competes; it extends to its scope, that is, with whom and where it competes. Being creative about the scale of operations, the range of products and services, the geographic markets served, and the channels of distribution is the hallmark of the entrepreneurial organization in general and the aspiring rejuvenator in particular. "The key for us is to pick—very accurately—where we want to compete." So said a senior manager of GM at a seminar in London on the subject of GM's competitive determination to re-assert the values of creativity that had made the auto company the world leader. Even if GM finds it does not have the resources to compete across the board, the implications for less well-resourced enterprises are obvious. The smaller organization *must* be creative in making its choices if it hopes to catch up to the leaders and become a rule breaker and exemplar. And if the leaders themselves are alert to the possibilities of strategic innovation, by themselves as well as by others, the task for the contender is that much harder.[1]

Hotpoint's rejuvenation exemplifies the value of creativity in the choice of scope, for the firm broke almost every rule in the tradition of its industry. When the leaders were operating large-scale plants and industry pundits were pointing out the disadvantages it faced in its smaller plants, Hotpoint built plants of only half the perceived minimum efficient scale. Hotpoint broke the conventional rules about distribution. While its rivals courted the chain stores and ignored the dwindling small "independent stores," Hotpoint did the opposite, courting small stores and incurring the wrath of larger chains with its pricing and distribution policy. Finally, while rivals were expanding their penetration in foreign markets and observers were arguing that the industry was essentially European. Hotpoint deliberately cut its exports and focused exclusively on the United Kingdom, where its choices helped it become the strongest brand. It changed the rules of the game, forcing others to follow or take account of its policies. Now Hotpoint is moving ahead to change the rules again, using a variety of cross-border alliances.

Edwards High Vacuum was also creative in its choice of scope. One of its first moves toward rejuvenation was to stop selling complete systems of high-vacuum technology and sell only basic pumps. This move defied conventional wisdom, which believed that profits lay in selling systems, not components. The retreat from systems allowed Edwards to conserve its resources and focus on building new steps for its strategic staircase, from which it later created an industry leadership position for an expanded geographic and product territory.

Courtelle, the producer of acrylic fibers, was creative in its approach to its range of products. Industry tradition was to offer standard products in large lots differentiated principally by levels of service and technical specification. Courtaulds altered the differentiation to one based on a wide variety of dyed fibers offered in small lots. Its redefinition of the range permitted Courtelle to steal a march on its competitors and allowed it a platform on which to build substantial capabilities for improvement.

Choosing the scope of the organization is critical too for new entrants, and many of the most successful organizations have started their lives by selecting a novel approach. Benetton, the once maverick textile firm and now European leader in the sale of clothes for young people, broke several conventions, one of which was scale of outlet. It offered a limited range of items through boutiques. This sales approach was a radical departure, for industry wisdom suggested that mass markets in the garment trade were best captured by large outlets offering a wide range of items.

Wal-Mart, also had a novel and creative approach to scope. Unlike Benetton, it chose to operate large stores located in small U.S. towns where it avoided most of the other chains. Its choice of scale and position and its decision to avoid direct confrontation were critical decisions that helped Wal-Mart attain much of its initial success.

Our rejuvenators first grew their competitive advantages in a novel way on a small and restricted scope that they could defend more easily against competitors. Only when this was successful did they move to broadening their offerings, sometimes building a truly global organization with a wide product range sold through many different channels. This sequence of selecting, building, and leveraging is significant.

Our claim that the rejuvenating organization has to rethink its scope is a step beyond those who advocate downsizing and selling off parts of the enterprise. While downsizing is often a feature of the first stages of rejuvenation, most of the literature on downsizing fails to stress the importance of finding a new creative approach to defining the territory. To be sure, internal factors are important, and we deal with them in Chapter 6, but all our rejuvenators realized the value of rethinking scope as part of the drive to create new advantages.

Creativity regarding the scope of a business requires a careful assessment of many factors. We group these under four headings: *tastes* of customers and consumers; *technology* trends and opportunities; *competitors'* behavior, particularly their blind spots; and the current *capabilities* and resources of the business. Exhibit 4.1 visualizes these forces and this chapter focuses on the first three. Assessing the internal capabilities and resources of the organization and their impact on the changing scope of the enterprise are dealt with in later chapters. For the moment it is sufficient to note that mature organizations trying to rejuvenate are typically deficient in capabilities and resources.

Analysis of external forces often reveals clear ground rules for making choices about the proper scope of a business. For example, in many European and international markets, taste and technology changes point to markets becoming a series of national and international niches. For rejuvenating organizations that lack the resources and capabilities and the confidence to surmount a full global challenge, the choice may lie between a national approach or a narrow international niche. In international markets, the creative manager needs to sense the loose bricks of the competitors, assess his or her own organization's capabilities, and gamble on one of the options.

Analysis after an event is often easier than before it, when skill is required to judge which are the vital issues. By considering four questions in turn: scale, product range, geographic location, and channel, we show how our rejuvenators and entrepreneurial organizations read

EXHIBIT 4.1 FORCES AFFECTING THE SCOPE OF REJUVENATORS

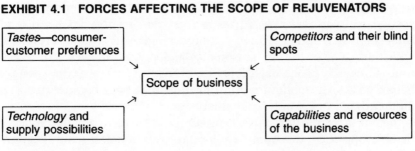

data in unusual ways to yield remarkable strategies for building success. We also note that the strategic choice about the scope of a business is not a one-time event. Changes in the firm's capabilities or in economic factors force a periodic reassessment. At the end of the chapter, we address the triggers for reassessment.

CREATIVITY IN CHOOSING SCALE

Entrepreneurial organizations are creative in their choice of scale, and many have used a novel approach as a platform from which to build and leverage advantages. The importance of novelty is most obvious for successful entrants that aim to break the established rules of the game. Their activities yield important lessons to all, for like rejuvenators, the new player is often short of resources and lacks an established reputation.

Benetton had a novel approach to size. Traditionally, retailers aiming at mass markets have built large outlets to exploit scale and scope economies. Since much of the cost of a retailing operation lies in running individual stores, the economics of large units is attractive. Such units have lower costs per square foot, and the potential for generating multiple purchases from customers' shopping trips is high. Moreover, many consumers are attracted to a wide range of merchandise, like to economize, and therefore appreciate low prices.

Benetton's innovation was to develop and adapt for the mass youth market small outlets that traditionally sold high-priced merchandise to a limited clientele. Benetton's small outlets were, and still are operated by partners, reflecting the firm's strategic network philosophy, and they helped create an image of exclusivity and fashion in the target audience. Costs were controlled by simple, effective approaches; outlet design was carefully tailored to show goods to best effect, yet it used low-cost fittings and inexpensive equipment. In addition, inventories were kept low so that the total capital employed was small relative to turnover. By using the partner system, Benetton also reduced labor costs. Local partners avoided restrictive labor regulations because of their small size, and instituted flexible arrangements to staff the shops, which are subject to high seasonality and swings in sales. These factors—unusually good image, low capital cost, and low operating costs—helped make the policy of limiting unit size cost competitive and differentiated it from larger competitors.

Benetton could not have been successful had it not developed a flexible approach to supply appropriate to its small-scale, fashion-oriented retailers. Its information and rapid response factory systems permitted the whole organization, including the retailers, to minimize its finished goods inventories, which, in the fashion sense, are perishable. Retailers, although required to place orders of a minimum monetary value, can be flexible about which colors of products they accept and when they accept them.

The Italian government has played a paradoxical role in Benetton's history. In Italy small stores benefit from an advantageous tax policy. Outside Italy such advantages are fewer. Yet the Benetton formula worked well elsewhere in Europe and several Asian countries, showing that its concept was founded on a few simple fundamentals.

In Exhibit 4.2 we remind readers of the four factors. Benetton's choice of outlet size capitalized on the tastes of youth, exploited hitherto ignored aspects of technology, and reacted to limited resources by employing franchising and developing a supply chain to cope with pressures on the outlets. Of course Benetton's strategy bears much similarity to that adopted by McDonald's in the fast-food industry, but there were substantial differences too. The concept of franchising fast food through small outlets required many refinements before it could be applied to mass fashion markets. Benetton, a leader in its own right, is finding other clothing firms emulating its approach.

Hotpoint used a novel approach to scale as a base for creating its competitive advantage. In the early 1970s, Hotpoint was a medium-size player in the European appliance industry. In the eyes of many industry observers, its modest scale was a disadvantage. Contemporary studies conducted in the United States and the United Kingdom suggested that each doubling of plant size would reduce costs by between 7 and 10 percent.[2] With European leaders operating plants more than twice its size, and U.S. leaders with plants more than four times its

---

EXHIBIT 4.2   FOUR FORCES INFLUENCING BENETTON'S CHOICE OF OUTLET SIZE

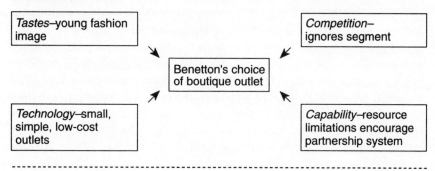

---

size, Hotpoint seemed to be in a precarious position. To outsiders, including government policy advisers, the course of action seemed obvious: build larger plants.

Chaim Schreiber, who joined Hotpoint in 1974, realized that the firm's costs were out of line with those of the competition, that building larger plants would not be a panacea, and that in any case Hotpoint lacked the resources for the latter. Its existing cost base was so poor that even doubling plant scale would not secure profitability, especially in an industry plagued with excess capacity, in which demand was not growing and many leaders were unprofitable despite their supposed cost advantage. Schreiber persuaded his managers to reduce costs without altering the basic plant configurations. With improved labor practices, quality, and other aspects of the manufacturing process, productivity rose by between 10 and 20 percent. Although there was no increase in scale, output rose through better productivity. The discrepancy between the industry leaders and Hotpoint narrowed.

In a process described in Chapter 8, Hotpoint decided to leapfrog its rivals to move out front. Once more it sought to alter the rules of the game. It built a new plant, but again chose a modest scale, incorporating a process new to the European appliance industry: using prepainted steel. This process, which had been introduced in other industries, eliminated the expensive paint shop, reduced the capital and labor required for the plant, and increased flexibility. (For instance, the factory could then produce different color machines in small lots, an impossibility in a traditional plant.) The new process required an entrepreneurial and responsive organization, which had been developed in the productivity drive. This technological experiment gave Hotpoint a cost position close to the best in the industry as well as flexibility, at a modest capital commitment.

Its wisdom in the choice of scale can be appreciated by the fact that Hotpoint epitomized a new trend in the industry. Exhibit 4.3 is a diagrammatic representation of the scale and cost position of a large number of European appliance plants in 1984. (For reasons of confidentiality, individual plants cannot be identified.) The less productive large-scale plants with capacity of more than a million units a year were typical of the Italian factories of Zanussi, Indesit, and Philips which accounted for a significant proportion of the European industry. Hotpoint's washing machine factory was the second most productive, with a scale of only 500,000 units a year, half the believed minimum efficient scale of a million units. Some firms of the scale of Hotpoint were rivaling its efficiency, and one was better. All adopted Hotpoint's approach, albeit in their own fashion. Only the Germans, whose data are privileged, operated large plants efficiently. Although much better than

EXHIBIT 4.3   PRODUCTIVITY AND PLANT SCALE, 1984

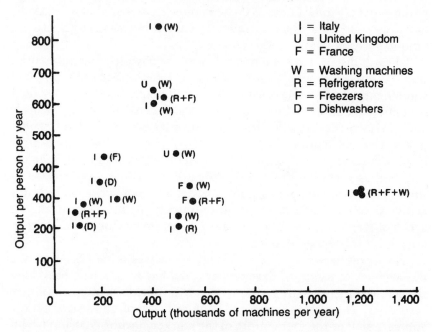

Sources: Survey data. C.W.F. Baden-Fuller and J.M. Stopford, "Globalisation Frustrated," *Strategic Management Journal* 12, no. 7, 1991: 493–507.

the Italian operators, the Germans did no better than Hotpoint despite their larger size and greater capital investment.

CREATIVITY IN CHOICE OF RANGE

Almost all our rejuvenators redefined their product ranges, but Edwards High Vacuum experienced perhaps the most dramatic response to its changes. At the time of its crisis, Edwards was supplying vacuum technology, in the form of pumps, complete systems, and ancillary services, principally to the U.K. market. Popular wisdom in many sectors held that the real profits were to be made from selling systems and that components, such as the pump itself, would become commodities. The managers at Edwards thought otherwise. In their minds, the problem was that Edwards was not good at producing either components or systems, so they took the unusual step of dropping systems to concentrate on the pump. "If we cannot make the component pump properly, we do not have a hope in systems," they argued. For more than ten years Edwards concentrated its energies on the basic vacuum pump. Not only did it produce a better component than that of its rivals, but it established a basis for industrywide differentiation, creating a unique position in the world market.

Edwards discovered what many now see as obvious, that differentiation is often possible for a commodity component. Each OEM (original equipment manufacturer) customer had different needs, and each final customer had further differentiated needs. Because there was primary and replacement demand, the opportunities for differentiating the pump were substantial. In addition, many customers wanted a high-quality durable pump, and few if any competitors could meet the demands of users such as those in the silicon chip business. By devoting its limited resources to making pumps better and more cheaply, Edwards achieved considerable progress quite quickly. It managed to build a series of steps on its staircase of advantages from which to deliver an assault on worldwide markets.

There was, however, a price to pay. Focus was achieved by cutting out avenues of technical development that had to be added back later to meet the increasingly stringent demands of new customers in new territories. The effort to accelerate the addition of more steps on the staircase slowed the momentum of the market assault. With hindsight, one can see that Edwards had to face up to an essential trade-off. Without the sacrifice of resources that assumed high value later on, there would probably have been insufficient progress on the basic pump to give value to those resources at any time.

Courtelle adopted a novel approach to range in its acrylic fiber business. As noted in Chapter 3, it was an industry leader but enjoyed only marginal profits in a sector plagued by excess capacity. Its owners, Courtaulds, threatened the unit with closure if profits did not improve. Traditionally, Courtelle's industry differentiation was based on technical specifications, and organizations delivering better technical capabilities got the better price. As all producers possessed this capability, price premiums were eroding. Such differentiation gave only the smallest increments in profits.

Courtelle broke the rules by redefining the basis of differentiation, offering a range of colors. The organization invested much effort, but only a modest amount of money, in increasing its active color range in stages to several thousand. Lot sizes were reduced from around one ton to tens of kilograms and the order cycle shortened from as long as months to days. Most expected small rewards, but the result was striking. With a marketing campaign, the business was transformed. Profitability soared. Customers welcomed the new flexibility as it gave them a cost advantage in their downstream markets. Dyeing fiber during the production process yielded better colors at a lower cost than dyeing finished (ecru) fiber. Redefining the range and the market position so as to exploit the color capability was the basis of Courtelle's transformation.

Courtelle's willingness to explore the technological possibilities driven by appreciation of unfulfilled customer desires and the blind spots of competitors created this novel strategy. None of the major fiber competitors had thought to offer colored fibers in small lots, thinking this impossible, or unprofitable. In time, when Courtelle's successes became clear, the competitors copied. But the time gap was long enough for Courtelle to have reaped substantial profits and established itself as the industry innovator.

CREATIVITY IN GEOGRAPHIC TERRITORY

The choice of geographic territory is often closely tied to the choice of the range, and a creative approach to the issue can form the basis of rejuvenation or a growth path. The question of geography is most pertinent to those dealing in international markets, or against international competitors. They realize that the reduction of visible and invisible barriers to world trade and transport costs, and the convergence of information technology have made most markets more liberal and more open. But these changes do *not* indicate that "global" strategies are the only way forward.

Free movement of goods and services does not make for homogeneous tastes and preferences. Despite the emergence of global brands, global marketing, and even global fashions, there are many markets in which differences in taste between and even within countries make a global approach risky and suggest that gains to rethinking are high. Culture, history, language, climate, wealth, and income are some of the sources of differences between geographic regions. A product that is a certain seller in New York may not be so attractive in Milan, or even in California. Those who do business in North America are aware of great regional differences in the tastes of consumers. There are even larger differences among European countries. Germans' attitudes to pork differ from those held by the French, who in turn differ from the British. The differences extend to clothing, cars, and most other goods and services.

Differences in tastes have to be addressed. An entrepreneurial organization that has coped with variety at low cost has an opportunity to exploit its newfound advantages and the resources to tackle its

91

challenges. For such firms, simultaneous representation in the Triad markets of North America, Japan, and Europe, together with a wide product range, makes sense.[3]

In contrast, mature and less capable organizations should perceive that coping with taste differences is a capability they must build if they are to compete over a broader strategic territory. The greater the number of markets and the greater the potential range of product types that may be demanded, the greater are the knowledge base and skills the organization may have to acquire to deal with local market differences.

We have noted two successful rejuvenators' responses to this complexity of range and territory. One is to restrict operations to a local geographic market and to serve and exploit it to the full. Another, and quite different, approach is to seek out niches across the world which have great similarities despite the fact that they are in different cultural environments. The mature organization aspiring to rejuvenate with limited resources is advised to tackle the most limited market sustainable and compatible with the loose bricks of the competitors. Edwards limited its pump range and chose the global niche. The story of Hotpoint, which chose the local market option, is most instructive.

Hotpoint and Washing Machines in Europe

Hotpoint's creative approach was to ignore the siren calls of globalization of geography, products, and distribution and focus on selling only a limited range of machines in the U.K. market. The geographic focus and the product focus reinforced each other, for with limited territories, the range could be narrower than that of more expansive rivals. To understand why, in retrospect, Hotpoint's strategy can be judged wise, it is necessary to appreciate the complexities of the European market.

Before the start of its rejuvenation in the 1970s, Hotpoint was an unsuccessful business with a wide product range, including small appliances sold in many European countries. Its strategy was similar to that of most of the industry leaders, particularly Electrolux, Philips (now Whirlpool), Merloni, and Candy, which to a greater or lesser extent operated in many different country markets. These strategies reflected the prevailing view of the industry leaders, namely, that the market was both European and homogeneous. Their view was based on the projection of their past successful strategies, the belief that scale was important—not just in production, but also in branding and distribution—and that, crucially, the elimination in tariffs between European countries and the convergence of media would make consumer tastes more alike, eliminating the complexity caused by serving so many markets. Some of them also thought that their policies would make the market homogeneous. Their views were largely wrong, as we show by examining the case of the humble washing machine.

First, there are substantial differences between American and European consumers. The typical North American household has a large washing machine in its basement or laundry room. European and Japanese houses are not as large, and many people live in apartment buildings without communal areas. Consumers in these countries are used to having quiet, compact machines in the kitchen. Although these essential regional differences are the most obvious, there are others not as obvious but equally important.

Consumer preferences within Europe vary substantially and are as great today, if not greater, than they were in the 1970s, when Hotpoint acted. The map of Exhibit 4.4 describes major European appliances, and Exhibit 4.5 summarizes a few key points for washing machines in particular. It seems that the French—like the Finns and Norwegians—prefer top-loading units, the British front-loaders. The Germans prefer machines which spin at high speeds, the Italians, Austrians, Swiss, and consumers in other southern European countries, prefer those which spin at lower speeds. These preferences are manifested in buying behavior. It is said that German consumers believes that a washing machine must be capable of spinning at very high speeds and therefore place low value on those which do not have this feature. They also believe in ecological features such as cold fill and minimum water cycles. In contrast, Italian housewives believe that high-spin-speed machines can damage clothes and some go to the extreme of refusing to purchase machines with such a feature. British households have large water heaters, so purchasers typically buy machines with hot and cold fill. Many British consumers also believe that machines which use little water do not clean clothes and therefore do not value ecological features.

National differences in taste are not new, having been noted by Ted Levitt when he studied the market in the 1960s.[4] The difficulty for a Pan-European producer, however, is that the differences can vary over time. Whereas Levitt assumed that taste was primarily determined by nationality and was also static, the evidence shows considerable volatility. In the early 1970s, the French preferred front-loaders and the British, top-loaders. Today, the two have exchanged positions. Worse yet is the emergence of many new segments of demand, not all of which are nationally unique.

In common with many other consumer markets, European appliances show all the symptoms of an explosion of variety, much of which is idiosyncratically driven at the country level. Demand for variety has

EXHIBIT 4.4 DIVERSITY OF CONSUMER PREFERENCES IN THE MAJOR DOMESTIC APPLIANCE MARKETS

1 The British Isles (UK and Irish Republic)

Washing machines: 98 per cent are front loaders (compared to 29 per cent in France). 50 per cent have top spin speeds of over 1000 revs/min (in Italy 400–500 revs/min is typical). Most machines use hot and cold water, whereas most continentals fill with cold only.

Tumble dryers: 38 per cent operate by draining water off rather than by condensation.

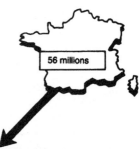

61 millions

Dishwashers: 40 per cent are fitted, the highest level in Europe, compared to 35 per cent in Germany and 5 per cent in the Iberian Peninsular.

Freezers: 69 per cent are upright models, compared to the Euro-average of 37 per cent; the British do not purchase super-insulated freezers to the same extent as the French and the Germans.

Fridges: 68 per cent have a split level or two-group cooling system; the same trend is apparent in Germany (Euro-average: 51 per cent).

Micro-waves: 56 per cent of households own a micro-wave (Euro-average is 26%) and the proportion of those operated electronically is also high at 62 per cent (Euro-average is 25 per cent). There is a distinct preference for high capacity models.

Cookers: most are single source (i.e. all gas or all electric).

2 France

Washing machines: 71 per cent are top loaders (2 per cent in the UK).

Tumble dryers: unique to France are top loading dryers (35 per cent of sales).

Dishwashers: 35 per cent are fitted, a relatively high level.

56 millions

Freezers: 30 per cent are super-insulated. The main reason for this is to conserve food longer in the event of a power cut.

Fridges: household penetration is high at 97 per cent. The French use much fresh produce and therefore use large refrigerators with capacities of 250/300 litres.

Cookers: top temperatures are high at 240°/280° (Euro-average is 180°/210°). This is due to culinary traditions and a preference for meat that is quickly fried over a high heat. 32 per cent of cookers use both gas and electricity, compared to the Euro-average of 7 per cent. Distinctive to France is the use of pyrolysis (50 per cent of ovens and 15 per cent of cookers use pyrolysis).

3 The Iberian Peninsular (Spain and Portugal)

Washing machines: in contrast to the UK, half use cold water washes and 70 per cent run at temperatures of less than 40°C.

Dishwashers: only 5 per cent are fitted, compared to 40 per cent in the UK. The further south one goes, the more that free standing ones become popular. 25 per cent are wider than 45cm, the standard width.

50 millions

Freezers: household penetration is the lowest in Europe at 12 per cent (Euro-average is 45 per cent). This is due to the large consumption of fresh foods.

Fridges: most have large capacities of 250–450 litres in order to store the large amount of fresh foods consumed. This is the only market where multi-door fridges have proved to be at all popular.

Micro-waves: the level of household penetration, at 2 per cent, is the lowest in Europe, where the average stands at 35 per cent.

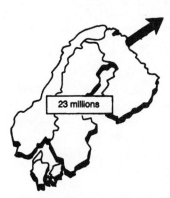

4 Scandinavia (Sweden, Norway, Denmark and Finland)

Market in general: there are two main consumer concerns: the environment and safety. The standard height of goods is 90cm compared to the rest of Europe where it is 85cm.

Washing machines: 36 per cent are top loading compared to the Euro-average of 27 per cent but in Finland top loaders account for 70 per cent of the market.

Freezers: the level of household penetration is high at 40 per cent. A large number of freezers are super-insulated.

Cookers: there is a high level of penetration of microwaves at 41 per cent, a profile that exactly mirrors that of the German sphere of influence. Electricity is the dominant source of power. Cookers do not tend to be fitted, as the concept of fitted kitchens is not well developed.

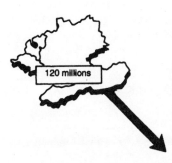

5 German sphere of Influence (Germany, Benelux, Austria and Switzerland)

Market in general: concern for the environment is extremely high. 65 per cent of households have fitted goods, compared to a Euro-average of 22 per cent.

Washing machines: there is a preference for environmentally-friendly machines and higher spin speeds.

Dishwashers: household penetration of 35 per cent is the highest level in Europe.

Freezers: 60 per cent are super-insulated, the highest level in Europe (in France the figure is 30 per cent and in Spain and Italy there are none).

Cookers: 80 per cent are electric, the highest level in Europe (this compares to 50 per cent in the UK and 10 per cent in France).

Micro-waves: 43 per cent have small capacities of 20 litres or less.

6 Italy

Washing machines: most Italians wash at average temperatures, but spin speeds tend to be low at 400–500 revs/min. Demand is strong for stainless steel vats.

Tumble dryers: household penetration, at 1 per cent, is the lowest in Europe, compared to 14 per cent in France, 24 per cent in Germany and 36 per cent in the UK.

Refrigeration: household penetration of freezers (22 per cent) is lower than average; the high level of consumption of fresh produce explains the predominance of high capacity refrigerators of 200–350 litres.

Source: Thomson SA (TEM Division).

EXHIBIT 4.5   CONSUMER PREFERENCES IN WASHING MACHINES

Feature	France	United Kingdom	West Germany	Italy
Loading	Top	Front	Front	Front
Spin speed	Medium	Medium	Fast	Slow
Filling	Cold	Hot	Cold	Cold

Source: Consumer surveys in Europe, 1986–1988. See C.W.F. Baden-Fuller and J.M. Stopford, "Globalisation Frustrated," *Strategic Management Journal* 12, no. 7, 1991: 493–507.

been increasing. Exhibit 4.6 shows that for the United Kingdom the number of models and brands has proliferated: between 1976 and 1987 the number of models increased fourfold to 201, and the number of models per brand more than doubled to nearly six.

EXHIBIT 4.6   MODELS AND BRANDS OFFERED IN U.K. WASHING MACHINE MARKET

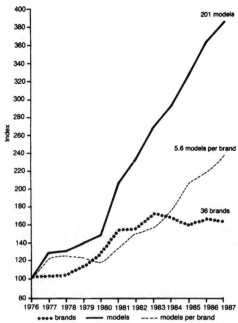

Sources: U.K. Consumer Association reports and trade association statistics: see C.W.F. Baden-Fuller and J.M. Stopford, "Globalisation Frustrated," *Strategic Management Journal* 12, no. 7, 1991: 493–507.

These taste and geographic variations were exacerbated by such differences in each country's retailing practices as the kinds of outlets and methods of display. For example, the Germans, French, and British had the benefit of large supermarket-type retailers, which permit consumers to examine displays and inspect goods at leisure without being disturbed. In contrast, most stores in Italy were small and cramped and offered little opportunity for browsing. Therefore, distribution displays that were popular in one country were often useless in another.

Not only displays had to be modified: selling methods had to change too. Sales support levels considered essential in one country were unacceptable elsewhere. For example, retailers in parts of France expected appliance producers to supply trained demonstrators for their products; in other areas, for example, the major U.K. electrical chains, retailers would not allow such people into their stores.

The highlighted differences between the major bands of consumer preferences in each major country hide the diversity of submarkets and subcategories. Local markets, ethnic groups, and the like continue to grow in importance despite the attempts of retailers and producers to limit individuality.

Hotpoint's genius was to recognize that the explosion in variety caused by taste and distribution differences between countries could be exploited and provide the basis for rejuvenation of the firm. It bet that the benefits of scale were overrated and noted that most of its rivals, which had adopted a Pan-European strategy, were having trouble and seemed almost overcome by the complexity of the challenges they faced owing to the diversity of markets.[5]

Hotpoint was not the only firm to adopt a "national approach." Thomson, the major French appliance firm, restricted itself to the French market. Thomson's choice appears to have been deliberate, especially as the parent company was well aware of the dynamics of global businesses. A major part of the Thomson portfolio is the manufacture and sale of electronics goods.

The national approach was not the only alternative to the Pan-European strategy of the major players; Miele, the German firm, had adopted a Pan-European niche. It successfully sold very high-priced and high-quality machines in all European countries. This niche showed a consistency in product characteristics and market channels not apparently shared in the mass markets. Exhibit 4.7 summarizes the three competing approaches to the market.

Hotpoint by its choice could devote resources to resolving systematically the many dilemmas it faced in its local territory. In particular, it has been able to deal with issues of quality and reliability, flexibility in the face of volatile demand, and speed of new product introduction,

----

EXHIBIT 4.7   THREE CONTRASTING APPROACHES TO THE EUROPEAN APPLIANCE INDUSTRY IN THE 1980s

Pan-European	National mass markets	International niche
The market is homogeneous, and current differences in purchasing habits reflect the diversity of offerings, not underlying tastes.	Consumers in different countries are different, and their purchasing habits reflect their choices and those of retailers.	Consumers in different countries are different, but there are some common groups, particularly those in the premium market.
Scale in production, logistics, and branding gives Pan-European firms an advantage.	Scale is overrated. In the mass market, country focus is critical. Long logistics chains across borders are hard to manage.	Scale is overrated. For premium markets, it is possible to build a brand on small country volumes if quality is emphasized and delivered.

----

and it has allocated considerable resources to forging close links with its distributors and retailers in anticipating and influencing their needs. This strategy, discussed in greater detail in the following section, made it the envy of the industry. As a senior executive of a major rival said at the end of the 1980s, "Despite its small size, Hotpoint is a formidable player. . . . We may be global . . . but we are not yet strong enough to take on Hotpoint."

In 1989, Hotpoint moved again to change its choice of scope. (As we point out at the end of the chapter, choices need to be modified and the position of all organizations has to be fluid and not set in stone.) The subsequent activities of Electrolux and other firms had altered the economic scene. Partly in response to changes in technology and partly in response to competitive pressures, Hotpoint formed a joint venture with General Electric (GE), America's largest appliance firm. Nominally Hotpoint has moved from a local producer to global scale in one jump; the reality is different. The aims of this joint venture are to coordinate the transfer of technology and ideas between the two sides of the Atlantic. As yet there are no product flows, and there is certainly no attempt to integrate marketing approaches. Thus Hotpoint and GE are becoming global in a different way from their competitors in Europe.

CREATIVITY IN DISTRIBUTION AND PURCHASING

Hotpoint and Benetton are two players that effectively "changed the rules of the game" in their industries because of their novel approach to channel and supply management. Hotpoint's actions demonstrate how powerful the influence of a rejuvenator can be.

The traditional policy of appliance producers selling in the United Kingdom has been to focus efforts on selling to chain stores. This policy seemed logical given that the distribution of major appliances has traditionally been dominated by a few large chain stores. Independent stores, that is, outlets not affiliated with multiples and typically smaller in size, have been on the decline. In 1960 they had between 30 and 40 percent of the market, but by 1975 this figure had fallen to 14 percent.[6] The decline has been exacerbated by the producers' policy of granting large discounts to chain stores, which has widened the competitive gap between small and large stores. Hotpoint used to be one of the many firms that courted the chains and granted such large discounts. The volume of purchases from the chain stores was an incentive along with their potent threat of refusal to stock a brand if discounts were not given.

After Schreiber's arrival, Hotpoint's managers, perceiving the need to adopt a novel distribution policy if they were not to be further squeezed by the chains, decided to woo the independent retailers. Although the volume of purchases from each individual outlet was small, the number of outlets and potential volume of purchases were large. Hotpoint speculated that having comprehensive distribution through the smaller stores would give a significant marketing advantage, for it seemed that many consumers browsed and examined machines in the small stores, yet made their purchases at the chains where prices were lower.[7] Hotpoint's innovation was a price-support scheme promising small retailers that if they were undercut by a chain store, Hotpoint would help them match such price cuts.

The mechanics of Hotpoint's distribution scheme were necessarily complex, but the effects were simple. The small stores became keen to stock and promote Hotpoint's products, and the resulting push from a large body of retailers greatly boosted the demand for the Hotpoint brand. While Hotpoint's policy was acceptable to some chains, many were combative and disinclined to submit. Their managers tried to stop carrying Hotpoint machines, and some even took Hotpoint to court for its new price-support policy. In the ensuing fray, Hotpoint, to its surprise and pleasure, found that consumers were on its side. Chain store managers who refused to stock Hotpoint appliances were confronted by irate customers who wanted to know why Hotpoint, the most widely distributed brand, was not available in their outlets. Managers who found themselves losing trade, pressured their senior managers to give way to Hotpoint. Under these conditions, the chains, one by one, acceded to Hotpoint's new policy.

Hotpoint's policy altered not only the firm's position but also the balance of power in distribution channels. Other manufacturers found that Hotpoint commanded unusual attention among distributors. Rival brands accustomed to distributing through only a few outlets found themselves at an increasing disadvantage to Hotpoint. While not forced out of the market, they found that the balance of profits had shifted. Many competitors delayed reacting, perhaps because they were spread more widely over Europe and so were less flexible or perhaps because they failed to appreciate the impact of Hotpoint's policy.

As noted in Chapter 3, Benetton's approach to supply and distribution management was radical to its industry. We have already discussed Benetton's unusual policy of partnerships through special outlets; of equal importance was Benetton's upstream supply linkages. The resulting strategic network allowed Benetton to dominate an international niche by retaining great flexibility of response to local differences.

RESPONDING TO GOVERNMENTS

Creativity in dealing with governments also affects businesses. For some, government is a benign force outside the scope of the firm, but for many, government at a local, state, or transnational level can be an interference. Courtelle's story shows the power of creative thinking when a company is confronted with a transnational institution during a crisis. For U.S. firms, which will have to deal with the North American Free Trade Agreement, the example of Courtelle may be especially pertinent.

Courtelle in the early 1980s found itself in an industry plagued by excess capacity and with most of its major money-losing rivals receiving substantial government subsidies. National governments felt powerless to help as the industry was clearly Pan-European, so the European Community (EC) felt free to enter the fray. Vicomte Etienne Davignon, the EC commissioner and architect of a steel crisis cartel, called a meeting of the heads of the leading man-made fiber producers. Such meetings, designed to achieve an "orderly reduction" of excess capacity in the industry, were billed as favorable to the producers. The EC, as a transnational institution, was not subject to the antitrust laws of the various member states, and felt able to take this unusual step. Courtelle, a lead producer of acrylic fibers, was among the participants at the meeting.

The conventional wisdom was that a crisis cartel was the only way forward. "Market forces" seemed to work too slowly; negotiating around the table, beloved by politicians, appeared a better approach. The talks lasted some years, and progress was very slow. When lack of profit threatened the future of Courtelle, its management withdrew from the talks. This move incurred the anger of several influential politicians, who debated imposing draconian sanctions, but the gamble paid off. The talks collapsed and the market adjustment mechanism slowly started to deliver substantial capacity reduction.

To appreciate why the talks made matter worse, not better, it is necessary to review the reasons why the other participants were still in the market.[8] It seems that most came to the meetings in the hope that some other firm would deliver the capacity cuts, and each therefore shelved its own plans for closure. This belief was strongest among the state-owned firms, which believed that if the privately owned players like Courtelle were forced out of the market, they would benefit. When collective decisions were made on withdrawing capacity, many state-owned players did not implement the agreement, believing that non-compliance would not be punished severely. The collapse of the meetings precipitated a crisis, and rivals such as the Italian state-owned firms were forced to act individually. When they reduced capacity, the excess was slowly eliminated.

Smart rejuvenators realize that managing government relations or using laws proactively can help shape a firm's environment. Few are in Courtelle's situation at the European meetings; usually the opportunities are more modest. Most exploit government regulations in more traditional ways to facilitate their own causes. Richardson found that its efforts to expand in Germany were frustrated by local regulations framed to suit local manufacturers. By threats of court action, citing European legal principles of mutual recognition, it was able to facilitate negotiations and surmount local barriers.[9] Cook, the steel casting manufacturer, has used the article on state aid in the European treaty to its advantage.[10] It took the Spanish government to court and won an injunction to stop it from subsidizing competitors in Spain that were exporting castings to the United Kingdom. Cook also lobbied the U.K. government and the European Community to alter various schemes involving steel to its advantage. It strongly believes that government policy can be influenced by company initiatives.

TRIGGERS FOR MARKET CHANGE

Changes in any of the four forces outlined earlier should trigger a reassessment. Tastes, technology, and competitors are constantly in flux; the many drivers to these changes are mostly outside the influence of firms. They can exploit these changes by anticipating them and operating ahead of the competition, and in some cases may even be able to drive and shape the changes.

It is difficult to establish the extent to which any of the firms we studied managed to shift consumer or customer preferences. If any succeeded, it was probably Benetton. With its highly visible advertising and publicity, it has created a household name and image. Interestingly, this international niche is not homogeneous in its attraction. The people to whom Benetton appeals in Italy are younger than those in Scandinavia. The characteristics of would-be customers differ slightly from country to country.

Other attempts by firms to alter tastes in their direction have been less successful. Many executives of European appliance producers claim that consumer tastes are only marginally influenceable. Thomson (TEM) of France likes to illustrate this point from its own attempt to create and cater to a Euro-taste. It set up a joint-venture microwave oven factory to supply the German and French markets, which at first successfully supplied similar models to its target customers. However, consumer and retailer preferences took the upper hand, and demands for differentiation forced Thomson to adjust its product lines.

It is popular to say that greater differentiation is inevitable, but a word of caution is in order. History suggests that the trend could sharply reverse. In the early years of the automobile market there was great variety. Homogeneity came late, with Henry Ford. Since then variety has only slowly crept back in, becoming more popular in recent years. Seesaw trends are more obvious in European appliances. The early 1960s saw a great variety of appliances offered. The convergence of models and designs occurred in the late 1960s and early 1970s. Since then, as noted earlier, the trend has been divergent. Perhaps it will swing back.

Few of our rejuvenators have created new supply capabilities; rather, they have been masters of the difficult craft of synthesizing and exploiting what has been available elsewhere. None of the innovations, including Hotpoint's paint-free factory and Benetton's partnership, are wholly new. But what is impressive is the organizations' ability to adapt ideas from elsewhere.

Hotpoint's experience provides a lesson for many managers whose industries are dominated by large-scale players. It shows the limitations of the Fordist mentality and of believing that low costs can be achieved only by building ever larger operations. While experiences of the 1980s have reduced the numbers of those who subscribe to such views, there is a strong feeling in chemical companies, the automobile industry, banks, and other service organizations that because large scale has proved successful in the past, it is the only route to lower costs for the future.[11]

There have also been long-run swings in the area of supply capability. The recent trends in downsizing plants and service units seem set to continue as the labor force becomes more multiskilled and flexible machinery costs little more than specialized equipment. However, the economies of information management and logistics, increasingly important costs in the value chain, suggest a trend toward new notions of scale. General trends are difficult to foresee; what is clear is that in each sector factors are emerging which make it essential for organizations to reassess their strategic choices from time to time.

TRIGGERS FOR CHANGING STRATEGIC SCOPE: NEW CAPABILITIES AND RESOURCES

When and how often must an organization reassess its choice of territory? The start of a rejuvenation process is not the only time for reassessment. In their path to industry leadership, organizations find that they have improved their capabilities. As a rejuvenating, or any other, organization catches up with the leaders, and as it builds additional steps on its strategic staircase, it must reassess its position. Its proven ability to conquer a small territory or range suggests the possibilities for leveraging the advantage over a wider sphere.

Any extension of strategic scope calls for the ability to be flexible, and it is this capability which must be built into any extension or redefinition. For geographic expansion, the necessity to "think global but act local" is a guiding motto that has become almost a cliché in international management. Even though the general idea has been talked about in numerous books, beginning with the analysis of C.K. Prahalad and Yves Doz,[12] most established multinationals have found it extraordinarily hard to put into practice profitably. There are enormous behavioral obstacles. Perhaps helped by the fact they were relatively unencumbered by history, all our rejuvenators found that their skills in providing variety at low cost allowed them to expand their territories successfully. They could adjust parts of the product range to local variation without causing additional costs in their increasingly international supply systems.

Richardson initially limited its operations to kitchen knives sold principally in the United Kingdom.[13] Its first moves outside U.K. markets were tentative. In the early days quality was not good, and speed of reaction was poor. As capabilities improved, senior executives visited a German trade fair and the organization began to respond more entrepreneurially to inquiries from other countries. Its success at fulfilling export orders and tackling and conquering the U.K. market forced Richardson to reassess its position. It realized that it had developed the flexibility, speed of response, and levels of service required to conquer export markets where, despite the distance, it could beat local competition. It therefore increased its export efforts, engaging more foreign agents and managing them systematically. The results were greater sales and profits.

The big jump came when Richardson was acquired by McPherson's, which turned over to Richardson management its knife factories in other parts of the world. Richardson's managers, forced to rethink their approach, rose to the challenge. Instead of organizing each part locally, management moved quickly to make Richardson an integrated, substantial multinational producer with a portfolio of merchandise and brands. The challenge meant enforcing a high world standard of quality, product design, and speed of service, all at low cost. The move was almost faultless: the organization found that the skills it had developed when it was small in scope were applicable and transferable elsewhere, and that its capacity to be entrepreneurial and effective allowed it to fill the missing gaps easily. Perhaps the significance and creativity are more apparent when one realizes that few of Richardson's competitors have adopted the multinational approach. Richardson's strategy involved a wholly different direction; the firm's choice of territory, albeit partly thrust upon it, was a creative path to the global market.

Richardson's moves, described in more detail in Chapters 8 and 9, show that the strategic choices of how and with whom to compete have to be changed over time. They also demonstrate the pattern of starting with a limited territory, moving on to build new competencies on the staircase, then leveraging on a larger scale.

We have mentioned that Benetton also extended its strategic territory. It replicated its Italian success first in nearby countries in Europe, then further afield. Its capacity to respond quickly to market trends was an admirable discipline in making its foreign investments work. While the detailed skills required to respond to fashion are different from those required to run a multinational retailing network, the concept of responsiveness at low cost was common to its choices. Benetton's expansions overseas brought some problems, the most obvious of which have been in the United States. There the firm's early bold moves were less successful. The difficulty in finding franchisees to subscribe to the Benetton ethos according to American contract law, the tariff barriers to imports from Italy, and the structure of competition led to disappointing performance. Since then, Benetton has changed its policy and utilized joint-venture partners in most of its moves outside Europe, a practice that has been particularly successful in Japan.

Building new levels of capability has not always led to geographic expansion. Hotpoint's original success in the washing machine and refrigerator markets in the United Kingdom was clear evidence of progress up a strategic staircase. Hotpoint's initial move was product extension into dishwashers. It first sourced the product from Bosch-Siemens in Germany, then set up its own U.K. plant. Geography came later, and it was an approach by GE Inc. to its parent company, GEC Ltd., that led to the setting up of a joint venture between Hotpoint and GE's European appliance sales operation. It has continued its product extensions, buying the Creda company, adding stoves and another brand name to its U.K. range.

Being creative about strategic territory requires a special approach. On the one hand, there is a need for careful analysis to understand the basic economics of the market; on the other hand, there is a need for upside-down thinking and an ability to challenge convention. Doing something differently does not mean doing it perversely. As we have demonstrated, the rejuvenators, by accident or design, have hit on policies that captured real economic opportunities. These policies removed the loose bricks from the competitors' defenses and gave the rejuvenators an opening.

All organizations need to be vigilant, and creativity is fostered best when firms have as their goal the building of an entrepreneurial organization. Managers in the entrepreneurial organization are committed to experimenting with new methods. They are also committed to collecting the high-quality data on which careful analysis to justify such creativity can be justified. The characteristics of such organizations are examined in the next chapter.

NOTES

[1] Many ideas in this section draw on C.W.F. Baden-Fuller and J.M. Stopford, "Globalisation Frustrated," *Strategic Management Journal* 12, no. 7, 1991: 493–507. See also C.K. Prahalad and Y.L. Doz, *Multinational Mission* (New York: Free Press, 1987), and G. Yip, *Total Global Strategy* (Englewood Cliffs, N.J.: Prentice-Hall, 1992).

[2] See, for instance, J. Hatch, *Competition in the British White Goods Industry 1954–1964.* Ph.D. diss., Cambridge University, 1970, and F.M. Scherer, *Industrial Market Structure and Economic Performance* (Skokie, Ill.: Rand McNally, 1973).

[3] K. Ohmae, *Triad Power: The Coming Shape of Global Competition* (New York: Free Press, 1985).

[4] Theodore Levitt, "The Globalization of Markets," *Harvard Business Review*, May–June, 1983: 92–112.

[5] At the time of Hotpoint's decision, Philips' large appliance division, now owned by Whirlpool, was Europe's largest producer, operating factories in many different countries. At one time Philips had been very successful, and although it was still more profitable than Hotpoint, its profits were declining. Its geographical spread has been accompanied by a spread along other dimensions. Philips not only sold the full range of large appliances—washers,

refrigerators, stoves, and vacuum cleaners—but also put the Philips name on others—televisions, electronics, and small appliances. It was clear, in hindsight, that Philips—and now Whirlpool—found its global spread difficult to manage. Far from reaping large and rewarding benefits, it has found that the difficulty and complexity in coordinating marketing, inventory distribution, and design across the continent of Europe outweighed the advantages of having large production units, each concentrating on a particular appliance. Philips's difficulties were further compounded by the way it has historically looked at and measured its share. By its own measures, it was one of the largest players in Europe (and through Whirlpool, one of the largest in the world), yet its European share has been dispersed over a large territory: in every local country apart from the Netherlands, its position has been weak, never number one, giving a misleading picture of its acceptance and importance in each national marketplace.

In the early 1970s, Electrolux was beginning to buy its way to European leadership. It, too, had a broad geographic spread, with plants in many countries and particular concentrations in Scandinavia and northern Europe. Its market share was unevenly distributed, with only a modest position in Germany, but much more significant local shares in northern countries. (Subsequent to Hotpoint's crisis, Electrolux bought White, with a significant position in the United States, and Zanussi, with a significant position in Italy.) Electrolux's product range was wide, stretching from stoves, refrigerators, and washers through vacuum cleaners. Electrolux's expansion has been more successful than that of Philips, but not always as profitable as Hotpoint. It coped with complexity by delegation and autonomy at the local level, an approach midway between the Philips and Hotpoint strategies.

⁶ Percentage share of the market taken by chain stores and independents in the U.K. appliance trade.

	1960	1965	1970	1975
Specialist chains	45–55	58	60	59
Department and similar stores	5–10	10	10	14
Independent appliance stores	30–40	26	21	14

Source: AGB market survey data, census data, and authors' sources.

⁷ Some chains were able to reduce their prices even more by offering minimal sales assistance.

⁸ More details are available in J. Bower, "Management Revolution: The Response to Global Glut," pp. 19–39, and R.W. Shaw and P. Simpson, "Rationalisation within an International Oligopoly: The Case of the West European Synthetic Fibre Industry," pp. 75–94, in C.W.F. Baden-Fuller (ed.), *Managing Excess Capacity* (Oxford: Basil Blackwell, 1990).

⁹ The principle of mutual recognition has changed the rules of the game in the European Community. No longer do other EC producers need to be bound by local rules in the country where they are selling if they can prove that they satisfy the regulations in the country from which they export. Under mutual recognition, if a company has legitimated its product in one European country market, it cannot be kept out of another. This principle was first promulgated in the case involving Cassis de Dijon, and further discussion of its consequences appears in N. Colchester and D. Buchan, *Europe Relaunched* (London: Hutchinson, Economist Books, 1990).

¹⁰ Ibid., Article 90.

¹¹ The large-scale operation gains its benefits from using specialized labor and machines. To obtain the capital benefits of specialized machines, the equipment needs to be fully utilized, which is difficult if the output is inflexible. Technological changes have closed the gap between the costs of specialized and flexible machines. As designers of machines have altered their processes and electronics has taken over, specialized machines are often programmed generalized machines. Using more flexible machines allows an organization to build a small factory

at only a small capital-cost penalty. Moreover, the real cost differences may be even smaller, for it is much easier to keep a small flexible production line busy than a large inflexible one.

The labor-cost advantages of large operations are also diminishing. Most people do not like to work in large units organized along Fordist lines. Charles Chaplin's depiction of the drudgery and repetition of a production line is an overstatement, especially in modern multi-skilled operations, but there is a grain of truth in the message. Strike activity, industrial unrest, and even accidents are positively correlated with size of establishment, with larger establishments experiencing more of all of these. The real cost of multiskilled labor in small operations is often not much greater than that of many large operations using less flexible labor.

[12] Prahalad and Doz, *Multinational Mission.*

[13] There were also sales to its American owner, Hahn who owned a distribution network in the United States.

Chapter Five

The Entrepreneurial Organization

Like frightened rabbits caught in the headlights of an approaching vehicle, mature organizations often recognize that action must be taken, yet are so mesmerized that they cannot move. Death for the rabbit may be mercifully swift, but for a mature organization it often involves a long period of unexciting financial results and strategic failures until the deepening crisis forces bankruptcy, dismemberment, or takeover. Even though the organization as a whole may be frozen, it may contain bright spots; there may be excellent departments or groups. There may also be perceptive and active individuals who understand the need to take positive steps but cannot by themselves alter the course of events sufficiently to achieve a real change.

Why, even when some managers see the vehicle behind the headlights and recognize the signs of crisis, do some firms find it so hard to overcome their inertia? One reason is that a mature firm can become bedeviled by the multiple checks and balances that were originally put in place to help the organization run smoothly but later impede adjustment when the state of competition shifts. Individual perceptions can be ignored by the common will. Another is that past success can breed complacency, even arrogance, at the top and thus blind the enterprise to the sorts of market changes described in earlier chapters. Market leaders can dismiss others' innovations on such grounds as, "If we cannot make money by doing X, then no one can." Blinkered perception can lead firms to measure the wrong activities and permit managers to continue in blissful ignorance of impending doom. Just as has been said of control, "What gets measured gets done," so with strategy: yesterday's formulation of direction and priority determines which signals for change are recognized and which ignored.

If it is hard for mature firms to respond to crisis, it is much harder for them to recognize opportunities and emerging challenges before there is a crisis. In a state of slow change, individuals can do their little piece better: rendering bills more speedily or better engineering a particular part. But none of these separate actions will do much to transform the basic routines and behavior of the whole organization. The challenge for perceptive individuals is to transform their desire for action into a collective will and purpose. Clever diagnosis and perceptions of dynamic strategies alone do not provide the basis for effective management in dynamic markets: competitive battles are never won by brilliant individuals alone.

To break out from stasis, the mature firm needs to start building an *entrepreneurial organization* capable of combining strategic and organizational innovations. The goal is to assume the characteristics of the successful entrepreneur. It was Joseph Schumpeter who long ago pointed out the vital role of entrepreneurship—the finding of new combinations of resources—in organizations. The individual entrepreneur is able to take risks, innovate, and make progress both in good times and in the face of adversity. The same abilities are pervasively evident in some vibrant organizations. The entrepreneurial organization can deploy its strengths to the extent that it changes the structure of competition in its industry the way Schumpeter suggested.

Canon Corporation provides a good illustration of what an entrepreneurial organization can achieve. Famous as a leading producer of cameras, Canon decided to explore the possibilities of entering the photocopier market. Many years of patient building of new capabilities were needed before it could make significant inroads into the market dominated by Xerox. These capabilities included imaginative reconceptualization of the means to manage access to customers and the purpose and design of the machine itself. Though many of Canon's successes were seemingly bold and imaginative leaps, close inspection of what was actually done shows that rapid progress at any one time was usually the result of combining separate capabilities that were built earlier. One small detail of machine design makes the point. A team was set up to resolve the critical problems surrounding maintenance of the photocopier drum, which was the source of 90 percent of all its problems. The answer, which seems in hindsight to be almost trivial, was a disposable drum that the user could replace without the assistance of a skilled technician.[1] Because a team-based approach had already been put in place as a dominant value in the organization, this solution was not only identified but put into practice in a surprisingly short time. This was, of course, but one of many innovations that helped put Canon into a winning position in the photocopier market.

Marks and Spencer, the U.K. retailer, has also demonstrated an extraordinary capacity to innovate collectively. Limited in growth potential in its traditional market by high market share and threatened by the trend to small boutiques by firms such as Benetton and Next, it moved from being a clothing store to dominating one segment of the food trade as well. It has captured the number one position as the innovator of fresh prepared foods, identifying and then satisfying this newly created segment. Its shelves are filled with fresh foods ranging from simple salads to complete meals, many of which could be described as gourmet. To achieve its purpose, Marks and Spencer has had to organize supply chains completely different from those traditional to the food industry. It had to pioneer new packaging, new processing, and new ideas of customer service with great attention to quality. All this has required change because handling fresh, prepared food requires far higher standards than those required in handling clothes or fresh unprepared and frozen foods. These standards have subsequently migrated to other parts of the organization to improve the service delivery of stores handling both fresh food and clothes.

The critical question is how such abilities and organizational characteristics are created, for they are not God-given. The building process extends far beyond the work a single person or even a single function. It takes time and courage to sense the possibilities for sustained building and to embed the necessary perspectives and values throughout the organization: there are no quick fixes. Progress in gaining a clearer understanding of markets affects progress in building capabilities to deliver new strategies, and progress in building greater capabilities affects perceptions of opportunity and broadens the sense of the scope of future possibility.

In this chapter, we concentrate first on defining the attributes, or capabilities, discernible in organizations that have achieved the status of corporate entrepreneurship. These attributes can be used to identify the range and scope of the ambition needed in any firm committing itself to a path of rejuvenation. At the end of the chapter, we indicate some of the milestones along that path as the attributes are created and deployed ever more widely throughout the fabric of the enterprise. These milestones provide a first look at the more detailed agenda of capability building that is discussed at some length in the rest of the book.

For a flavor of the argument, we concentrate on the experience of the successful rejuvenators in building new, multiple capabilities in stages. Some were created sequentially, some together, as we suggested in the notions of building a strategic staircase. Some capabilities seemed to be prerequisites to providing a "platform" on which others could later be built. In all cases there was an essential determination to experiment, to work where necessary by trial and error, and to learn from both success and failure.

A significant finding was that the entrepreneurship required for renewal is similar to that required for industry leadership. For all our rejuvenators, whether or not they became industry leaders, the virtues of individual entrepreneurship were usually first developed in small teams, a form of corporate venturing. But the rejuvenators went further to avoid the common problem that much of the worth of such ventures remains trapped within a separate, often small unit that is isolated from the main business.[2] They realized that organizational renewal requires a more far-reaching form of entrepreneurship, one which crosses internal functional and hierarchical boundaries. A few firms carried their renewal forward to the point where they transformed their industries and initiated what we call *frame-breaking* change; here entrepreneurial activity had to encompass the whole organization and extend down the value chain.

Our finding firmly destroys the myth that renewal requires a wholly different approach. To be sure, the actions differ at various stages, and we detail these differences in the following chapters, but the underlying thrust is common. We found that, in each stage of rejuvenation, individual entrepreneurship, renewal, and frame-breaking change, many of the organizational attributes most clearly visible at the end had been present earlier, but in attenuated form. The process of building, then, is one of holding clear a sense of the ultimate goal as a guide for making conscious and consistent investments in the supply side of strategy to match the needs of ever more stretching competitive demands.

DISTINGUISHING FEATURES

What features distinguish the mature from the entrepreneurial organization?[3] All the enterprises we observed were multifaceted and complex with untidy features, making simple classification difficult and dangerous. Some themes appeared to stand out, and we were much struck in our research by the mind-sets of the managers we spoke to. It seemed to us in many cases that actions reflected company philosophy. Poor performers often reflected narrow, defensive, and parochial thought. Typically, these thoughts reflected linear, top-down, mechanistic views of the world. In contrast, dynamic organizations exhibited a more positive approach, which was aptly summarized by the founder of Matsushita Electric. He listed many of the key attributes that, in our view, are the desired result of transition from maturity to the entrepreneurial organization.

We are [Japan is] going to win . . . The reasons for [Western] failure are within yourselves . . . For you, the essence of management is getting the ideas out of the heads of the bosses into the hands of labour . . . For us, the core of management is precisely the art of mobilizing the intellectual resources of all employees . . . Only by drawing on the combined brainpower of all its employees can a firm face up to the turbulence and constraints of today's environment. This is why our large companies give their employees three or four times more training than yours, this is why they foster within the firm such extensive exchange and communication.[4]

Central to Matsushita's observation lies teamwork, and indeed a strong orientation toward teamwork is at the heart of the whole idea of the entrepreneurial organization. Teamwork, however, needs to be explained and explored, for, if improperly deployed, it can have many negative features. Moreover, teamwork by itself is not a sufficient goal. Many organizations do have teams, and many spend much time cultivating them, but this does not ensure entrepreneurial behavior for the enterprise.

We identified four other essential features (see Exhibit 5.1). First is a high level of aspiration about future possibilities, particularly an ambition beyond the limited horizon of the immediate task—at all levels of an organization. A firm that sets out to be less than the best in its industry seldom has the spur to reach for innovations that might propel it ahead, let alone the capacity to defend its position against more ambitious rivals. Second is the freedom of groups to conduct experiments and the recognition that the consequences of experimentation may be failure. As all scientists know, it is only by experiments that knowledge can be tested. Many have labeled this feature "proactiveness." The third feature is the capacity of individuals and teams to learn; learning encompasses many aspects, including new skills, new data bases, and new systems, all of which are required to harness

----

EXHIBIT 5.1   FEATURES OF THE ENTREPRENEURIAL ORGANIZATION

Teamwork in all parts of the organization
Aspiration to achieve more than the immediate task
Experiments to explore what is feasible
Building capabilities to learn and adapt
Recognizing and resolving dilemmas

----

the results of experiments and to challenge the basis of the established hierarchy. The fourth feature, really a culmination of the other three, is the capacity of the organization to recognize and resolve dilemmas posed by unfolding events, a subject explored in earlier chapters.

This list does not attempt to capture all the features of innovative organizations. It is, however, strongly suggestive in highlighting key features we suggest as the *minimum necessary* conditions for true corporate entrepreneurship.[5]

TEAMS

A key feature of an entrepreneurial organization is teamwork. Teamwork requires assembling people with differing skills and perspectives to resolve seemingly insoluble problems and clearly identify opportunities and threats. People who share similar backgrounds, such as accounting or mechanical engineering, and similar tasks commonly work together. But teamwork among people with differing skills within a single function is difficult to achieve. Electronic engineers do not work easily with mechanical engineers, nor do financial experts with accountants. Effective teamwork that goes beyond the single functional or office boundary is even more elusive.[6]

Richardson was able to bring together different skills within a single function—engineering—to solve a common task. Engineering combined electronic knowledge and skills with its long-standing mechanical engineering skills. Traditionally, everyone perceived the manufacture of knives as a mechanical problem. Yet Bryan Upton, the managing director, was determined to try new ways of resolving what he considered an impasse to improving the process. To do so he hired electronic engineers, who bought new perspectives to old problems. By creating teams of existing engineers and shop-floor workers, the business discovered simple but radical ways of bettering its product, which, contributed to a staggering improvement of productivity by nearly thirty-five times over a few years.

Teamwork across functions was evident in Hotpoint, one of whose early examples is striking. Hotpoint's washing machines often broke down, and customers were becoming upset with the poor levels of reliability and service. The company had always sought solutions for this problem without involving two important departments: production and service. Customer service staff were separated from production physically and in the organization chart. Because the company plant was old, senior managers suggested that the quality problem could be resolved only by investing heavily in new machinery and new, expensive systems. When Chaim Schreiber, the new chief executive, arrived, he instructed service engineers to work with the production department. They pointed out to the production department that many of the failures in the washing machine could be traced to a few basic causes; the production department then realized that a few simple changes to basic procedures could reduce the number of failures. At a negligible cost of a few meetings and a simple work program, Hotpoint was able to reduce its fault level substantially.

Combining skills and perspectives across organizational boundaries can also be effective. Wolsey, a U.K. knitwear company in the Courtaulds group, which also rejuvenated, provides an excellent example of the effectiveness of bridging vertical boundaries, in this case with an agent. Wolsey for years had been selling its knitwear to the Scandinavian and Danish markets through agents, yet had failed to heed what those representatives had been telling the company. Contentment with selling to the agent only what it produced, rather than involving the agent in the marketing and design functions of the business, was one of the many features that contributed to a steady downturn in Wolsey's business. One day the senior managers, deciding to listen to what a very successful agent had to say, observed that he was building a wholly new type of business. From a previous focus on selling knitwear, the agent had expanded into selling a wide range of midpriced, midfashion garments, including knitwear. His new approach represented a radical change, and the results were evident in greater sales, greater profits, and greater visibility. Wolsey, too, began to change its approach and discovered to its surprise that working with the agent allowed it to achieve higher profits and greater sales as its core product, knitwear, was adapted to the particular style and color needs of each foreign market.

The startling feature of the entrepreneurial organization is the frequency with which effective teamwork is used to cross the boundaries that all too often separate the functions, territorial units, and layers in the hierarchy. These teams have to supplement, not destroy the traditional skills and competence that are the essence of the organization. Here lies a major difference between mature and entrepreneurial organizations. In mature businesses, where there is extensive use of them, teams, are confined within functions or used for routine tasks, seldom for solving problems. For example, nurses and doctors in traditional hospitals, are used to working as teams in all manner of routine operations and medical treatments, yet only in forward-looking hospitals do they work together in other contexts and with administrators. Entrepreneurial organizations use teams to resolve difficulties and explore new ways to proceed, particularly activities like providing better customer service. Such teams often require participants to cross traditional divides of hierarchy, function, and geography. The shop-floor operative has to work with the accounts clerk, the nurse with the lab assistant, the salesclerk with the customer repair staff.

Making Teams Work Effectively

Teams and teamwork are not the same thing, for it is hard to make teams work effectively, and equally important, ensure that results are implemented. Effective teamwork demands that people reconcile opposing tensions of individuality and collectivity and requires trust, sharing, and reciprocity. Further, the vital team needs a strong sense of common purpose, without which difficult trade-offs can seldom be judged consistently. That sense of consistency is a necessary ingredient to permit the building of new capabilities and to allow members to acquire and deploy new skills. Serious obstacles must be overcome before the tension between individuality and collectivity can be managed productively. Not only do many managers instinctively prefer to exercise personal authority, if only as a crucial part of making their mark for promotion, but most organizations still prefer individual measures of performance and accountability. There are also risks to be guarded against. The wrong kind of teamwork can lead to groupthink, which can stifle individuals' initiatives, erode their specialist skills, and blunt the drive for innovation.

Since publication of the original edition of this book, we have read the perceptive 1993 study by Jon Katzenbach and Douglas Smith and found that their observations mirror ours in the rejuvenators we studied. They show in detail how many successful U.S. firms, such as Motorola with its cellular phone business, have relied on effective teamwork to confront and surpass global competitors. Their general conclusions about the opportunities and pitfalls in building what they call high-performing teams provide the reader with a gold mine of insight into the processes involved.[7] In what follows, we emphasize some of the issues we found to be especially pertinent if the power of teamwork is to be released. We place teamwork in the wider context of the entrepreneurial organization, where the results of one team's performance have to be used by others if full competitive benefits are to be realized.

Consider first the elusive issue of trust. Functional experts may have to reveal scarce and valuable expertise to those outside their normal domain and risk the seeming loss of status when others discover that the barriers to picking up a working knowledge of a subject is not so great as many experts claim. Functional experts may also have to reveal their ignorance of how to solve problems, leading to potential

116

loss of face and even of power. Related to trust are sharing and reciprocity, both of which are necessary to problem solving. Sharing skills and knowledge not only is essential but also threatens individual power bases and forces people to recognize that what they hold most dear may require modification. Reciprocity requires individuals to refrain from being exploitative and unreasonably opportunistic. In a world of collaboration, any one party can hold to ransom the rest of the group by offering collaboration, then at the last moment refusing or raising the fee for the necessary vital ingredients to complete the job.[8]

Trust is not easy to establish and make durable, especially in organizations where exploitative behavior prevailed in the past. Trust is particularly difficult between different levels of an organization, where seniors have the power to dismiss juniors, but juniors have little opportunity to curtail abuses by seniors. For this reason trust often goes side by side with senior executives' open willingness to alter their views upon pressure from juniors. Besides trust, sharing, and reciprocity, there must be respect for expertise and competence. Bad teams can come up with plans that do not work because expert advice was ignored and functional skills bypassed. This may be because the team did not have the correct skills, which may lie elsewhere in the organization or outside it. Either way, they need to be utilized by the team.

Establishing true teamwork often takes a long time, and operating in teams may appear to slow down the process of decision making and action, involve more people than apparently necessary, and consume immense amounts of valuable time. This can be justified only if the quality of what is accomplished is, and is seen to be, better.

To help make teams effective, many mature or paralyzed organizations must rethink how they train and reward their staff. Systems that rewarded individualism have to go because they fail to measure commitment to the team. They have built-in mechanisms that discourage collective entrepreneurship. Instead, new reward systems that encourage individual effort, provided it is collectively employed, are necessary. Some organizations undertake individual assessments but use the results of teamwork as the basis for rewards. Others abolish individual assessments altogether and reward only teams. Many entrepreneurial organizations use formal training to support team initiatives. Edwards High Vacuum believed in training its staff to work together, considering this strategically important, not an option pandering to the desires of the personnel function.

Relocating people can also help foster greater degrees of teamwork, for people in disparate locations often find communication difficult, especially in the early stages of building teams. Creda found that the integration of design and production was greatly enhanced when its design department was moved to the floor above the factory, and entry was via the shop-floor area. Shop-floor workers can intercept designers to show them how badly—or well—designs fit into production systems. Designers debate half-formed ideas with technicians before launching them. Teamwork of the best kind is evident here: informal interactions and meetings, prompted by need, generated mutual respect, under-standing, and sharing and swept away unnecessary, time-consuming meetings and formality. Some organizations relocate departments but fail to generate this sort of teamwork, for proximity is not always enough.

A vital team needs to combine the benefits of mutual trust, respect, and a shared sense of purpose. It also needs to have a built-in mechanism for dissent to combat the insidious pressures of groupthink that famil-iarity can breed. The combination puts great stress on the nature of leadership. It must be legitimate for team members to disagree, to advocate new ideas, and to do so without deflecting the team from its common purpose. How to judge when the signals for change should be recognized and acted upon is an elusive skill for the team, but is evident in many of the high-performing teams we observed. They achieved results no single member thought was possible, precisely because there were individuals who could make necessary judgments and persuade their colleagues to change, even when there was little more than an ill-defined sense of a challenge.

These attributes of successful teams raise the vexatious question of who leads a team. In many cases, a leader exists by virtue of appoint-ment or recognized expertise. Yet we found that in the most successful teams, it was not always clear who was leading the team at any one point. All members could contribute leadership ideas, leaving the "offi-cial" leader with the role of orchestrator. Furthermore, in an entrepre-neurial organization, a skilled scientist or marketer who is a leader in one team may have to become a follower in another. Individuals need to understand the virtues and values of such flexibility and transfer the learning from one team to another over their careers. The same applies on a larger scale for the organization as a whole, for the notions of orchestration and development of all resources are a distinctive attribute of rejuvenated businesses, as we show in later chapters. The virtues of teamwork on a small scale must be replicated across the organization if the effects are to permit the business to reach for frame-breaking innovations and go beyond the achievement of limited prog-ress that does little to transform the whole.

The teams that survive in mature organizations are usually lingering vestiges of behavior that was driven out by the onset of maturity: entrepreneurial organizations create new teams all the time. The essential difference is that entrepreneurship demands that energy be focused on meeting challenges. Change does not always have to wait until there is a financial crisis. The excitement of working to defeat a problem can act as a powerful magnet to pull together people of different backgrounds and reinforce the values of reaching for stretching goals. But how are the challenges to be identified? The ability to spot early signs of both crisis and opportunity is an important part of leadership. That ability seems closely tied to managers' ambitions, an issue to which we now turn.

ASPIRATIONS

In many mature businesses we heard the words *it cannot be done*, meaning that some new target or goal was unattainable without massive investments and long time delays. In sharp contrast, reaching out for a better solution was a key feature of all innovative organizations. Such ambitions can be grandiose or quite modest. Komatsu, the Japanese producer of earth-moving equipment, had a mission to *encircle Caterpillar*, its larger U.S. rival. This vaunting ambition helped Komatsu's managers create multiple teams desirous of finding innovative solutions to their competitive challenge. Among other entrepreneurial organizations we also found high levels of ambition, but it was rarely directed at the competition. Generally, the ambition seemed more prosaic and earthy. For example, at Richardson, Jerry Hahn, the chairman, telephoned Bryan Upton, the managing director, with this message: "Bryan, we've got a project to work on. All we have to do is to develop a knife that doesn't need sharpening."

Although not initially directed at challenging world markets, it was certainly an ambitious target. At the time the challenge seemed incredible, for as every child knew, knives became blunt through use. How could a firm invent a knife that never needed sharpening? The organization accepted the chairman's challenge, set up teams, and within less than a year developed a prototype of the world's first knife to attain that goal. That achievement was possible because the challenge harnessed and provided the spur to develop further the skills in grinding technology that had earlier been advanced by electronic engineers. Mass production followed shortly, and the knife was offered with a twenty-five-year guarantee. Now the Laser knife accounts for nearly half of Richardson's worldwide sales, and with copies from rival businesses, they account for at least 10 percent of the world knife market.

Challenges from the top are not the only kinds of aspirations found in entrepreneurial organizations, and they are not even the most common. We found that within departments or work groups there was the same sense of pushing for a new goal, countering the idea that it cannot be done. Of course beliefs are closely related to aspirations. One cannot easily aspire to a challenge that lacks credibility; on the other hand, if the challenge is believable, there can be real excitement. We have already recounted the story of Canon and the team that solved the maintenance problem in photocopiers; there are many other examples in other organizations. Most such goals focus on simple objectives, such as achieving near-perfect quality without major capital investment. When challenges are credible and perceived to be based on extensions of existing capabilities, action can be swift and effective.

Making credible the challenges from high aspiration depends to a considerable degree on the will to win in the teams and throughout an organization. If people truly believe they can succeed, they are moved to search creatively for the means to do so. Why then do so few businesses devote managerial effort to ensuring that the will is there in the first place? One possible answer is that the climate of determination is set by those at the top, and that all too often senior managers are more concerned with finding excuses for poor or indifferent performance than with finding ways to overcome obstacles. This was one of the dimensions of managerial belief we identified in Chapter 1 as distinguishing the mature business from the dynamic one.

Beliefs and Actions

Just how widely beliefs and aspirations can vary within a single industry was well documented in a detailed study of executives in the major appliance industry undertaken by our colleague Sebastian Green (see Exhibit 5.2).[9] In poorly-performing mature businesses, many managers believe that external factors drive their businesses' performance and that failure is someone else's fault. Pointing at intense and unfair competition from abroad, the failure of government to provide protection, the fickleness of customers, the overbearing power of suppliers and buyers, they are keen to fasten the blame on *anyone but themselves.* They avidly read books on industry analysis, which describe stable, unchanging environments. In their eyes, the industry's economics or government policy is the deus ex machina that explains failure and justifies their paralysis.

By contrast, most managers in strategically innovative businesses believe that the organization controls its future. They believe not only that success is a consequence of their own actions (not surprising) but also that all the setbacks they experience are the consequence of their own decisions. Action goes hand in hand with belief. Strategic innova-

---

EXHIBIT 5.2   BELIEFS OF INNOVATIVE AND LESS INNOVATIVE ORGANIZATIONS IN THE MAJOR DOMESTIC APPLIANCE INDUSTRY

Beliefs of the less innovative	Beliefs of innovators
Imports are from unfair competition.	Importers have new ideas and suggest areas where we are inefficient.
Service is a profit center and products are bound to fail.	Products must not fail: service is a signal of failure.
Stagnating demand is the government's fault.	We compete with everyone for the consumer's budget.

Source: M.R.S. Green, "Beliefs, Actions, and Strategic Change: A Study of Paradigms in the U.K. Domestic Appliances Industry," in *Papers and Proceedings of Academy of Management Conference*, New Orleans, August 1987.

---

tors want to change their environment and refuse to accept the fatalistic beliefs of the less innovative. In Exhibit 5.2 we contrast just a few of the beliefs of managers in the appliance industry.

Managers in the less innovative businesses believed that products would always go wrong and that consumers could be blamed for many of the failures. This was particularly obvious when consumers did not follow installation instructions (perhaps using incorrect plumbing) or "misused" machines (for example, children using a washing machine to clean football boots). But the innovative businesses believed that product failures were always the business's fault, a symbol of the firm's inability to design and make a foolproof and fail-safe product, so producing foolproof, fail-safe machines became a goal. If the consumer put shoes in a washing machine, it was the duty of the manufacturer to ensure that the machine did not break down but either worked or invoked a safety switch.

Like all businesses, most of the strategic innovators we studied made mistakes and suffered setbacks. For example, some of their new ideas failed the market test or their new solutions to old problems were not as reliable as anticipated. Unlike many, they always sought to remedy their failures rather than fastening the blame on others. This sense of purpose and responsibility seems to have helped them find positive responses to seeming failure—to find the silver lining in the cloud—rather than to write off a mistake as something never to be repeated.

Once again we emphasize the point that in the innovative organizations, it was the ability of groups to identify high ambitions which distinguished them from other businesses. One could find individual managers with high ambitions in all mature businesses, but their views were not collectively shared, and no sense of excitement or challenge was evident.

EXPERIMENTS AND PROGRESS

Stagnating organizations need to perform experiments, and learn from them, if they are to succeed in rejuvenation. The instigation of experiments and the related learning must start at the top and permeate every level and aspect of the organization. Experiments are crucial for innovators, for they seek more effective and efficient new methods. New initiatives in an organization can take many forms. Some involve adopting, without significant modification, a best practice from some other business; some involve reattempting, again without change, something that was previously tried. But the most exciting initiatives do more. They conjure new possibilities that teamwork or prior research has suggested. This mixture of the tried and the untried, what is certain and what is risky, is the essence of experimentation. Exhibit 5.3 captures some of these ideas, which are elaborated below.

Richardson's use of optical and electronic devices in a mechanical production plant was both unconventional and radical. Most of the basic notions were individually well known in other contexts, but their combination represented a challenge to the conventional thinking in the organization and resulted in tangible and immediate benefits. It was one series of experiments, some of which did not work, that achieved the goal of higher quality at lower cost. Canon's idea of the disposable drum for its photocopier was another challenge to convention: an experiment in making and servicing photocopiers.

Experiments need not be intentional: they can be accidental. But in these cases, there must be a recognition that something of potential worth has been discovered and that there is freedom to follow up. Marks and Spencer demonstrates the lasting value of such freedom. Its overarching goal is to deliver quality and service to the customer. It discovered an interesting feature reputedly by accident when it sold out its fresh foods early one Friday afternoon. The first reaction of the managers was that they had failed to serve their customers, but the customers' reactions were different. They became convinced that the food the following day would be really fresh, so more of them came to buy. Instead of admonishing and reimposing the old system, the business moved to a policy of deliberately limiting stocks to reinforce the message that freshness was ensured.

The nature of necessary experiments varied greatly according to

EXHIBIT 5.3   CONTRASTING DECISION MAKING IN MATURE AND ENTREPRENEURIAL ORGANIZATIONS

Decision making in mature organizations—a linear process

Top management believes that its role is to assemble data that have been collected from below, decide what is to be done, produce a coherent plan, and *tell* the rest of the organization what to do. Typically there is little feedback.

Data collection → Planning → Action
    Data collection → Planning → Action
        Data collection → Planning → Action
            Data collection → Planning → Action

Decision making in entrepreneurial organizations—a looped process

Top management believes that its role is to encourage others to experiment. Plans are never fixed but subject to adjustment. Progress typically proceeds as a series of experiments, sorties, and attempts to solve problems. Feedback with assessment and adjustment are crucial.

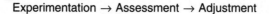

Experimentation → Assessment → Adjustment

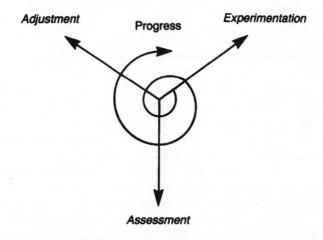

where a business stood in its path toward rejuvenation and frame-breaking change. At very early stages, as we show in greater detail in subsequent chapters, the experiments were typically small in scale and limited to work within a single team or a single function. They were designed to explore possibilities without incurring great risk for the business as a whole. Later experiments were undertaken on a grander scale. For example, Hotpoint challenged all industry conventions by building a major appliance factory without a paint shop. Benetton challenged conventions in the garment industry by enhancing its original concept of late dyeing with the development of sophisticated inventory management systems and computerized point-of-sale systems, thus enabling it to manage its stock and better respond to retailers. These larger experiments represented actions to deploy and combine capabilities *already* created by earlier, more limited exploration and success.

Experimentation always requires risks. Serious issues must be resolved before a business can hope to find a better future by trial and error. Whose risk? How much risk is acceptable? When should risks be run? There are no general answers to such questions, yet we found dynamic firms sharing a common feature in their approach: they consciously worked to create a climate within which managers had some degree of freedom to try.

Freedom to Experiment

Creating an environment in which to experiment often means breaking down traditional hierarchical decision-making procedures. Although hierarchical views of the world are contrary to corporate entrepreneurship, chaos must not be allowed to rule instead. With chaos there is no progress; instead there must be a climate in which there is freedom to experiment within a common purpose. Whose freedom is involved? Whose common purpose? The second question is easy to answer, for we have discussed the role of stakeholders' aspirations and group ambition. Couched in terms of a general strategy, the sense of common purpose has to be built, and as we show in later chapters, top management has a crucial role here. Whose freedom? We are clear that we mean the freedom of the individual and the small team to undertake those actions which they genuinely believe may help to achieve a goal. The freedom is one that exists without fear of reprisal should an experiment fail. Clearly every team has a difficult balance to maintain, for progress can be made only by taking risks, but without jeopardy to the organization.

Freedom to make mistakes, as opposed to undertake foolish activity, is essential if progress is to be made. The organizational climate must make failure legitimate. The implications of this observation pose a profound challenge to conventional planning and investment decision behavior. If there is no failure, there is no experimentation. The desired result of the myriad of small experiments is that some will fail. No right-minded finance director sanctions a project that seems doomed to failure; no manager risks the career-limiting behavior of proposing a failure. The paradox can be resolved only by procedures that set appropriate responses to outcomes and ensure adequate learning from both success and failure.

Let us first consider the problem of traditional hierarchy. In mature organizations we commonly observed that those upstairs rarely praised success and inevitably punished failure. This meant that individuals did not raise their heads above the parapet to try new procedures even if the chance of success was high. In innovative organizations the opposite occurred, with success praised and failure permitted (within limits) rather than punished.

Changing information systems and removing levels of hierarchy were common features of the rejuvenators. In the stagnating businesses we observed, many senior and junior managers had a hierarchical view of how organizations should work. They believed that initiatives and ideas should come down from the top of the organization. In the words of one, "Top managers are supposed to think strategically; others are supposed to act," and in the words of another, "The role of top management is to identify when a crisis exists, assemble the necessary data for the planning process, decide what is to be done, produce a coherent plan or vision of the future, and *tell* the rest of the organization what to do."

Hierarchical views of management are associated with the rational school of thought.[10] This school believes that the managerial task is to act logically and sequentially. It also believes that the brains of an organization reside at the top, among senior executives, and that only they can and should make crucial decisions.[11] Top-down thinking is the enemy of the entrepreneurial organization, and the belief that plans must precede action discourages experimentation and learning.

In the entrepreneurial organization, progress is not the result of carefully detailed steps emanating from top management. Rather, top management sets a broad agenda that subsequently involves the whole organization in both formulating and implementing new strategies.[12] The steps are a series of sorties and attempts to solve problems, which may involve new forms of organizing, new ways of undertaking tasks, new team construction, new routines, as well as new investments in physical assets. In learning organizations, middle and lower echelons of management are also involved in the experimental process. They may even initiate experiments without the direct involvement of top management. Within some broad guidelines of limited scale, entrepreneurial organizations can sanction a form of "bootlegged" experimentation hidden from top management as legitimate and desired behavior.

Ideas to identify and drive experiments forward are at a premium. Nicholas Hayek, who has masterminded the remarkable rejuvenation of much of the Swiss watch industry and is well known for his development of the Swatch, is clear on this point. He is fond of saying, "I like people who put a crazy idea on the table every day. I don't like to hear 'that's not possible.' " In his drive forward, he had to replace defeatism with determination and optimism. He also had to demonstrate that much conventional thinking could be turned on its head. For example, he concentrates manufacturing in Switzerland, the most expensive country in the world. To counter criticism that he would do better to move his supply base to low-cost countries, he replies, "CEOs must understand this point. If you can design a system in which direct-labor costs are 10 percent of the total costs, it is cheaper to build mass-market consumer products in the United States than in Taiwan or Mexico."[13] But to be able to do the same in Switzerland, Hayek had to create a whole series of innovative systems linking the elaborate web of local suppliers to an efficient central, integrated system. That required novel ideas from many people.

To permit experiments to be started, many entrepreneurial organizations have altered the financial tests they must meet. Rather than rely on careful calculations of a project's internal rate of return as the principal criterion, they recognize the difficulty of forecasting all future cash flows. Especially for small projects, such as Richardson's trials with new optoelectronic controls of grinding, primary attention is focused on the total cash involved and the potential for gains beyond the dimensions of the initial experiment. Risk is managed by meticulous attention to controlling costs and watching progress carefully to help judge when an experiment is to be aborted or expanded. For larger projects, such as frame-breaking experiments, while financial disciplines are important, they are only part of the full set of tests used to sanction a project.

Planning or Experiments?

There is a singular difference between organizations that use targets and plans to run themselves more efficiently and those driven by plans. In the first, plans are employed flexibly to ensure that the right steps are taken at the right time; in the second, the organization driven by documents and inflexible promises can all too easily lose touch with changing competitive needs. Planning as scheduling is essential: the production department must schedule its needs so that purchases can be coordinated; the personnel department needs to know future requirements so that people can be hired; the finance department needs to know when to expect cash and when bills have to be paid.

"Targets, not plans, are critical in driving our business forward. Moreover, these targets must change as competition shifts. The changes, though, are *additive*," said one chief executive of a rejuvenated organization. Planning in the form of targets to be exceeded rather than forecasts is vital to making a business go forward. By contrast, formal planning, as in thick books outlining in detail what should happen for the next five years, is not only contrary to the idea of experiments, but also a senseless activity in a changing, turbulent environment. The construction of forecasts that commit an organization to detailed courses of action over long time horizons is not nearly as valuable as the existence of careful analysis of possibilities. The latter is closer to the idea of experimental behavior and the climbing of the strategic staircase in ways that permit innovation.

One managing director of an appliance company aptly summed up our point when he said:

> I have difficulty forecasting the next six weeks, forecasting the next year is almost impossible, and the idea of long-range projections is absurd. It is true that my masters [at the group chief executive level] require projections [of all the financial numbers], so I give them what they want, but I also tell [the chairman] that they are meaningless.

The problem with forecasts, he told us, was that perhaps unwittingly they merely projected yesterday's events rather than tomorrow's requirements. The critical need, he explained, was continuous improvement. Thus, his organization had clear, stretching goals for many capabilities, especially customer service, frequency of product innovation, and cost reduction. He concentrated on monitoring progress of these measures, rather than trying to plan for profits and market share, which he regarded as the consequence of getting the input resources right in the first place.

Another managing director at a successful pump company said, "We never plan here." Yet sitting next to him was a planning director, who agreed! That planning director had a formal responsible function, but his job was to consider possibilities, not to produce thick formal directives. They both understood that the business did not rely on formal annual plans and forecasts as a basis for future decisions. They did have stretching targets for all parts of the organization. One was to reduce radically the length of time it took to send their products from design to market; another was to deliver better service to customers in a meaningful and demonstrable fashion.

Freedom to experiment alters traditional conceptions of authority and of priority measures. It allows organizations to challenge the conventions of their history, their industry, and their surroundings. It emphasizes continuous adaptation rather than discrete initiatives. It also recognizes that, unless control measures reflect these priorities, the illusion of accounting profits can blunt progress in the ways we indicated way back in Chapter 1. Taken together, all these issues add up to a different conception of how businesses should be run. Pushing back boundaries can occur only if an organization learns while maintaining the necessary disciplines for efficiency.

LEARNING

Few managers today deny the benefits of learning or indeed of what has become the new buzzword, the "learning organization." We prefer to use the term, "entrepreneurial organization," because, like Peter Senge,[14] we regard critical learning as going beyond the acquisition of individual skills or the procedures embodied in the typical management development program. Teamwork, aspirations, and experiments are key features of entrepreneurial companies, but they have to translate possibilities, beliefs, and discoveries into tangible results. The results of experiments and achievements by others provide a constant challenge to managers' mental models of the world around them. Mature and static organizations usually react negatively to suppress the results of those experiments which challenge deep-seated beliefs and to find reasons to discard information that may require the manager to alter behavior. Entrepreneurial organizations have a positive and dynamic approach: they learn from experiments of all kinds.

The goal of the entrepreneurial organization is to command and deploy an ever expanding base of knowledge, where knowledge is regarded as a stock of expertise, not merely the command of information. Just as René Descartes could say of the individual, "It is not enough to have a good mind . . . the main thing is to use it well," so for organizations. Expertise has to become the property of teams, not individuals, if the benefits are to be of competitive and lasting worth. Many of the experiments we observed in rejuvenating businesses had the quality of helping to accelerate the speed at which the teams could learn, thus allowing the knowledge to become a competitive asset (see Exhibit 5.4).

Although steps and experiments may be formulated with limited data, it is the careful collection and analysis of feedback data, that permit collective learning and innovation by deploying fresh knowledge.[15] Analysis and skilled interpretation form a central pivot for adjustment, which is critical at all levels. This is never easy, for many experiments produce ambiguous results. Attempts to improve routines can often start by making things worse in some directions while improving matters in others. For example, attempts to improve quality often result initially in higher costs, especially where cost includes labor time. The full benefits of low cost and high quality may take a

---

EXHIBIT 5.4   LEARNING IN ORGANIZATIONS

The mature organization	The entrepreneurial organization
Experiments are on-off.	Expermients lead to action and further experiments.
Plans are designed to remain constant over the longer term.	The results of experiments must be allowed to challenge even the most sacrosanct plans.
Skill development is defined in terms of individuals' current tasks.	Skill development must balance future possibilities with current needs.
Investment in information and data is less worthwhile than investment in tangible assets.	Investment in information is nearly always worthwhile if it can be turned into team-based knowledge.

---

little time to materialize, and require routines to be modified several times. In the learning business, the adverse results of a single experiment are never used to reject new possibilities; rather, a whole series of small experiments is undertaken to create new opportunities.

Richardson had to experiment with many kinds of steel and knife serration before it succeeded in finding the formula for the Laser knife. Scottish knitwear producers had to experiment constantly with their new machines before they could create variety at low cost. Edwards had to wait almost five years before its new information system could deliver real savings. However, in each case, the returns were high relative to the costs of the experiments.

Loop learning is also necessary where the results of experiments create new routines. Again at Richardson, the shipping clerk experimented in the arrangement of the shape of knife packaging and negotiated a reduction of approximately fifty cents in shipping cost per container. The benefits did not end there, for they led to a feedback loop between the design department responsible for packaging and the shipping department so that a routine of identifying future cost savings could be instigated.

In the entrepreneurial organization, the results and analysis of one experiment are also used as reasons to start another. It is transparent that this approach is vital, for singular success in one area cannot sustain an organization in a changing environment. In Creda, successful approaches in one part of the factory have been translated to new initiatives along similar but not identical lines in another part. The shops of the Benetton organization trade many ideas among themselves, as a means of encouraging and developing better ways of doing business.

The successful Scottish knitwear firms regularly call meetings of their agents to discuss possible ideas in their respective territories, to gather new ideas for future progress. By contrast, many mature businesses take a hierarchical approach to spreading good news, with groups of senior managers attempting to filter and select. This discourages spontaneity and experimental behavior.

The values of experimentation have to become pervasive to provide the motivation for managers, especially those in the middle, to learn. As psychologists tell us, old dogs rarely have difficulty learning new tricks; they more often have difficulty convincing themselves it is worth the effort.[16] Besides, as Karl Weick observed, "If people want to change their environment, they need to change themselves and their actions—not someone else . . . Problems that never get solved, never get solved because managers keep tinkering with everything but what they do."[17] A key element is *how* the planning processes involve those who carry out the actions. People and teams at many levels have to understand how even humble activities are affected by and in turn affect others in the enterprise. With that understanding, they can begin to move away from concentrating on their own patch to helping build the enterprise as a whole. That understanding can often be gained only by learning from experiments with the process itself.

Experimentation alone is not enough for these purposes. It also has to be linked to the sorts of diagnosis of competitive dynamics we described in earlier chapters. The sense of purpose that helps to foster team learning has to be linked to competitive reality. The goal is "holistic" thinking by managers at many levels. Perceptions of broad, external changes, challenges, and possibilities have to be combined with the mastery of the small details of effective performance if necessary new combinations are to be identified and put into practice. A simple example that we saw repeated many times illustrates the heart of the issue. One manufacturer of sophisticated machinery recognized the need to improve its information system if it was to deliver a strategy of more flexible production. A comprehensive system was developed for many functions, including human resources: immediate answers were available to such questions as precisely how many people had what levels of skill, years of experience with what equipment, and so on. The guiding values for the data architecture of the system, however, were set by financial controllers and technical experts whose perspectives were narrow and parochial. The system could not recognize that cost competition from other countries was changing the center of gravity of the industry to the extent that incremental improvements in performance at home were insufficient for survival. The information system drove the strategy, not the other way around. Information was confused with intelligence and the types of expert knowledge that mark the effectively entrepreneurial organization.

Learning and Copying

There is a distinction between learning and copying. At best, copying can lead a business to yesterday's best practice. Learning to do better can put one out in front. Obviously, the sensible business utilizes discoveries of others, but always seeks to improve on them. Moreover, the entrepreneurial organization recognizes that it has to balance the desire not to reinvent the wheel with the realization that what works well in one place may not be best in another context.

Richardson used learning instead of copying many times. For example, when Upton first went to Japan, he saw state-of-the-art technology in use, which revealed the enormous gap between his business and the leaders. He also recognized that he could not take his organization to a world position in one leap: the business lacked a skill base and understanding. He therefore set out to catch up but not to copy. Twenty years later, at the top of its industry, Richardson is still concerned to learn. It buys the latest and best machines, but immediately seeks modifications that will make them even better.

Organizations that learn quickly can in time overcome many deficiencies of a poor starting position and lack of initial resources. An organization needs to be smart: it has to be able to experiment and learn.[18] Like a scientist, the organization needs evidence about what does and does not work to obtain better ideas about what to do next.

Learning and Perspectives

Experimentation is a powerful mechanism for changing perspectives, but it is not the only one. Executives are influenced by competitors, by rivals, and by hearing about new possibilities from academics, consultants, and others. All of these can alter the perceptions of what can and should be done. Learning organizations are willing to change even their sacrosanct beliefs, but mature organizations try to remain constant regardless of the possibility that plans may turn out to be wrong. It seems that mature business would rather do a wrong thing well than admit that their course of action could be flawed.

De Geus has described how the strategic planners at Shell used mental images to encourage their executives to alter cherished beliefs and change their contingency plans. Shell constructed scenarios of the future, based not on forecasts, but on possibilities, then asked its managers to act out what they would do in such situations, and analyzed the results. Many managers realized that previous thinking and contingency plans were flawed and that they would have to rethink the future if they were to withstand an oil shock. Although changes meant admission of mistakes, the organization set up new routines. In 1985, one of its scenarios was a price of $15 a barrel of oil when it was selling for $28. The exercise proved to be vital when oil prices subsequently plunged to $10.[19]

Such experiments to affect managers' mental models underscore a central theme of preceding chapters. How you perceive the competitive environment affects how you act. There is no point in investing in learning and additional information if the old blinkers determining priorities are kept in place.

Learning and Skills

Reframing perspectives is not enough: entrepreneurial organizations have a different approach to investment in skills and human capital. We found that rejuvenating organizations typically invested as much if not more on retraining and bringing new skills to their labor force as they did on capital equipment, and several spent far more. We are not the first to emphasize the value of a skilled work force in any successful organization, yet our message is different from many which have gone before. We argue that although they are often required, new skills usually change as the organization learns. For these reasons, many dynamic businesses invest heavily in generalist and adaptable skills to complement the specific skills and training they need to accomplish today's tasks.

At Edwards, customers who wanted to place an order were traditionally dealt with by several different departments: one quoting order time, another dealing with part specification, still another dealing with delivery. Inquiries revealed that it was preferable for the business and the customer if many of the questions and issues could be resolved at the same time by the same person. It was agreed that one telephone clerk should be able to tell a customer whether a part was available, how long it would take to produce it, find out when and where it was required, and ascertain whether the order was needed so the customer could repair a broken machine or merely desired to replace its stock. The new approach required wholly new skills, some general and some highly specialized, from the clerks running the system. To make it work, the organization had to invest in training.

In many plants we observed experiments with line operators changing tools and undertaking simple repair tasks formerly performed by special staff. Such changes in procedures allowed the line operators greater control over their environments, reduced delays and downtime, and reduced the numbers employed in the plant. However, the new procedures required that the skills of the line operators be upgraded, and that they have new perceptions of their roles in the organization.

Changes in managerial behavior were equally frequent. In many mature organizations we observed that the finance and accounting staff saw their roles as controllers and monitors of the system. After experiments, some organizations found it helpful to involve these managers more closely in the active side of the business, setting prices and helping devise strategy. To make these changes work, the managers from both areas had to learn about each other's functions.

It is the changing rules of the game which ensure that a business must take a positive approach to generating new skills to handle new procedures and systems and demands of changing rules. Variety at low cost, total quality control, fashion at low cost, speed at low cost, all make new demands. What passes as a skill in one era may be less valued or even unacceptable in another. Thus, to implement innovations, organizations have to create and build new competencies.

Learning and New Systems

Investment in new systems, new data bases, and new knowledge is a vital complement to new skills. It is also necessary for development of effective entrepreneurial behavior. Whereas product and process innovations require some systems to be altered, innovations in strategy require radical changes in all systems.

The need for new systems and data bases was obvious in many major appliance companies. In the old order there was little variety; appliances were white and had standard sizes and features. The successful players were those which designed a product with features attractive to the largest class of customers. Now appliances come in a variety of sizes (particularly refrigerators and freezers), are made with a wide variety of features (for instance, low-spin-speed washing machines for Italy and high-spin-speed for Germany), and individual preferences are emphasized (for instance, many appliances are available in a variety of colors). The new order requires information capable of identifying details on small groups of customers and their preferences. Leading organizations realize that effectiveness requires a business to gather and manage detailed data on its markets.

In another industry, one business realized that its old costing system could not be adapted to cope with a wide variety of outputs, nor could it be adjusted to reflect the fact that the cost of manufacturing one type of product depended on the numbers of other types of product manufactured. In many instances the old system produced erroneous figures that suggested misleading courses of action. Costs could be ascertained only by building a new system from the ground up. Pricing systems also required changes, for the firm was no longer dealing with a few products in a relatively simple way: it had hundreds of customers in many countries who required billing in various currencies, and each customer needed a special service or product. New systems were required to master this complexity.

Of all the challenges facing a mature firm as it attempts to become a learning organization, the need to stimulate new kinds of behavior and thinking is perhaps the most pressing. Progress here permits the firm to conjure new possibilities and start investing in new skills and systems. These support innovation and improve efforts to make the business more competitive.

RESOLVING DILEMMAS

It was Charles Hampden-Turner who drew our attention to the importance of seeing many managerial problems as dilemmas to be resolved, rather than choices to be made.[20] What do we mean by dilemmas, and how do entrepreneurial organizations differ from mature ones in the way they tackle them? We start with a simple example.

In the past, U.S. auto manufacturers regarded high quality, like reliability, and low cost as irreconcilable opposites. In their eyes, high-quality cars had to cost more, and cheap cars were necessarily unreliable. Managers talked of the quality car segment and mass segments, and considered them to be different. By viewing quality and low cost as opposites, the U.S. companies approached business in a compartmentalized fashion; in contrast, the Japanese were holistic. As U.S. auto executives now realize, the Japanese saw the situation as a challenge to make cars more reliable *and* cheaper. The Japanese, to be sure, have not fully resolved the dilemma—their cars do rust and break down and are by no means perfect—but they have made progress. The Japanese have also bridged the gap between markets. Toyota, essentially a mass car producer, is successful in producing and selling the Lexus, essentially a luxury car belonging to another segment.

The idea of dilemma resolution is not exclusive to Japanese car producers, or even to Japanese producers generally. Many successful Western businesses are also able to reconcile opposites. In particular, the entrepreneurial businesses we studied nearly always proved themselves adept at both recognizing and resolving dilemmas, which we suggest is the essence of the difference between entrepreneurial and mature businesses.

Charles Hampden-Turner tells the story of Hanover Insurance, a rejuvenated New England insurance company that transformed itself from obscurity to one of the most successful in the industry.[21] It was able to reconcile many dilemmas, some of which were peculiar to its industry, some of which were general. One worth alluding to was the natural tension that existed between the head office and the branch offices. Like many organizations, its branches consider themselves to be special cases, whereas the head office wants each branch to be directly comparable to the others. This fight between the desire for local autonomy and centralism is classic, and sometimes the struggle gets out of hand, for example, when a branch refuses to allow a head office representative to visit. But Hanover seems to make the tension mostly productive; its managers successfully integrate a diverse empire, with each branch negotiating its own variations yet adopting to the general rules: "localism: branch initiatives coached, guided, and celebrated by mentors."

We contrasted the approaches to dilemmas among both mature and entrepreneurial organizations and found that, in general, entrepreneurial organizations sought to resolve dilemmas, whereas mature organizations saw them as places to make choices. The differences were noticeable. For example, in many mature businesses we saw alternate drives of extreme kinds, first toward cost cutting and then toward quality. In the first round, as profits fell, investment would be cut, people thrown out, and cost reduction seen as a single goal. This often produced some financial rewards but a situation in which quality declined precipitously. Top management, recognizing the dangers, would then institute a quality drive: quality was raised as the champion, and costs were forgotten. In the drive for quality, costs were added back and the original situation was restored, or worse, lower quality and higher costs resulted. Mature organizations, when they take action, seem to rush from one extreme to another. In entrepreneurial organizations there were oscillations to be sure, and achieving improvements in one goal often meant short-term sacrifices. For instance, improving quality often involved hiring new people to resolve problems, which led to rising costs, but then came a drive to reduce costs without sacrificing the raised quality level.

The entrepreneurial behavior to resolve dilemmas was typically built slowly, for the necessary skills, values, and attitudes could not be created overnight. Just as we indicated for the conduct of experiments, small problems were confronted first. As confidence grew, larger dilemmas could be tackled. In Exhibit 5.5 we show the results of a detailed study of dilemmas, as defined by executives in three British appliance businesses. One firm, Hotpoint, had made much more progress than the other two, allowing it to tackle larger problems and reap far greater financial rewards.

EXHIBIT 5.5   RESOLVING DILEMMAS POSED BY ECONOMIES OF SCALE AND FLEXIBILITY

Open-ended interviews were conducted among a group of executives from three British appliance companies: Hotpoint, Creda, and Thorn. Hotpoint and Creda were both successful, profitable, vibrant businesses; Thorn was perilously close to extinction despite its substantial market share and long history. These interviews revealed similarities among their perceptions of the challenges they faced but widely differing abilities to cope with them. The most universal dilemmas elicited from these interviews follow.

Teamwork
The needs for the division of labor and expertise appear to run counter to the need for collective effort. Can we both be differentiated and integrated?

Freedom
The needs of the enterprise for security appear to be at odds with the uncertainty of the environment. Can we plan, yet be flexible?

Flexibility
The desire of the customer for variety appears to be at odds with the need to produce long runs of products and avoid costly model changes. Can we have scale and flexibility?

Customers
Customers want individuality, but the system needs to cater to large groups. Can we be mass marketers, yet cater to many niches?

Technology
There is tension between introducing new technology as fast as possible and simultaneously allowing workers and managers to feel they control their destiny. Can these be resolved?

Parental relationships
The division has a desire to shape its own destiny and keep and grow its own resources, yet the parent company wants control and cash to fund other projects elsewhere. Can these opposing forces be reconciled?

In tracing these dilemmas, we first asked managers to identify the challenges, then drew up a simple cross diagram to depict the opposites. In Exhibit 5.6 we show the case of flexibility and product range. The executives noted the tensions between wide product ranges to serve the customer and narrow ranges to lower cost and help the organization. There was also natural tension between economies of long runs (what they described as economies of scale) and the need for flexibility. In the cross diagram, it seems that businesses have chosen differing positions and none seems to dominate. However, we then asked the managers to rank themselves and their rivals (on a 1–10 scale) in a simple box diagram that identified the opposites as dilemmas which could be resolved. Here we could plot real differences. It can be seen that Hotpoint was clearly ahead in its ability to combine scale and flexibility and that this was recognized by rivals. Exhibit 5.6 shows that Hotpoint has resolved one of the industry's dilemmas. Similar diagrams showed that it was ahead on others.

EXHIBIT 5.6   RESOLVING THE DILEMMA POSED BY ECONOMIES OF SCALE AND FLEXIBILITY

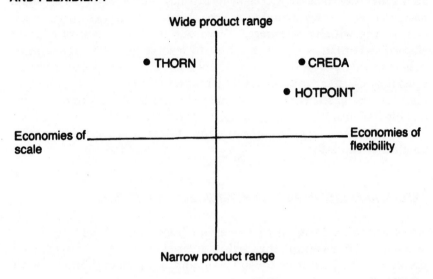

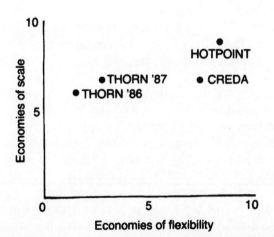

Source: Adapted from Charles Hampden-Turner and C.W.F. Baden-Fuller, "Strategic Choice and the Management of Dilemma: Lessons from the Domestic Appliance Industry," Centre for Business Strategy, Working Paper no. 51, London Business School, 1988.

All businesses must resolve a host of dilemmas, and many wonder if trying to resolve one set of dilemmas makes others worse. Typically, an organization faces some tasks of urgency and so needs to focus its resources, yet battles are inevitably fought on many fronts. Fortunately, one finding which has emerged from our study and that of Charles Hampden-Turner, is that the ability to resolve one dilemma appears to help businesses make progress along other dimensions. For instance, several businesses we studied found that tackling the problem of flexibility at low cost nearly always helped them to give better value to customers without raising prices, and greater value (profits) to the parent organization without sacrificing independence (needing a great amount of capital).

EXTENDING ENTREPRENEURSHIP BEYOND LEGAL BOUNDARIES

Ambition to build an entrepreneurial organization should not be restricted to actions within the legal boundaries of the firm. As many have discovered in their drive toward frame-breaking change and industry leadership, a more stretching goal is that of harnessing the resources of suppliers and buyers. As noted in Chapter 4, Hotpoint has invested in making its dealers more entrepreneurial, with gains to both its independent outlets and to Hotpoint.

Toyota's relationships with its subcontractors exhibit many of the signs of corporate entrepreneurship. Close collaboration exists between the center, Toyota, and the periphery, the subcontractors, concerning all aspects of the business, from car design through final sale. At the design stage, input and discussions with subcontractors help shape the project; just-in-time production systems and shared total quality control ensure that the whole system is optimized; and close links with sales allow subcontractors to anticipate demands. Because Toyota has built many features of corporate entrepreneurship with its subcontractors, it does not have to own all productive units. Independent ownership can coexist with close collaboration and teamwork.

Strategic alliances where there is a clear entrepreneurial center, extend the benefits of corporate entrepreneurship across the value chain. As we said earlier, "systems" approaches knit the strategic purpose of diverse units into a seamless web and call into question the need to own resources in order to benefit from them. Networks allow the center to suggest opportunities to experiment, in partner firms. Almost all of McDonald's successful new products were initiated by franchisees but developed and exploited by the center.[22] By making such initiatives, McDonald's is able to increase the rate of innovation and bring benefits to the whole system. Likewise, Benetton uses its partners to create ideas that are further developed in the center and then exploited throughout the group.

All such developments to extend the scope of the "competitive space" are in the spirit of corporate entrepreneurship. They are designed to resolve a major dilemma touched on in Chapter 3, namely, how to make hierarchies and markets coexist, enjoying the benefits of extra resources without the risks of ownership. In looking for solutions, innovators like McDonald's, Toyota, Benetton, and many others discussed in this book recognize the value of team relationships with their partners in which aspirations and knowledge are shared, but freedom is retained to experiment within the common purpose.

FROM MATURITY TO ENTREPRENEURSHIP

In this chapter we have proposed that the values and attributes of the entrepreneurial organization usually associated with individual entrepreneurs and new entrants should also be shared by other types of firm. It is possible to be large and long established and still display the vitality of innovation. Key features such as teams, aspirations, freedom to experiment, learning, and dilemma resolution are clearly visible in some leaders like Shell and GE, which have managed to find and deploy new combinations of resources as a means of retaining leadership.[23] Some organizations, like the Swedish multinational ABB, have first reacted to others' innovations, started processes of renewal, and only later created new capabilities to the extent that they could proceed to change the basis of competition for their industries.[24]

We have depicted the achievement of an entrepreneurial organization as a goal, or end state, for businesses setting out to break free of the trap of maturity and indicated that the crucial ingredients of organizational capability can be built. The overriding competitive purpose behind internal building is that of enlarging the competitive space that can be managed. The more leverage the internal organization can gain from scarce resources, the greater are the challenges it can profitably address. And if the same process is extended beyond the legal boundaries of the firm, that space is further enlarged.

The singular feature of all our rejuvenators, whether or not they reached a position of industry leadership, was that they built corporate entrepreneurship in stages. Their managers recognized that renewal is the intermediate stage between maturity and industry supremacy, not something different. In sharp contrast, many of the mature firms that failed had top managers who thought that entrepreneurship was a luxury to be added later. They wrongly assumed that renewal could be accomplished more quickly without the characteristics of experimentation, teamwork, learning, and dilemma resolution.

In Exhibit 5.7 we identify three stages in the process of transition from maturity. Obviously, we oversimplify the reality of messy progress, but the simplification allows us to suggest the agendas for management. The boundaries separating each agenda were always fuzzy and it was not always clear how priorities were assigned among competing agendas to focus actions. The break from a state of maturity was almost always tentative, for the possibilities for progress were seldom precisely clear to the chief executives. They had to feel their way forward in ways that could back up their initial hunches. We label this agenda as one of sensing, for top managers had little hard information to help them make their initial choices. Renewal could not begin in earnest until there was sufficient evidence from the early experiments that the scope of the endeavor could be enlarged.

In this process the top team had to become galvanized to the point where the members shared the enthusiasm and ambition of their chief executive. The first steps of sensing and galvanizing are the topics for

----

EXHIBIT 5.7 BUILDING ATTRIBUTES OF CORPORATE ENTREPRENEURSHIP

Primary agenda for management	Signs of change: "sensing"	Renewal: "galvanized at the top"	Frame-breaking: "deepening understanding"
Team orientation	Limited	Top team: extensive within functions	Many lateral and vertical teams
Aspirations beyond current resources	Individuals and isolated teams	Top team and individuals	Corporate ambition widely disseminated: growing understanding
Experimentation	Sporadic	Many small-scale initiatives within functions	Larger firmwide initiatives
Learning capability	Intuition, informal	Investment in information systems	Formal and informal processes
Capability to resolve dilemmas	Not explicitly addressed	Resolution within functions	Firmwide resolution

----

Chapters 6 and 7. In Chapter 8 we explain that the full achievement of frame-breaking change, in which larger investments could be made without undue risk to affect the state of competition, was often long delayed until renewal had proceeded a long way down the organization. This effort can lead to industry leadership. Some of the businesses we studied have yet to reach the end state, though they have made sufficient progress in rejuvenation to secure their place in their industries, at least for now.

Exhibit 5.7 summarizes how the features of entrepreneurship spread through our rejuvenating organizations over time.[25] In the early stages of sensing and galvanizing, entrepreneurship was mainly an individualistic or small-group activity, with the top team leading and others helping. At the later stages, entrepreneurship became more widespread, pushing up from the bottom as well as down from the top.

Finally, we address the question of assisting those who wish for a clear guide as to where exactly they are on the map. Measuring the extent of progress in building all these attributes of entrepreneurship is a notoriously difficult task, for different managers in the same organization can hold quite different perceptions about what is going on. We found it helpful in our research to use a simple questionnaire to give us clues about progress. Because individuals used different scales and different starting points for assessment, any quantitative scoring of the results is of dubious value. Yet we found that teams of managers could productively debate their differences to help them to build a stronger common understanding of both their current position and the direction for progress. That debate often yielded data on critical incidents, and the extent of differences in perception suggested how far the values and skills had migrated from one part of an organization to another. The Appendix that follows reproduces our questionnaire in the hope that readers will find it useful as a diagnostic tool in their own organizations.

APPENDIX

Measuring Attitudes and Progress

Here we lay out the simple questionnaire that some managers have found helpful in guaging the extent of their progress. The focus is on managers' expressed desires to create some or all of the characteristics of the entrepreneurial, learning organizations we have described in this chapter.

Thinking about the questions posed in the charts that follow is probably just as important as answering them. The questions challenge managers to face up to the problems involved in moving from maturity to vitality and in maintaining that vitality. The questionnaire has a double purpose: first, it can provide an inventory of the attitudes and perspectives held by individual members of a team; second, the results of the individual scoring can form the basis for productive group discussion of the extent to which a team acts as one and the extent of differences of opinion that are either divisive or the spur to further progress.

The questionnaire is divided into four parts, each focusing on a set of interrelated issues of corporate entrepreneurship. It addresses the following questions:

1. How important is the use of teamwork in the organization? Are the teams better developed laterally across the functions or vertically across layers of the hierarchy? Can the development of teamwork foster individual entrepreneurship or are the two mutually incompatible?
2. Is there a clear sense of shared purpose, and if so, is it shared widely in the organization? Has the development of greater clarity and sharing of purpose enhanced or constrained the freedom of individuals and teams to experiment with new initiatives?
3. How well has the business developed its capability to gather and interpret data on external and internal events? Has better information enhanced the ability to learn from experience and make better progress, or does the organization constantly reinvent the wheel?
4. Is strategy set within the limits of current resources, or is it based on the clear recognition of the need to build new capabilities? How well has the organization learned to manage the dilemmas that inevitably accompany attempts to chart new avenues of progress?

There is no "right" answer to any of these questions, for all organizations possess elements at either end of the scales of possibility. The issue is discovering the right balance among competing forces. We have found that debate among team members can help in the search for a balance that meets the needs of competition at any one moment.

The questionnaire invites readers to respond to questions about their business or organization by placing a mark on a line that has no formal scale.

Self-questionnaire

1. *Teams and progress*

Do you make extensive use of interfunctional teams for new initiatives and problem solving?

Functional isolation   Some teams   Extensive teams

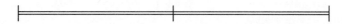

Do you use interhierarchical teams for new initiatives or problem solving?

No communication   Usually one-way   Extensive two-way
                                             dialogue

Has teamwork driven out individual initiatives, or does it allow them to flourish?

One excludes the   They coexist   Teamwork
   other   encourages
                                           individualism

2. *Freedom to experiment and common purpose*

To what extent is there a clear sense of purpose (often called a strategy)?

Chaos, constant   Fuzzy picture   Clear uniting
   shifting

Is it shared?

    Among a few   Moderately extensive   Wholly understood
                                                             by all

Has this common sense of purpose prevented, or does it encourage *individual* initiatives?

    Strategy constrains   Strategy is neutral to   Strategy encourages
                              initiatives   initiatives

Has the common purpose enabled collective experiments *among* functions and groups?

    Strategy constrains   Strategy is neutral to   Strategy encourages
                              initiatives   initiatives

3. *Feedback and learning*

How good are you at collecting relevant and valuable data on internal events?

Most internal reports   Some useful data, but   Crucial data collected
useless or misleading   many vital gaps   and disseminated

How good are you at collecting data on outside events?

   We know nothing   Some data, but   Extensive and good
about the markets of   difficult to collate   data
   crucial interest

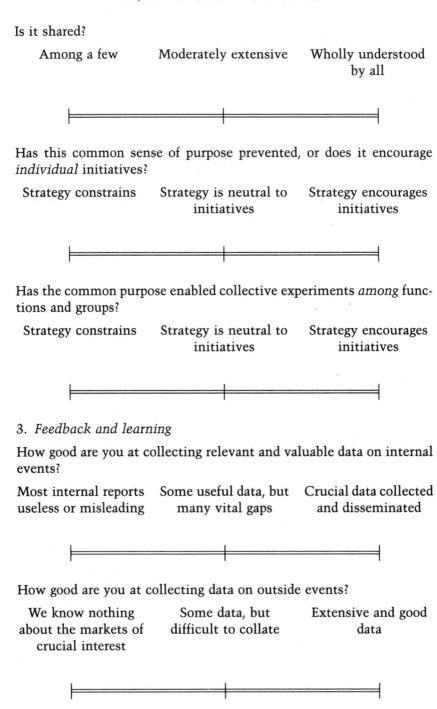

What has happened when you have gathered data or made initiatives? Have you learned, or are you constantly reinventing the wheel?

Never learn: mistakes   Learn, but also forget   Care taken to learn
often repeated   from the past

├──────────────────┼──────────────────┤

Has the learning helped progress or was it negative?

Feel powerless: past is   Neutral   Learning is vital to
a millstone   progress

├──────────────────┼──────────────────┤

4. *Aspirations and innovations*

Would you say that your organization has aspirations that exceed its present assets and capabilities, or do you feel that there is complacency?

Complacency   Aspirations match   Aspirations exceed
resources   resources

├──────────────────┼──────────────────┤

All organizations face imponderable problems. Some are very good at finding innovative and creative solutions. For example, in the car industry it was thought to be impossible to reconcile high quality and reliability with low cost, yet the Japanese found a way. Marks and Spencer also found ways to market food as a premium product, simultaneously addressing many quality issues.

How does your organization react to seemingly impossible dilemmas?

Ignore them: assume   Oscillate madly from   Work creatively and
that they cannot be   initiatives to   effectively to resolve
resolved   depression   them

├──────────────────┼──────────────────┤

NOTES

[1] We have borrowed this vignette from I. Nonaka, "The Knowledge-creating Company," *Harvard Business Review*, November–December 1991: 96–104.

[2] Relatively few firms can base their entire corporate strategy on setting a climate for pervasive and continuous venturing to the extent that 3M has, and relatively few can learn from their success in one part of the firm to affect other parts. For a thoughtful review of both the opportunities and pitfalls in corporate venturing, see Zenas Block and Ian C. MacMillan, *Corporate Venturing: Creating New Businesses Within the Firm* (Boston: Harvard Business School Press, 1993).

[3] Many of the ideas in this chapter are dealt with more formally in J.M. Stopford and C.W.F. Baden-Fuller, "Creating Corporate Entrepreneurship," *Strategic Management Journal*, forthcoming. We explain how our ideas fit into the substantial literature. An early version of the chapter appeared in J.M. Stopford, and C.W.F. Baden-Fuller, "Organizational Strategies for Building Corporate Entrepreneurship," in P. Lorange, B. Chakravarthy, J. Roos, and A. van de Ven, *Implementing Strategic Processes* (Oxford: Basil Blackwell), 1993.

[4] K. Matsushita, "The Secret Is Shared," *Manufacturing Engineering*, March 1988.

[5] Many people have argued that the extent of corporate entrepreneurship depends on the nature of change in an industry and that firms in slow-moving industries need not abandon the disciplines and efficiencies of an entrenched hierarchy. Our evidence is that "maturity," as measured by overall growth rates, masks the underlying dynamic.

[6] Our observations support the writings of R.M. Kanter, who has argued forcefully that managers add value by working in teams across traditional boundaries of the firm. See, for instance, *The Change Masters: Innovation and Entrepreneurship in the American Corporation* (New York: Simon & Schuster, 1989).

[7] J.R. Katzenbach and D.K. Smith, *The Wisdom of Teams: Creating the High-Performance Organization* (Boston: Harvard Business School Press, 1993).

[8] See C. Sabel, "Studied Trust," in T. Romo and R. Swedberg, eds., *Human Relations and Readings in Economic Sociology* (New York: Russell Sage, 1992).

[9] M.R.S. Green, "Beliefs, Actions and Strategic Change: A Study of Paradigms in U.K. Domestic Appliances Industry," in *Papers and Proceedings of Academy of Management Conference*, New Orleans, August 1987.

[10] For an explanation of these views, see H. Mintzberg, "The Design School: Reconsidering the Basic Premises of Strategic Management," *Strategic Management Journal* 11, no. 3, 1990: 171–196.

[11] See, for instance, N.M. Tichy, *Managing Strategic Change* (New York: Wiley, 1983). A.D. Chandler's famous thesis, *Strategy and Structure: Chapters in the History of the American Industrial Enterprise* (Boston: MIT Press, 1962), was partly responsible for this view. For a review of the history of these ideas, see also G. Morgan, *Images of Organization* (Beverly Hills: Sage, 1986).

[12] H. Mintzberg and J.B. Quinn have studied change processes in organizations. They observe that most firms undertake dynamic strategizing with emergent plans, and many small steps. See, for instance, H. Mintzberg and J.A. Waters, "Of Strategies Deliberate and Emergent," *Strategic Management Journal* 6, no. 3, 1985: 257–272, and J.B. Quinn, *Strategies for Change: Logical Incrementalism* (Homewood, Ill.: Richard Irwin, 1980).

[13] For a full exploration of Hayek's approach and philosophy, see William Taylor, "Message and Muscle," *Harvard Business Review*, March–April 1993: 99–110.

[14] Peter M. Senge, *The Fifth Discipline: The Art and Practice of the Learning Organization* (New York: Doubleday Currency, 1990).

[15] Our findings are in accord with many newly emerging pieces of research from writers. See C. Argyris, *Overcoming Organizational Defenses: Facilitating Organizational Learning* (Boston: Allyn & Bacon, 1990), R.M. Kanter, *The Change Masters: Innovation for Productivity in the American Corporation* (London: Allen & Unwin, 1985), and E.H. Schein, *Organizational Culture and Leadership* (San Francisco: Jossey-Bass, 1985).

[16] K.W. Schaie and J. Geiwitz, *Adult Developing and Aging* (New York: Harper & Row, 1982).

[17] Karl Weick, *The Social Psychology of Organizing*, 2d ed. (Reading, Mass.: Addison Wesley, 1979).

[18] See Argyris, *Overcoming Organizational Defenses*, Kanter, *The Change Masters*, and A. De Geus, "Planning as Learning," *Harvard Business Review*, March–April 1988: 70–74, and "Strategy as Learning," Stockton Lecture, London Business School, May 1990.

[19] See De Geus, "Planning as Learning." De Geus also reported on the behavior of birds to show how collectiveness is important. Robins are solitary birds in the United Kingdom, and only a few robins learned to peck open the tops of milk bottles left on doorsteps. In contrast, tits go about in large groups; when some tits discovered that milk could be drunk from the top of milk bottles by pecking at the tops, the successful tits were observed by others, and learning about the possibility spread quickly.

[20] See Charles Hampden-Turner, *Charting the Corporate Mind* (New York: Free Press, 1990), and Hampden-Turner and C.W.F. Baden-Fuller, "Strategic Choice and the Management of Dilemma: Lessons from the Domestic Appliance Industry," Centre for Business Strategy Working Paper no. 51, London Business School, 1988.

[21] See Chapter 4 of Hampden-Turner, *Charting the Corporate Mind.*

[22] For an account of McDonald's development, see John Love, *McDonald's: Behind the Arches* (New York: Bantam Books, 1986).

[23] For details on Shell, see De Geus, "Planning as Learning"; for GE, N.M. Tichy and R. Charan, "Speed, Simplicity, Self-confidence: An Interview with Jack Welch," *Harvard Business Review*, September–October 1989: 112–120.

[24] For an account of developments in ABB, see O. Brandes and S. Brege, "Strategic Turnaround and Top Management Involvement: The Case of ASEA and ABB," in P. Lorange et al. eds., *Implementing Strategic Processes: Change, Learning and Co-operation* (Oxford: Blackwell, 1993), pp. 91–114.

[25] For more details on the technical data collation, see J.M. Stopford and C.W.F. Baden-Fuller, "Creating Corporate Entrepreneurship," *Strategic Management Journal* (forthcoming).

Chapter Six

The Crescendo Model of Rejuvenation

Is rejuvenation really possible?[1] How does a business paralyzed by years of turmoil and failure and constrained by limited resources create a vibrant organization committed to entrepreneurship? Unless the organization is frugal and produces some short-term results, it risks losing support from its many stakeholders. But short-term results alone are not enough; longer-term survival must be sought. A start must be made to initiate a form of entrepreneurial behavior that increases the chances of durable recovery. As one chairman said, "We have put in new controls and financial disciplines that have stanched the hemorrhaging, cut costs, and returned us, temporarily, to profit. That's the easy part. Getting some momentum going is much harder."

Edwards was almost broke in the early 1970s, but fifteen years later it was the second largest vacuum pump maker in the world, and arguably the most profitable and most dynamic. At the start of its rejuvenation, BOC, its parent, had put it on the "sell" list and restricted reinvestment to less than the depreciation charge. Almost everything Edwards needed in terms of cash and resources had to be built from within. Only when Edwards had demonstrated profitability and viability did its parent allow it funds on a large scale.[2]

Hotpoint was almost broke when Chaim Schreiber took command in 1974. Ten years of hard work, first with Schreiber and then with Geoff Samson at the helm, converted one of Europe's worst-performing appliance firms with an appalling product failure rate into a shining star envied by all the industry leaders. Although it was part of the GEC group, its parent firm gave Hotpoint almost no cash and little other support until it had demonstrated profitability. Years of bad results had robbed Hotpoint of credibility, and GEC had little confidence in the value of spending money on it.[3]

Not only individual business units get into trouble; whole organizations need to rejuvenate and seem able to do so on limited resources. The Weir Group was in such bad shape in the late 1970s that it entered into the Bank of England's "lifeboat" scheme.[4] This allowed Weir protection from its banks, giving it time to reschedule its debts. A decade later, Weir, and particularly its pump division, posted a sequence of record profits; it had been rebuilt through its own resources and ingenuity.

When Bryan Upton became managing director of Richardson in 1966, the firm was small, broke, and part of the smokestack and rust bowl of Sheffield. By the end of the 1970s, when others were going bankrupt, it was one of the most profitable and fastest-growing firms in the industry. In 1990 it was staking its claim as the world's largest, most profitable, and most innovative producer of knives. Upton did not benefit from a rich banker or a strong parent; he had to generate the resources from within.[5]

Komatsu, the Japanese construction equipment firm, was in bad shape in the 1960s and early 1970s with poor productivity, poor quality products and service, and little hope of expansion beyond its protected domestic market. Despite extremely limited resources, it managed to haul itself from near oblivion to become the world's second largest player and challenge Caterpillar for leadership in the earth-moving equipment business; it is now Caterpillar's turn to rejuvenate.[6]

THE CRESCENDO MODEL

We regard building corporate entrepreneurship as the essential ingredient for lasting rejuvenation. As we suggested in the previous chapter, the task is difficult and often subtle. To ensure that all the attributes of entrepreneurship are diffused throughout an organization, the business must avoid the "quick fixes" so beloved by many. As we explain at great length later in this chapter, massive capital investment programs, aggressive but shallow attempts to force total quality management, or reengineering, or "cultural immersion" are usually ineffective if undertaken with insufficient attention to the issues we raised. The quick fix rarely delivers any long-term sustainable reward for, like the Tower of Babel, it falls if its foundations are insecure. The way forward must carry the whole organization to be self-sustaining.

Rebuilding a mature organization takes time; it cannot be done with a leap. It is, for example, seldom clear at the outset, because of information gaps, just where the business should be headed. Even when the direction has become clear, the details of the twists and turns in the road ahead can remain fogbound. Experimentation is necessary to test the feasibility of ideas. Too early commitment to a new direction can be unduly risky. A way has to be found to build consistently and to link newfound strengths before real and lasting transformation can be achieved.

While there are many routes mature businesses might take, the experience of Edwards and others can be distilled to identify one path that we feel is more sure than many others. It is a four-stage renewal process, an orchestrated crescendo. Crescendo is a musical term meaning "a gradual increase in volume." Our renewal process is also gradual, requiring many steps over many years. The crescendo has to be managed and momentum for change established to allow businesses to reach for ever more challenging targets.

In this chapter we address the question of how businesses can get started and shrug off the stasis that has plagued so many mature firms. To place that start in context and show where we are headed, we begin with a brief summary of the overall model: details are spelled out in later chapters.

Four Stages for Rejuvenation
1. Galvanize: create a top team dedicated to renewal.
2. Simplify: cut unnecessary and confusing complexity.
3. Build: develop new capabilities.
4. Leverage: maintain momentum and stretch the advantages.

Galvanize

Although it seems obvious to begin by creating a top team dedicated to renewal, this vital stage is often overlooked. Rejuvenation is not the fixing up of a few activities or functions that have gone awry; it is the process of changing every part of an organization and the way its functions, territories, and various groups interact. No individual, not even the chief executive, can alone achieve this magnitude of change, but at the start it requires leadership from the top team. Such commitment carries important positive messages to the whole organization, for without that commitment those who labor in the firm become demoralized or frustrated.

To galvanize the top team, the agenda for action needs to be drawn up carefully. At the start, detailed plans of action are neither necessary nor wise. Instead there must be a broad understanding of the issues and a belief that progress will be achieved only by many small steps. There is serious danger in the early stages that top management will either try to buy its way out of difficulties with overgrandiose schemes, such as investing in expensive state-of-the-art technology that few in the organization understand, or spend too much time chasing culture change programs and not enough time initiating action.

Simplify

Simplifying the business helps change managers and workers' perceptions of what has been wrong and what new actions are required. Like clearing the rubbish from an overgrown garden, cutting some activities is a necessary precursor to building something new. Removing outdated control systems and incorrect data helps eliminate the causes of resistance to change. Simplifying the business concentrates scarce resources on a smaller agenda and so increases the chances of gaining positive results in the short to medium term. Simplification also signals to outside stakeholders—owners, suppliers, customers, bankers, and employers alike—that something positive is being attempted.

Actions to simplify the task and provide focus for the effort are no more than temporary measures. They must be regarded as work to provide a "beachhead" in complex industry structures that can be defended while work to build new strengths can proceed.

Build

In the third stage, which overlaps the second, the organization must set about building new advantages for later deployment as the business breaks out of the beachhead. It is at this stage that corporate rather than individual entrepreneurship must be developed. Beginning with raised aspirations to do better and resolve old problems, in the course of time new challenges need to be articulated, which will help all to work to a common purpose. That purpose, expressed in terms of visions and a direction for progress, is typically phrased in terms that all can understand. Making progress along the chosen path requires managers to experiment and to discover what can work and what fails.

Experiments, of necessity have to be small at the start: resources are limited, knowledge about possibilities uncertain, and the risks seem immense. As some experiments pay off, momentum should increase to the point where major investments in new technology for delivering the product or service may be required. Learning may also start slowly, though ordinarily some parts of the organization progress more quickly than others. Over time the organization must invest in deepening existing skills and acquiring new ones, developing new systems, data bases, and knowledge. Alongside these initiatives, teamwork must be developed, first on a small scale to deal with essential tasks but then growing across the whole organization and extending along the supply chain. The momentum created helps build the values that underpin the crucial ingredient of the will to win.

152

Leverage

The final stage is leveraging advantages and maintaining momentum. As the organization grows in competitive strength, it can expand the sphere of its operations into new markets, new products, and new parts of the value chain. Leveraging capabilities can be by acquisition, alliances, or internal moves so that the business can extend its new-found advantages to a much wider sphere of activities. Pressures for expansion must be balanced against the danger of too much complexity slowing down the pace of innovation and forcing the organization to a standstill.

We label the rejuvenation process a *crescendo* to emphasize that the four stages are not discrete steps but rather activities which merge into each other as the magnitude of change increases over time. The reality of all organizations is messy, confusing, and complex. In the building of corporate entrepreneurship, activities in one department or at one level of the organization may proceed faster and more effectively than others. Moreover, organizations do not rejuvenate only once: they may need to do so repetitively. The challenges of one period may be resolved, but those of the next may again require organizational change.

The rejuvenation steps are summarized in Exhibit 6.1. The arrows are drawn as lines, though in practice progress is usually made in loops of learning. The dance to the crescendo of music is the samba. *One step back to take two steps forward* describes how organizations pro-

---

EXHIBIT 6.1   CRITICAL PATH FOR CORPORATE RENEWAL

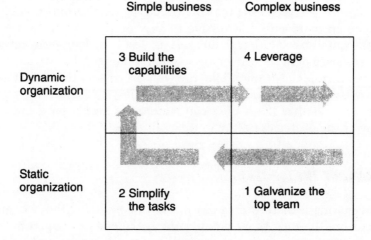

ceed—and it is exactly what happens with simplification and building. Let us use an analogy: renovators of old buildings know full well that the plaster has to come off the walls if a rotten structure is to be repaired. So it is in mature organizations that appear to be well run but suffer from deep-seated difficulties. While fixing the structure is not the same as demolition, it is rarely possible to fix it without spoiling the decorations. Removing the surface may reveal much that is in good shape and can be retained, but the surface must be uncovered if the real extent of damage is to be revealed and essential repair work undertaken.

We emphasize that in the early simplifying stage of renewal, cutting may have to be radical. The contraction can be tangible, for example, cutting out parts of the product range, geographic territory, or stages of the value chain; it can also be less tangible, for example, eliminating systems and procedures. Even profitable activities may have to be dropped if they distract attention and deflect resources from building the new "core."

In building, progress is best achieved by many small initiatives, because resources are limited. Small steps spread the risks and prevent the organization from betting everything on one initiative. As rejuvenation proceeds, the risks become better understood and progress more secure, allowing the steps to get bigger. Small steps also allow the organization to encourage initiatives from below and help build an entrepreneurial culture. Whereas instructions for surgery are imposed from the top, it is the bottom-up flow of ideas and actions that accelerates the convalescence and return to fighting fitness.

We stress that organizations need a long time to rejuvenate. It takes years to build a truly entrepreneurial company. Like builders of houses, who spend almost two-thirds of the cost and time below ground digging foundations and preparing the site, effective organizations that aim to become entrepreneurial also have to sink deep foundations; rushing for the quick-fix solution is unlikely to result in long-term rewards. Our proposed path to recovery may seem prolonged, but we suggest it is often the quickest route. Like the walking path to the mountaintop that twists and turns and appears to ascend only by degrees, the gradual slope ensures that the walker can maintain a steady pace and avoid many of the obstacles on the route of direct assault.

GALVANIZING THE TOP TEAM

Rejuvenating a mature organization is impossible without commitment from the top. As we pointed out at the end of Chapter 5, many mature organizations show signs of life with innovative actions being taken in parts, and include many able individuals who are committed to change. Entrepreneurial individuals generally labor in isolated groups. They are unable to make the connections essential to altering the path of the organization, for that requires linkages across functions and territories, which cannot be achieved without the backing of top management.

Initial moves are often made by a new chief executive, and in all the firms we studied, the CEO played a vital and decisive role.[7] The effective ones, however, did not act alone; they all realized the importance of teams. Although we found several instances where a single charismatic leader originally undertook almost all the leading, the charismatic leaders always built teams. As a manager of one rejuvenated firm told us, "When I arrived, I heard that we are doing things because [the CEO] says so. Now it is noticeable that there are no obvious power plays."

It is fashionable to claim that "we work as a team," even when this is not so. One of our failed firms was run by a talented but misguided chief executive who was depicted by his successor as old-fashioned. He talked about teams but did not really believe in them; his meetings were about what had happened, not examining possibilities. As a result, initiatives were pigeonholed and ignored. Moreover, even in board meetings he held down those who had ideas. He spent most of his time complaining about the fact that things had not improved and managed to demoralize his colleagues. Some progress did occur and for a time results improved. But the managers were neither unified nor committed to rejuvenating the organization and proved unable to generate any momentum. The potential for progress was dissipated by failed teamwork at the top.

Building a top team dedicated to change provides continuity and reduces the risks that the process will falter if one person leaves. In several of our organizations the chief executive changed without loss of momentum. At Hotpoint, Schreiber started the process of rejuvenation, Samson followed and improved, and Bruce Enders carries on the work. At Courtelle a chief executive changed during the relevant period. These were cases of continuity. Edwards was less fortunate. In its early years there was a stream of chief executives and during one period of almost a year early in the process, there was no chief executive. The fragile team, lacking effective leadership, could make no progress and tended to accept compromise rather than face up to necessary hard choices. On arrival, Danny Rosenkranz found effectively no strategy and no team and had to build both. Promotion was his primary means of building a top team, which proved sufficiently robust that its momentum for progress could be maintained with only part-time leadership for the year it took to find a successor. Edwards's experience shows that it is the whole team, not the chief executive alone, which matters.

Effective top teams span all the key functions. Rejuvenation involves changing the way in which the functions work and the way in which they relate. An effective top team must have a real understanding of the functions so that it understands what is technically possible, what is required by customers, suppliers, the work force, and other stakeholders. Without shared knowledge within the team, there can be no intuition, which is vital for the business.

The need to involve the key functions also ensures the involvement of the vital power brokers of the organization. Functional or territorial heads carry weight in getting things done. They can influence the perceptions and actions of their group, perhaps because of their position but often because of their background and skills. Unless they are involved in the early stages, the power brokers may sabotage or slow down the process through misunderstanding and lack of appreciation.

For rejuvenation, all members of the top team must share an understanding of the problem. An effective top team avoids vacillation, does not seek outsiders to resolve its problems (although they may help), does not look for a quick fix or shirk dealing with immediate issues. In short, many rocks and whirlpools have to be avoided. To sidestep these hazards, the team must believe that there is a crisis, that action has to be taken, and that the action must extend throughout the organization. Only where there is real common acceptance of these three priorities does the top team feel empowered to start the process of rejuvenation. Achieving consensus is not easy, so we examine the issues. (See Exhibit 6.2.)

Sensing the Need to Start

What triggers actions that can lead to rejuvenation? Why is correct sensing so critical to generating a sense of urgency? Earlier we discussed the difficulty of recognizing crises in a form that can lead to action and the even more serious problem of using the recognition of an opportunity as a way of focusing energies to change behavior. It is one thing to bring together a top team, quite another to have it share, collectively, a sense that change is imperative. We use the word sense advisedly, because at the earliest stages only rarely does hard data indicate a clear direction; information by itself seldom "proves" or "disproves" any action.

Consider what can happen when managers sense the signals for change. They may seem so vague that they are effectively ignored. They may point to solutions that are beyond current capabilities, they can provoke responses of general concern, but the actions are little

---

EXHIBIT 6.2 GALVANIZING THE TOP TEAM

Limiting perceptions	Galvanizing perceptions
The problem we face is temporary.	There is a crisis and the issues are major and fundamental.
We must move slowly to avoid upsetting the existing order.	There is a sense of urgency. Change must be set into motion even if we do not know exactly where we are going.
It is someone else's fault that we are in trouble.	We must understand *why* we are in the mess, so that we, the top team, can lead the way forward.
The problems lie in specific areas of the organization; they are not widespread.	Firmwide change is needed across functions, territories, and hierarchy.
The financial figures tell us what is wrong.	We have to look behind the figures to find out where the markets are going and the needed capabilities.

---

more than tinkering with the symptoms. More precise signals can also be ignored, even when the solutions are within capabilities, because the team has yet to share a common will to respond. The issue of the urgency is also embodied in the message. Managers may feel that they have plenty of time and allow other agendas to preoccupy them. Alternatively, an urgent message may seem to be so complex that appropriate responses are hard to calculate.

We found that all the top teams of rejuvenating firms had experienced many of these difficulties before they could commit themselves to collective internal action. Often, we found top teams working to exhaust all the "obvious" actions before they could perceive the need to consider more radical approaches to transform the business as a whole. Rational calculations of partial response to complex challenges can be used, perhaps unwittingly, to perpetuate the inertia of maturity. The problem is exacerbated when the agenda is so complex that team members cannot agree on priorities. One board agenda had been so all encompassing that every action proposed by one functional director met a counterproposal from another. Though everyone worried about the firm's declining fortunes, managers could not agree on priorities, felt powerless, and drifted on the tide of industry fortune. It took the shock of looming bankruptcy to jerk them into collective action rather than go to the wall.

It is important to appreciate that the data in signals for change need to be interpreted for others, particularly when they are weak. Consider the assessment of competitors, so commonly undertaken by top management. Measures of competition may cover profitability, productivity, reliability, or customer acceptance. Generally, a few competitors are doing better on some if not all the measures, but many may be similar to a given organization and some may be doing worse. Should this fact be seen as a trigger for action or a signal for complacency? Unless someone has high aspirations and a sense of danger, complacency prevails. As we pointed out in Chapters 1 and 2, there are always those who believe that poor performance, be it in profits or some other measure, can be excused: "It is not our fault." Worse yet, competitor benchmarking studies can be used to justify the status quo. One mature firm that later went out of business went so far as to reject a study that indicated the need for a fundamental change of approach. In the words of one director, it was "obviously fallacious. If this was possible, we would be doing it already."

There are many other reasons why managers may fail to react to changing circumstance. Mature organizations can become trapped in an illusion bred of undue focus on accounting profits. Of necessity, accounting figures can register only what has happened, not what is about to happen; when confronted by "satisfactory" profits, many top groups ignored other signals indicating declining competitiveness. As Exhibit 6.3 suggests, the problem is that declines in competitiveness can precede declines in profits or profitability, often by a significant margin, maybe by years. The reasons for this are well known and the smart firm has many measures of competitiveness, which it watches carefully. The longer a firm ignores the warning signals of declining competitiveness, the more unprepared and unable to fight it is when the internal records catch up with market reality.

In the 1980s, Caterpillar made a serious error in believing that it was still successful in the earth-moving-equipment industry many years after signs indicated a serious loss of competitiveness measured by the benchmarking of costs and buyers' calculations of perceived value. Caterpillar's problem was that the weak signals of an impending crisis were drowned out by the false signals of a booming market and high profits. When the downturn in the market came, Caterpillar's profits collapsed and its competitor Komatsu moved ahead.

Similar misfortunes have hit U.S. automobile manufacturers. The first signs of lost competitiveness were evident even in the late 1970s. The Japanese were making significant gains in market share in the United States, consumer associations were rating Japanese cars as more efficient and more reliable, and writers like William Abernathy were pointing out failures in the U.S. companies' production processes.[8] However, it was several years before falling share had a large impact on U.S. auto company profits: the response was correspondingly delayed.

EXHIBIT 6.3   ACCOUNTING PROFITS CAN BE POOR INDICATORS OF COMPETITIVENESS

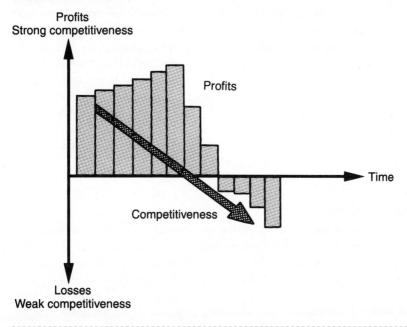

Like the U.S. auto manufacturers, Rolls-Royce Motors was lulled into complacency by strongly rising sales and profits during the 1980s and did not see the shifts that led to large losses in the early 1990s. In reacting to the crisis, management became aware that it had not paid sufficient attention to many internal indicators, such as an upward creep in costs and the break-even level, as well as external ones, including—ironically for a company famous as a symbol of quality—measures of relative quality and customer satisfaction. Explicit recognition of these failures and the development of a more rounded and appropriate set of performance measures helped Rolls-Royce Motors to move aggressively and quickly to restore profitability.

Missing the signals of decline is an old phenomenon: the textile companies of Lowell, Massachusetts, experienced strong growth in sales of cotton goods between 1830 and 1920, but despite rising sales after 1870, their market share declined rapidly as the southern industry grew. A crisis did not hit Lowell until 1920, when the market stopped growing. Its manufacturers suddenly collapsed, while its more efficient southern counterparts continued to grow. Yet for those who had cared to look beyond the familiar landmarks, the signs of failure were evident many years earlier.

Only a few of our rejuvenators did the obvious thing at the start, that is, establish measures that heighten the sense of urgency to deal with emergent problems before they become serious. Wise and successful organizations broaden their measures of performance to include specific indicators of relative achievement of financial and nonfinancial goals. A broader and more balanced scorecard helps top teams in general, and chief executives in particular, to anticipate where trouble might strike. It amplifies the weak signals that forewarn of danger and diminishes those signals which encourage complacency. If the top team does not anticipate it, the organization may be submerged and unable to retrieve itself when the real crisis arrives.

Triggers for Action

Sensing impending doom is not always sufficient to induce action. Although it comes late in the day, falling profitability seems to be the most common trigger for inducing a sufficient enough sense of urgency and crisis that actions to cure the roots of the problem can be instituted.[9] A financial crisis was the trigger for Hotpoint. GEC, the parent company, was exceptionally healthy, but it considered the losses of its subsidiary so catastrophic that it seriously considered closing the entire business. Lord Weinstock, chairman of GEC, appointed Chaim Schreiber as managing director of Hotpoint, reputedly with a mandate to close the business. Schreiber, who at the time was also running his family furniture business, had considerable power and influence in some quarters of GEC. It is said that he could interpret his broad mandate for radical action as he saw fit. In the event, he found sufficient signs of life and possibility that he ignored the mandate and decided to turn the business around.[10]

Must firms wait for a financial crisis before top managers do more than tinker with some of the parts? Though harder to do, it is possible for individuals to anticipate a looming crisis and initiate corrective action before it is too late or too expensive to try. It is relatively easier for that to happen when an individual has the power to act. The awareness may come first to shareholders, who appoint a new chief executive to carry the message, or the chief executive may be prescient. It is more difficult when the messages come from outside and are heard by individual managers without power. Dealings with suppliers, customers, bankers, and innumerable others can highlight the problem and stir up action within isolated groups. But when that happens, action to change business fundamentally usually has to wait until, as at Hot-

160

point, there is a chief executive who listens and buys into the possibilities.

In Richardson's case, the trigger for radical change came some time after the arrival of new managing director Bryan Upton. He was put in charge when the chairman and owner replaced the old top management team. Upton recalls that at the time his objective was to bring the firm up to best British practice. His trigger occurred later, after a visit to Japan, where he observed the backwardness of best British practice in the cutlery industry. This was his personal turning point: he knew that there would soon be a crisis. He set in motion precisely the action programs that were later needed to meet the challenge set by his chairman—the development of the never-needs-sharpening knife described in Chapter 5.

At Courtelle, the largest producer of acrylic fibers in Europe and second in the world, profits were the best of all firms in the European industry, but less than the aspirations of both the managers of Courtelle and those on the parent company's main board. Here was a clear case in which an industry's problems and the prospect of a hopeless market became a factor sparking off the search for new avenues. Another was lack of cash. The company received many traditional investment proposals that offered a reasonable return, but at that moment the parent had no money to spare. This was perhaps the crucial trigger which sparked a search for new initiatives, and hence new solutions.

In the case of Wolsey, the realization came only slowly and more from observing changes in the market and pressure from customers than any particularly bad financial performance. Wolsey had fallen from profit to break even, but in a seesaw business such as textiles this would not have been a real financial crisis. The team at the top found that some items on the agenda never seemed to get resolved and eventually decided that it had to reach for more ambitious goals if it was to find solutions.

We cite these four cases to indicate that it is possible to anticipate a real crisis. Those who have done so have been able to take positive action at less cost than would have been incurred had they procrastinated. In such instances, hindsight seems to show repetitively that the actions taken were less risky than a policy of standing still. But before the event, the risks may have appeared large.

Empowering Management
Bringing together a top team and making its members realize that there is a crisis is not enough to start rejuvenation: the team must believe that it has the power and the responsibility to do something. It is necessary that certain aspects of the problem are appreciated by the

top team: that the problem is not limited to a single part of the organization, that the quick fix does not work. The top team must also appreciate that it does not have to know all the answers before it can act. Its job is to chart the direction ahead and enlist the aid of others in finding durable solutions. It is tempting to suggest that the realization comes quickly, but the truth is that appreciation comes gradually.

Earlier chapters detailed how managers of mature organizations are often keen to fasten blame on others. Sometimes they blame the environment, poor demand, overfussy customers, adverse exchange rates, even the weather. Sometimes they blame the decisions of previous top management and sometimes the failure of current middle management to implement decisions made by the top team. While an element of blame may rightly be attached to these groups, in all cases top management showed insufficient appreciation of the issues at stake. Progress can take place only when team members appreciate the extent of a problem and realize that they, and only they, are ultimately responsible for its organization's failures. More important, only the top team can lead the organization out of its mess.

It is also common for senior managers to perceive that the problems, (and hence the solutions), lie in a single function or part of their organization. Blaming particular functions, territories, or groups is often unhelpful, as the crisis reflects failures of the whole organization. For example, when high-cost products are also poor quality, the production department is usually blamed. Such finger-pointing is naive, for rarely is production alone to blame for poor quality. It may be that production, not being told by the service department which failures occur most frequently, is trying to improve the wrong elements. Distribution may be at fault, damaging goods in transit. Purchasing may be paying insufficient attention to ensuring that suppliers provide quality components, and marketing may insist on designs that are difficult and expensive to produce. Quality at low cost can be achieved only when all functions work close y together.

Rectifying poor customer support and unnecessarily high costs requires close functional collaboration in service businesses as well as in manufacturing. For years British Telecom customers complained about the long delays and high costs associated with new telephone installation. British Telecom found that it could not improve the speed at which new telephones were connected without involving all functions. New orders were being processed too slowly because sales procedures were cumbersome and slow and not integrated with other departments. Accounting insisted on extensive credit checks before processing any order, which slowed the system, as opposed to checking credit while the rest of the system prepared the work. Line installation also proceeded along separate rules unrelated to immediate needs, and orders were often delayed because the service engineers were not coordinated. Every part of the organization had some responsibility, but none "owned" the problem.

The dawning realization that the problems are serious and that the causes extend beyond a single function to all parts of the organization is one step on the road toward taking necessary corrective actions. But before effective action can be initiated, hard choices among many alternatives must be made. Here the chief executive has the central role of holding the ring as people test their intuition against always imperfect data. Lacking hard evidence, a top team always has members with competing senses of priority. And lacking anything more than a common will to be positive, the debates can all too readily become unproductive without firm leadership.

CHOOSING EFFECTIVE ACTION

Some top teams choose to manage their way forward by exhaustive analysis of the alternatives they can perceive at the time of crisis. Others feel their way by trying solutions and discovering what does and does not work. Still others examine the experience of other organizations. And often all these approaches are combined. However choices are made, there are many false paths and blind alleys, which can seduce and lull management into thinking that it is effectively dealing with the issues at hand.

The steps that we suggest mark out the most effective path of action are in stark contrast to other actions we observed. Simplification involves cutting to conserve resources, revealing a new core, and pointing the way forward. The subsequent building, later described in detail, lays new foundations for the entrepreneurial organization and requires an extended time perspective. These measured steps contrast with the following alternatives, which many have taken and which fail to address key issues effectively: scrapping everything and starting afresh—rather than saving what is of value; looking to outsiders to alleviate a problem—as a substitute for internal action; vacillation among extreme directives issued by top management—paralyzed uncomprehending top management; large-scale investments in state-of-the-art technology and systems at the initial stages—quick fix or big hit; and culture change programs without parallel actions—denying that there is an immediate crisis. These issues, summarized in Exhibit 6.4, are discussed more fully below.

EXHIBIT 6.4 INEFFECTIVE AND EFFECTIVE EARLY STAGE ACTIONS

Ineffective actions	Reasons for likely failure
Scrap everything and start afresh	Denies that there is anything of value in the organization
Seeking outside support, e.g., government subsidies, cartels, tariff protection as substitute for action	Distracts the organization from internal action; preserves the status quo; delays and increases the crisis
Top-down directives that address symptoms, not causes	Destroys morale and fails to address interfunctional issues
Going for the big hit	Extremely risky, wastes resources, and does not build proper foundations; such investments should come later
Culture change programs without corresponding action	Denies the crisis and need for action: postpones the inevitable

Alternative approach	Reasons for possible success
Simplify: cut and build	Concentrates scarce resources
Set a climate for experimentation	Encourages innovation; enables cross-functional initiatives; builds new foundations

----

Scrap Everything and Start Afresh

Consider first the problem of those Cassandras who argue that it is hopeless to try to rejuvenate—better to give up without a struggle and go elsewhere. Their pessimistic views can be justified if *all* the alternatives are more costly and more risky. Only if all else fails must an organization be extinguished.

One U.S. company considered seeking the rejuvenation of an existing operation a waste of time. Instead of tackling the deep-seated problems in its Midwest plants, it moved the whole operation to the South, leaving its past behind. In so doing, the company abandoned many skilled and loyal workers who might have been capable of adapting to new working methods faster than it took to train a brand new work force and at less cost. The Japanese experience of buying U.S. facilities and doubling or trebling productivity within less than a year illustrates that the possibility of rejuvenation often exists. Their experience also confirms that faster returns may come from renewal rather than greenfield initiatives, a point often overlooked by those in a hurry to "get something going."[11]

Sometimes, to be sure, troubled organizations do not have the option of a clean start elsewhere. Even though they might wish to walk away, the owners may not be able to afford the exit costs. They may also face severe union opposition and the resistance of politicians and local government officials. In such cases, management is obliged to try to find a middle way, regardless of how many Cassandras argue that the effort will be in vain.

Seeking Outside Support

For years, many major European chemical companies, particularly the Italian giants, the French and Belgians, and even the British ICI, perceived the problems of their industry as being caused by government's failure to manage demand in the economy and allowing the Middle Eastern countries power over oil prices. In these firms, top management consistently lobbied governments for support to resolve their problems and failed to take internal initiatives.[12] ICI, one of the bigger culprits, was also one of the first to break out of the vicious circle and realize that internal action was necessary. A galvanized top management led the way, and ten years later, in better shape than many of its European counterparts, it is still trying to pull its organization around.

In the early 1980s, British Steel had long been one of the lame ducks of the British nationalized industries. It was broke and beleaguered by inefficient work practices. Management blamed the unions and successive governments for its problems. True, the government and the unions did have much to answer for, but the hollowness of the claim was showed up when a new top team brought the perception that something could be done to turn the organization around. The team was assisted by the changes in attitude promoted forcibly by Margaret Thatcher's government, but the hard work to regain success was more the result of internal efforts to change behavior. Many sacred cows were destroyed as British Steel raised its productivity many times, its losses were turned to profits, and managers at all levels realized that they were required, empowered, and able to take the initiative.[13]

Cook, one of the world's most successful steel casting firms, began its rejuvenation by ignoring its competitors' attempts to lobby the government for support. It realized that, at the early stages, it should devote its effort to putting its own house in order. The initial approach Cook adopted, which was not so unusual among companies we studied, should be contrasted with its current role as the industry's critic on government initiatives that hurt the industry. Cook has taken on this role since making great progress in rejuvenation.[14]

Lest we be accused of ignoring politics and reality, we fully recognize that all organizations have a role to lobby and put their case to government, and all need to watch and influence events.[15] However, we draw a distinction between this approach and those failing organizations which do nothing for themselves while waiting to be rescued by the white knight of outside support. The first puts the role of public policy in perspective, while the second fails in the duties of management.

Top-Down Directives That Address Symptoms, Not Causes

Many top managers seem to believe that issuing orders from the top and expecting immediate responses is the best way to start things going. As we explained in Chapter 5, this is unlikely to instill corporate entrepreneurship. As a sense of crisis looms, if statements from the top become hysterical, they can be met by inaction or lack of results from below. Vacillation is usually another sign that top management is not really in control and does not understand either the causes of a problem or how to respond effectively. Seldom can top-down directives do more than preserve yesterday's "formula."

For example, one company we studied identified that its competitors' products cost less and were of higher quality than its own. To compete, the company started cutting costs in a ruthless program that also cut out many of its quality assurance systems. Costs indeed fell, but so did quality. When customers complained, the company restored the quality checks and procedures it had eliminated. These helped, but the organization quickly found itself not back to where it had started, but worse off. It encountered higher costs and lower quality because of falling morale and confusion over its direction; meanwhile, competitors had moved further ahead. It took a major breakthrough in thinking to realize that the organization had to achieve higher quality and lower costs simultaneously. A new approach had to be built, and for that to happen the board had to learn to listen.

The issuance of directives for action without a sense of how to go forward can also cause paralysis. We were given an extreme example by a main board member in one large company. In this firm, the board, deciding it was essential to stop the organization's losses, ordered that certain factories be closed. However, the plant managers lower down did not detect unanimity among the board, nor did they understand the need for decisive action, and they effectively subverted the board's decision. The sabotage was occasionally quite effective; for instance, someone in the personnel office removed and hid the address list of the employees. This prevented implementation of the closure, as the company could not fulfill the legal requirement of sending layoff and dismissal notices to the employees' homes. Ultimately the board succeeded in its objectives, but had it conveyed a sense of unanimity and purpose, its actions could have been carried out more quickly and effectively.

Going for the Big Hit

The recognition that an organization is far behind in its capabilities can drive top management to seek a quick fix. At the beginning of the renewal process there is a temptation to spend money on modern capital by buying state-of-the-art factories, service delivery systems, or other forms of technology. Typically, consultants or other outsiders have suggested that such investments permit a firm to catch up with its industry leaders. Usually the investments are large, take several years to build, and commit the organization to a single unchangeable route for the future. There is often an absence of understanding in the organization of how the new technology works, and certainly a lack of appreciation for all the issues it involves. At the early stages of rejuvenation, big programs are dangerous, not least because most of the organization's resources are bet on a single course.

For the mature organization in crisis, the arrival of massive amounts of new capital, new computers, or new systems without a corresponding building of a skill base risks disasters. All our rejuvenators discovered, if they did not already know, that skills have to be built in tandem with investment in hardware. Without the proper skills and awareness throughout the whole organization, the investments are misused or underused. Little progress is made in delivering either financial results or building a competitive edge. Worse, the spirit of entrepreneurial enthusiasm with its characteristics of learning and experimentation may be repressed.

General Motors (GM) undertook a very expensive project in trying to catch up with Japan. Its top managers correctly identified the yawning gap between U.S. and Japanese auto producers in productivity and quality. However, they incorrectly thought that the best way to solve the problem was to invest in new machines without first instilling corporate entrepreneurship in their managers and work force. After spending several hundred million dollars on new plant, GM in late 1986 was still taking forty-one employee-hours to build a midsize car. Managers became disillusioned about the rate of progress. In the early 1990s the crisis was apparent, and although the investments had some effect, it seems that much money was wasted and precious time and momentum lost. In contrast, Ford was building its Taurus with just twenty-five employee-hours of labor. Ford had invested less in machines than GM, but paid more attention to teamwork.[16] It made more limited resources go further, achieved impressive payoffs, and had laid foundations for a stronger organization. Ford still had a long way to go—the new Honda plant in Marysville, Ohio, was taking about fifteen hours to build a similar car—but at least it was doing better than GM with its investments in robotics and high-tech gadgets.

The General Motors story is dramatic; few mature organizations have the same scale of resources. However, we observed many firms making similar mistakes by investing large sums in buying solutions, investing heavily in new technology, and the like, without changing their organization. Frequently such investments are underutilized, or worse, wrong. Expensive gear is often unnecessary; cheaper investments of a more modest nature are often all that is necessary.

We should make it clear that large investment programs can pay off handsomely when undertaken by firms that have gained entrepreneurial capabilities. When organizations have built their internal skills and processes, they can leverage new investments effectively. At the beginning of its rejuvenation, Richardson raised productivity many, many times with only modest capital investment. Such gains eventually became constrained by the lack of the latest technology; new investment was essential. By then, Richardson had built skills, and the organization was ready for a big investment; the gains were immediate, and the payback on expensive machines was ensured.

Culture Change Programs without Corresponding Action

If the big hit is dangerous because it squanders resources, takes unnecessary risks, and does not build a new organization, the culture change program goes to the opposite extreme. It is certainly true that mature organizations need to change their culture if they are to become entrepreneurial, but many mistakenly believe that the culture has to be changed before actions for improvement can be taken, or that culture change is sufficient in itself. A culture change program without action is very risky because it denies the existence of a crisis and takes the organization's attention away from the necessity for immediate action. Moreover, it fails to appreciate the most obvious fact that organizations change only through actions because actions reflect and alter beliefs.

Our finding echoes the observations of Tom Peters and Robert Waterman, who noted that effective organizations had a bias for action.[17] Their point was that unless action is taken, progress cannot be made. Their message is highly appropriate for rejuvenating organizations. We found a surprising number of firms investing heavily in changing the culture of their organizations without ensuring that deliberate progress was made in the specification of the actual tasks.

A major international professional service firm noted that its competitive position had slipped. After using a set of consultants, it decided that new structures and new systems were required; however, more than a year later little progress had been made: detailed operations in the departments had hardly been altered. The firm then undertook an extensive culture-change exercise with mission statements and awareness seminars. A year later a second review still showed little progress. Those laboring in the bowels of the organization had seen much talk but little action. The chief executive who had instituted the program was promoted to chairman after the real crisis came, and his successor set about making real change. No doubt, the initial culture-change programs helped a little in preparing the organization for the maelstrom of change that came later, but far too much time had been wasted. Had senior management really thought through the issues and recognized the weaknesses of the consultants' panaceas, it could have initiated action programs from the beginning.

In a major appliance company, senior managers in one section noted falling quality standards and a lowering of morale. They connected the two and rightly suggested that improving morale might help. However, their change program did not address the important issues. The initiatives focused on carpeting floors and introducing office plants, music, and a general "feel good" atmosphere. After years of no significant results, the business was bought by Electrolux, which quickly instituted effective change.

Rejuvenating a business does require a culture change, but change must be linked to action. Our research suggests that effective culture change requires managers to deal with tasks. Thus, abolishing the executive dining room at Edwards did help, but only because it reinforced other important initiatives dealing with productivity and quality. In many organizations, quality circles and the like are introduced, and it seems that those which work well are those which have short-term tangible goals as well as long-term ones.[18] Grand schemes for change without action seldom work.[19]

The Quick Fix: TQM or Process Reengineering

All our rejuvenators subscribed in one way or another to aspects of total quality management (TQM) and all have reengineered their processes, occasionally several times over. But what they did, which is described in the ensuing chapters, bore little relation to those peddlers of snake oil who claim instant results.

A few less careful proponents of TQM or process engineering (or the equivalent) portray complex philosophies as quick-fix solutions. They understate the investment in the time, energy, and effort required to yield results. In their desire for speed, they fail to stress the need to teach the organization the skills to ensure that the process can be continued and typically do not build a proper foundation for lasting success. Not surprisingly, recent surveys of organizations that took up the TQM fad in the 1980s show that many have been disappointed and stopped earlier initiatives.[20] To be sure, there have been successes, but we suggest that they have probably been organizations which were either far down the rejuvenation road or, like our mature firms, patient and persistent ones. We forecast the same for process reengineering.

Claims by consultants that process reengineering can deliver a tenfold improvement come as no surprise. Richardson improved productivity thirty-five times in its early stages! But boasts that such progress is achieved quickly do not ring true. Long before the recent fad, we observed mature firms attempting such rapid engineering without preparation and failing. Thomas Davenport, who has studied the IT-led process reengineering, makes these remarks supporting our position: "We know of no large organization that has fully implemented a major process innovation in less than two years. Ford's widely reported elimination of three-quarters of its accounts payable staff . . . took five years from design to full implementation."[21]

As we suggested at the start of the chapter, effective change requires organizations to avoid going directly from an old method to a new one, but rather to spend considerable time and effort coaching and changing the organization, its culture and beliefs, and its actions. Going back to our crescendo diagram, the big hit makes the dangerous and risky attempt to leap from a current situation to a fully entrepreneurial position without going through the intermediate stages of building the organization's abilities (see Exhibit 6.5).

THE WAY FORWARD

To go forward, the mature firm aspiring to rejuvenate must galvanize and build a top team committed to action. Crucial choices need to be made about the scope of the firm and how and where it will compete. In addition, action must be taken to start the building of entrepreneurship, which we assert is necessary for renewal and any higher aspirations. Some businesses have found that outside stakeholders can play a role. One such group is the top team of a business that is part of a holding company or parent organization.

Perhaps the most celebrated example of coaching behavior is that of Jack Welch at GE. He has galvanized many of his business units to achieve far-reaching change and succeeded brilliantly in raising sales and profits to the point where GE's market value has risen from eleventh place in the United States to second, behind only Exxon. He has established "work-out" sessions with groups of managers at many levels to get the messages across. Yet even his presence at many of these sessions has not succeeded in accelerating change in all. The same sorts of resistance we saw earlier are still observable in parts of

EXHIBIT 6.5 THE BIG HIT OR QUICK FIX VERSUS CRESCENDO

	Simple business	Complex business
Dynamic organization	3 Build	4 Leverage
Static organization	2 Simplify	1 Galvanize

The crescendo path of renewal

The mistaken quick fix

GE. Time may be on Welch's side, but there is always the fear that the momentum for progress will not be sustained because of the obstacles to getting people to own the ideas and values for themselves.

There may be a gap in cultural perceptions on these matters about what is and is not effective. Where many U.S. managers espouse the value of directives from the very top and point to the benefits of the resulting focus and speed of change, many we spoke to across Europe adopted a different perspective. Those whose job it was to look after a whole portfolio often preferred to work on encouraging managers to embrace the values of creativity, innovation, and challenge to conventions without specifying the actions or processes. Many set challenging targets, but some who regarded their approach as slower and harder to control, bet that the end results would be much more durable.

There is no way we know to resolve the issue of which is the superior approach. Both have good and bad points and both are dependent on the climate of attitudes into which such initiatives are introduced. The difference of opinion, however, serves to reinforce the point we made at the start of this chapter: real transformation of a business cannot begin in earnest without the recognition by its top managers that a new direction must be found.

The role of a galvanized top team of the business is to lead the way by ensuring that rhetoric matches actions on these agendas. The challenge such teams face was neatly captured by remarks of Akio Morita, the chairman of Sony.

> The innovation process must be set at the highest level of the corporation by identifying goals and priorities, and once identified these must be communicated all the way down the line. The targets you set must be clear and challenging, for you cannot wait for innovation just to show up at your company one day. But you need not, and should not, possess the entire solution to the challenge you set. You have to be sure . . . that the target you raise is realistic, though it might appear impossible.[22]

That message is well understood at Richardson and other businesses that have made progress. It is, however, a message that is extraordinarily difficult to put into practice. To start the voyage, most firms find that they have to concentrate on finding sites where specific progress can lead to superior performance before the values and practices can be extended to the corporation as a whole. This is the subject of the next chapter.

NOTES

[1] Many of the ideas in this chapter were explored in our earlier article, J.M. Stopford and Charles Baden-Fuller, "Corporate Rejuvenation," *Journal of Management Studies* 27, no. 4, July 1990: 399–415, which contains a full discussion of many theoretical issues.

[2] For more details see J.M. Stopford, *Edwards High Vacuum International*, London Business School, 1989.

[3] For more details see M.R.S. Green, *The Hotpoint Story: A Study in Excellence*, London Business School, 1987.

[4] Lacking any procedure akin to America's Chapter 11, the United Kingdom introduced a temporary measure early in the Thatcher administration to alleviate the difficulties in which many British then found themselves.

[5] For more details see R.M. Grant and C.W.F. Baden-Fuller, *The Richardson Sheffield Story*, London Business School Case Series, 2, 1987.

[6] For details see Christopher A. Bartlett and U. Srinivasa Rangan, *Komatsu Limited*, Case No. 9-385-277 (Boston: Harvard Business School, 1985), *Caterpillar Tractor Co.*, Case No. 9-385-276 (Boston: Harvard Business School, 1985), and Christopher A. Bartlett and Susan Ehrlich, *Caterpillar Inc.: George Schafer Takes Charge*, Case No. 9-390-036 (Boston: Harvard Business School, 1990).

[7] For an exceptional example of radical change implemented in an organization against the desires of the chief executive, see M.E. Beres and S.J. Musser, "Avenues and Impediments to Transformation," in R.H. Kilmann and T.J. Covin, eds., *Corporate Transformation: Revitalizing Organizations for a Competitive World* (San Francisco: Jossey-Bass), 1988.

[8] See W.J. Abernathy and R.H. Hayes, "Managing Our Way to Economic Decline," *Harvard Business Review,* July–August 1980: 67–77.

[9] Others have also found that financial crisis is a frequent but by no means universal trigger. See, for instance, P.H. Grinyer, D.G. Mayes, and P. McKiernan, *Sharpbenders: The Secrets of Unleashing Corporate Potential* (Oxford: Basil Blackwell, 1988).

[10] Sadly, Schreiber died before we started our research.

[11] The West German approach to rebuilding East Germany also has the appearance of trying to start afresh: old factories are demolished, workers dismissed, and the new owners act as if they are setting up greenfield sites. For an academic view of when it is best to start afresh, see M.T. Hannan and J. Freeman, "Structural Inertia and Organizational Change," in K.S. Cameron, R.I. Sutton, and D.A. Whetten, eds., *Readings in Organizational Decline* (Cambridge, Mass.: Ballinger, 1988).

[12] See J.L. Bower, *When Markets Quake* (Boston: Harvard Business School Press, 1986).

[13] British Steel's rejuvenation is not yet complete. At one time it was about the most productive large steelmaker in the world. However, its stunning rise to profitability has been reversed, indicating that there is more to be done as competitors have pushed ahead.

[14] See C.W.F. Baden-Fuller, "Competition and Cooperation: Restructuring the UK Steel Castings Industry," in Baden-Fuller, ed., *Managing Excess Capacity* (Oxford: Basil Blackwell, 1990), pp. 145-162.

[15] For a fuller exploration of the issues and imperatives in harnessing governments as partners in progress, see J.M. Stopford and S. Strange, *Rival States, Rival Firms* (Cambridge: Cambridge University Press, 1991); see also L. Tyson, *Who's Bashing Whom? Trade Conflict in High-Technology Industries* (Washington, D.C.: Institute for International Economics, 1992).

[16] See R.L. Shook, *Turnaround: The New Ford Motor Company* (New York: Prentice-Hall, 1990).

[17] See Thomas J. Peters and Robert H. Waterman, Jr., *In Search of Excellence* (New York: Harper & Row, 1982).

[18] See, for instance, R. Schaffer and H. Thomson, "Successful Change Programs Begin with Results," *Harvard Business Review,* January–February 1992: 80.

[19] See M. Beer, R. Eisenstat, and B. Spector, *The Critical Path to Corporate Renewal* (Boston: Harvard Business School Press, 1990).

[20] See, for instance, the studies by Arthur D. Little in the United States and A.T. Kearney in the United Kingdom as reported in *The Economist,* April 18, 1992.

[21] T.H. Davenport, *Process Innovation* (Boston: Harvard Business School Press, 1993), p. 12.

[22] Akio Morita, "The Innovation Lecture," London, February 1992.

Chapter Seven

Reduce Complexity, Start Initiatives

When Chaim Schreiber arrived at Hotpoint in 1974, he found a company that had grown both by mergers and by internal development to sprawl across many products made in numerous factories scattered across the United Kingdom and sold in a bewildering array of market segments at home and throughout the rest of Europe. It was unclear what the business was really about, and its reputation and market share were in decline. First, Schreiber decided to simplify both the business and the way it was run. His "keep it simple" prescription was readily adopted by most managers across the organization: "He wanted everything expressed in the simplest possible terms so that he could understand them. He did us a great service, because solutions to problems come much more easily when you think things through in a simple, logical way."[1]

Schreiber did more than reduce complexity; he also started initiatives. For example, he insisted that the service engineers talk to the production department. Thus production personnel began to learn at first hand which models of which machines went wrong, and how often, and how costly it was to repair mistakes. Before then, production had worked blindly, and efforts to improve quality had often focused on minor problems and ignored the important ones.

It appears that two considerations were at work in simplifying the Hotpoint business: one was the need to create a new core of viable activities that could provide a foundation for later construction; the other was to control the cash. To raise cash, Hotpoint sold its small appliance business, a perfectly sound operation that has subsequently prospered under new ownership. Hotpoint's export network across Europe was closed. Even though rivals, especially the Italians, were successful in exporting, Schreiber seemed to believe that, for Hotpoint at that time, the volume and value of exports was more than offset by the added complexity and consequent distraction for managers. His overriding concern was to focus his managers' energies on a single task: selling large appliances in the home market.

In the late 1980s, many U.K. knitwear firms debated exhaustively and repetitively the issue of how best to simplify. The nub of the problem was the same for all. Put crudely, each firm had two areas of business: old and new. The new business required the firm to produce short runs with many fashion and color changes. The prices were, according to internal records, insufficient to yield an adequate return. By contrast, the traditional business of long production runs of standard items was still yielding good margins. How should the firm best respond? Was the trend to shorter runs a portent of the future, something which captured taste changes, technical possibilities, and allowed firms to outperform their competition? Or was it merely a quirk in the market? Those who became convinced they were seeing the future being created by imaginative Main Street retailers knew they could not adequately serve both markets. For them the choice was obvious: their organizations should concentrate on producing variety and eliminate long runs. They would have to abandon opportunities for short-term profits, because they knew it would take time to build a capability to deliver variety at low cost.[2] The fact that in this instance the winners proved to be those who followed the signals for the newer business does not remove the difficulty of the prior judgment. Managers cannot escape from the puzzles that we discussed in Chapter 2 of how best to read market dynamics and must be open to the possibilities of seemingly nonrational reactions in the marketplace. These difficulties are helpfully illustrated by Paul Strebel who shows how so many turning points in industries have been created by rejuvenating firms and not by predictable shifts in economic forces.[3]

Simplifying and updating accounting systems was often a priority. Many traditional systems are expensive to run, waste many resources, and can force absurd decisions. For example, one company charged overheads on all domestic sales but not on foreign ones. This costing system was devised when foreign sales were insignificant and domestic business dominant and profitable. The subsidy to overseas sales was a "temporary measure" to encourage the exploration of new markets. In time, the overseas business burgeoned while U.K. customers became more price sensitive.

Because managers forgot that the procedure was a stop-gap device, the system was left in place. When domestic prices were raised to cover the cost of total overhead—on a declining proportion of the business—domestic sales spiraled downward. There were further problems. The system lagged because standard costs were calculated on the basis of the previous year's volumes. Thus, as U.K. sales shrank, costing became even more distorted and indicated small losses when large losses were in fact being incurred. The old costing system also created a strange distortion on foreign sales. Export prices were set at a small margin over marginal costs and profitable opportunities to increase prices were being missed. It took some time for managers to realize just what the problem was. Once they did, they were able to find a solution that simplified the system and allowed some freedom to price according to the market. The consequence was an increase in profits in both the domestic and the overseas markets.

These examples serve to introduce the main themes of this chapter, namely, that in moving from maturity toward corporate entrepreneurship, a top team should begin by simplifying its business and simultaneously start new initiatives. The two must go hand in hand: without simplification, the obstacles to changing the business may be insuperable; without new initiatives, building the foundations needed for the next phase of development is unduly delayed.

Both must be undertaken with a positive view toward making the business more exciting and capable of development. Though the short-term effects seem to be mere downsizing, the purpose is quite different. It is not a case of conceding positions in markets once and forever: it is a carefully calculated effort to rein in scarce resources so that they may be developed to the point where they can later be unleashed on a broader market, often much larger in scope than that formerly served poorly by the mature organization. If explained, this purpose can create excitement, provide managers at many levels with hope, and inspire them to make herculean efforts to change.

We start with the difficult issue of deciding where and what to cut. We go beyond the issues raised in Chapter 4, considering the importance of removing control systems, creating visibility, and gathering resources. We then look at some of the parallel initiatives that provide the hope. The two are linked by efforts to clarify the purposes of the enterprise and to establish the basic disciplines and values that will be needed to maintain coherence as complexity is later reinstituted.

RESTRICTING THE SCOPE OF BUSINESS

A business can be too complex along one or more of many dimensions: the number of products it offers, the number of markets it serves, and the number of operations it undertakes. The internal tasks may also become overly cumbersome in such forms as conflicting control systems, too many layers of hierarchy, or tortuous procedures. The resulting clutter can drown out signals for action, lull some managers into somnolence, and make the business unmanageable for others.

When a business is thriving and vibrant, diversity can give the organization strength, but when it is doing badly, diversity becomes the encumbrance we noted in Chapter 5. The menu of action to reduce the complexity to manageable proportions has numerous components, as Exhibit 7.1 summarizes. Most rejuvenators have found they had to work on three dimensions: the product-market scope; the information and control systems; and the priority tasks for key managers. Sometimes they tackled all three dimensions together, sometimes they took them in sequence, depending on the urgencies of particular circumstance. Some depended on top-down directives; others had to be worked out cooperatively with managers down the line.

One reason why diversity in maturity becomes an encumbrance is that it creates confusion and dissonance. We met no one who was able to claim that he or she could master all the data that crossed one's desk each day. We met only a few who could claim and provide some evidence to back their claim that they had a consistent and positive rationale for the selection criteria that filtered the data. We saw much evidence of the defensive routines that were highlighted in a provocative study of senior U.S. managers. One was cited as saying,

> I have to sort through so many issues at once. There are ten times too many. I use a number of defense mechanisms to deal with this overload—I use delaying actions, I deny the existence of problems, or I put problems in a mental queue of sorts. . . . .
> One of the frustrations is that I don't want to tell my people that

---

EXHIBIT 7.1 CUT AND BUILD TOGETHER

Remove complexity	Start new initiatives
Top-down directives	Bottom-up and top-down
Restrict the scope of the business and eliminate or simplify the systems.	Many small investments to build skills within the functions and improve the remaining systems
Establish new disciplines, standards, and values and set new priorities.	Initiate cross-functional communications and adapt the structures.
Reveal a viable new core that people can see.	Create a sense of excitement and possibility.

178

their number one problems have lower priorities than they think they should get.[4]

Cutting helps cure such paralysis. One manager in a rejuvenating firm said, "I found that I could begin to put my arms around the problems I had to cope with. The job was more manageable. I felt that I could do something." But cutting the scope of the task has to be supported by other changes that affect thinking. The managers knew that they had to create alternatives to the old, often deep-seated beliefs. They had to provide and articulate a rationale for their decisions.

To be effective in creating a launching pad for progress, simplification has to be accomplished in such a way that managers and technicians can see the whole, not just one part, of the competitive imperative. As Warren Bennis observed, "The more our work makes us specialists, the more we must strive to remain or become generalists in other matters. . . . All of humanity's pursuits are connected, after all, and we remain ignorant of those connections at our peril."[5] In the same vein, in encouraging managers to think across organizational boundaries, Rosabeth Moss Kanter argued:

> To see problems and opportunities integratively is to see them
> as wholes related to larger wholes, rather than dividing
> information and experience into discrete bits assigned to distinct,
> separate categories that never touch one another. Blurring the
> boundaries and challenging the categories permit new
> possibilities to emerge like twisting a kaleidoscope to see the
> endless patterns that can be created from the same set of
> fragments.[6]

Gathering Resources

Chapter 4 outlined some of the important criteria for redefining the scope of a business, emphasizing the role of the tastes, technology, and competitor loose bricks. In maturity, the organization's scope may exceed its capabilities—there may be too many things being done badly—and management has to limit its task. Some deck-clearing decisions are the relatively routine ones of contracting out minor activities, such as catering, cleaning, small construction works, and property management, which are not at the heart of how the business creates value. Such services may be better organized independently, perhaps with existing staff, for removing these activities helps the organization focus on its central task. More serious judgments have to made when deciding what and where to cut from the business's product and market scope. The simplifying process should remove the complexity that

179

paralyzes the business, conserve—or release—valuable and scarce resources, and signal to stakeholders that change is under way. These actions, as noted in Chapter 4, must be taken on the basis of identifying the new core, around which sustainable competitiveness can be reestablished.

Although we are by no means the first to argue that failing organizations need to simplify the scope of their business, we sharply disagree with many others about the rules for deciding what to cut. Management must avoid being driven solely by monetary indicators. The financial turnaround literature has espoused the principle of cutting out all money-losing units and keeping only those which are profitable.[7] Organizations in stable environments where the rules of the game have not changed may find this advice appropriate. But for mature firms trying to rejuvenate in turbulent times, the advice is dangerous. The core that remains after simplification must form the basis for the rejuvenated organization. It must not be a bag of currently profitable odds and ends that cannot be developed.

What should an organization do when it has little market data and cannot trust that which it has? If waiting for better data is unrealistic or unacceptable, should the organization be guided by internal records? Accounting data can be a poor guide to competitiveness and potential, as we illustrated by the knitwear story in Chapter 6. If internal systems were perfect and the market were stable, profitability figures would reflect future profit potential; but internal systems are not perfect and few markets are stable. Most organizations needing rejuvenation have inappropriate accounting systems that churn out many inaccuracies by failing to recognize, for example, interdependency among units. The definition of activities according to the organizational chart may no longer match the realities in the market. These are serious but not insurmountable problems. More important, the business has to address the changes in its industry, and in its position. Today's high-profit earner may be under strategic threat, and an operation that currently yields low profits may be where the long-term future lies. We argued in Chapter 4 that the mature firm often needs a new scope; it is better to focus on doing well the tasks that will be important in the future rather than freeze priority on those tasks which worked well in the past.

If the organization starts from a poor competitive position, perhaps losing cash, then stemming losses and cutting costs is obviously important. In many mature organizations, complacency has set in and costs have crept up. We were not surprised to find many examples where obvious waste could be eliminated, such as failure to practice economy in traveling and entertainment, failing to take advantage of obvious discounts in purchasing, and engaging expensive and unnecessary temporary help. Such cost savings may be significant.

Cutting costs and taking no other action may backfire. We stress the need to think about the causes as well as the symptoms of lost competitiveness. Taking action on the simplest stages of removing waste, eliminating jobs and other costs without the necessary accompanying steps of maintaining or reinforcing strategically important tasks, will not solve the problem of lost competitiveness and may make matters worse. Edwards would have gone wrong if its management had cut staff and spending without reducing and redirecting its scope. Cutting costs beyond the elimination of obvious waste without changing the organization and its systems can have the perverse effect of forcing down quality, service, and other factors important to customers, thus trapping the firm in a vicious downward spiral. The aim of simplifying is to reduce costs and increase competitiveness *simultaneously*.

Cash is often a key concern, so simplifying may extend to halting new large-scale projects. In most cases, shortages are caused by previous generations' squandering money, resulting in falling profitability. For example, one textile fibers business had two projects with an estimated internal rate of return of over 30 percent, and a payback of less than four years. But these projects threatened to absorb all the available cash and thus preempt any other initiatives. More important, they augmented only one function, production, and were designed to create scale-based efficiencies that reduced the firm's ability to respond to market change. The numbers seemed right, but the feel was wrong for reasons alluded to in Chapter 6. A new top management team emphasized the value of flexibility and canceled both projects. Seeking other initiatives, they soon identified five projects which together required only half the cash. Each project increased the flexibility of the business and the coordination between the functions, and offered good returns on investment. Not only could the firm invest in all the projects, but more significant, by conserving resources it could actively search for other initiatives that could add further strengths.

It is important to keep a balanced perspective when trying to conserve cash resources. None of the successful rejuvenating companies we studied expected to generate cash alone: they all saw the need to have a balance between short-term savings and long-term gains. More important, all saw the need to simplify and focus their business while conserving resources to create a new core.

Eliminating Unnecessary Systems, Controls, and Procedures

The old adage "What gets measured gets done" rings true for managers engaged in simplifying a business. The scope of potential cutting must extend beyond products, markets, departments, and businesses and include control and information systems. Unless the old measurement systems and data that produce false signals are jettisoned, old ways will persist. There must be a greater involvement of the people being measured so that the new focus can be held on priority tasks. Our recipe runs against the convention which, in times of crisis, suggests that more power be dragged into the center and new control systems be added. Why, therefore, our radical approach?

How can one grab people's attention to the point where they can see the need both for change in general and in their own behavior? The very conservatism of managerial thinking is a serious obstacle to changing organizations, as all managers readily recognize. The inertia of familiar routines and natural behavioral characteristics are powerful obstacles to change that are seldom removed by rational argument alone.[8] This hardly seems surprising, since the fundamental sources of resistance can be seen to lie in the realm of hidden beliefs, systems, structures, and data bases that litter any organization.[9] Despite much evidence on these matters, popular opinion and many textbook writers prefer to concentrate on rationality alone. In our view, part of the crucial process of simplification is eliminating hidden barriers so that organizational learning and experiments, unfettered by past shibboleths, can take hold. We have found that one way to grab attention is to change the measurement system. Let us explore why.

Data and theories drive organizational beliefs. Incorrect data are rarely caused by stupidity, but rather by beliefs and systems that reflect the pressures and needs of a previous era. These systems may have served organizations well under the old market rules of competition, but they become a menace when the rules of the game change. By providing misleading or incorrect numbers, the systems may perpetuate outworn beliefs and encourage organizations to make wrong decisions, or reinforce resistance to the "right" decisions.

Removing inappropriate controls and systems frees up valuable resources. As organizations move to more efficient factories, better service departments, and better logistics, overhead represents an ever greater proportion of total cost. Much of the overhead consists of systems, which collect both essential and redundant data. Many people are involved in producing reports, and an inordinate amount of time is spent in considering how to circumvent those which are not needed. By removing the unnecessary, the imperative to create new systems is brought sharply into focus and resources are freed up to define the needs of the future.

Why do these difficulties occur in the first place? We consider first the example of a failed accounting system that produced false costing data in an appliance business. This system led many in the firm to believe that short runs of products cost far more than they actually did, and that long runs cost less. Because of this, management avoided exploiting an important market segment and consistently ignored important trends. The old system was geared to calculating unit costs for long runs of a few standardized items; product changes were assumed to take place between production shifts and were costed on this basis. Over the years the business had changed; the runs had become shorter, the variants greater, and product changes were made within the period of a shift. Top management realized that they could not plan without the correct data, but feared that changing the costing system would take too long and be too expensive. Consequently, they compromised by throwing out the existing paralyzing systems and recognizing that each decision to produce a wider set of varieties had to take place in the absence of proper data: it would be a sort of "experiment."

A similar situation arose in another company, where the costing data sent signals to produce less variety when more was needed. Its distribution and marketing costs were computed by a single departmental average figure that prevented any analysis of profit margins by end user or market segment. Even production costs were difficult to compute as reports were formulated in terms of variance from a standard cost whose size was not easy to determine from the computer printout. The data had a logic: designed to promote plant efficiency, they instead impeded strategic change. The decision to specialize in certain end-usage segments had to be made on partial data, and was in effect a gamble.

In all these cases, the data that had been collected were not only wasting a great number of resources, but also impeding the process of rejuvenation. The problems were caused by *failures in the systems* rather than errors in data collection or stupidity. In some cases everyone knew for some time that the systems were giving false information. Yet until someone could explain what a new system should look like, the old routines prevailed. This posed a circular problem: it was impossible to describe what the new system should look like without knowing the new strategy. The only way out of the impasse was to destroy the old systems and encourage the staff to behave responsibly and entrepreneurially.

Identifying which systems to remove requires investigating the systems from top-, middle-, and lower-level perspectives. Often systems that look innocuous from above are in fact quite stifling when seen from below. The worst systems are often buried in the routines and subroutines of organizations and come from a previous era. The problems emerge the moment new experiments are launched. Questioning at all levels may be needed to identify where such subroutines occur and where action must be taken to neutralize them.

Telling people that their systems are wrong is not enough. Those at the lower echelons of the organization will fear that, if the experiment fails and the data systems remain, they will be blamed for the failure and find the erroneous data being used to accuse them falsely. In several firms needing rejuvenation, we found junior managers being reprimanded for failing to follow procedures, even though their new methods had caused profits to rise. The formal systems could not make the necessary connections between unsanctioned actions and the change in profits, whereas they did signal a failure to satisfy useless old procedures. When erroneous data and inappropriate systems have the power to impede necessary experiments, it would seem that uncontaminated entrepreneurial instinct might serve better.

Only top managers can remove outdated systems. Only they have the power and the perspective of the whole organization needed to undertake this vital work. Too often we found top management ignoring this important stage, then being surprised when plans were not implemented and things went wrong. Their problem, though, is that it is seldom obvious which system or which particular feature of a system has become obsolete to the extent that it provides an obstacle to progress. Discovery requires effort.

In one instance, a knitwear producer installed a new computer-controlled machine that cost four times as much as existing machines, and was even more expensive compared with depreciated book values. The worth of the new machine's lower changeover costs and faster changeover speeds could be realized only when it was used to produce a wide variety of output. Ideally, the new machine would have been used for high-margin short runs and the old machines for low-margin long runs. Practice, however, was far from ideal. The costing system recorded only that the time cost of the new machine was much higher than that of the old one.

The production department was given a cost reduction goal that contradicted top management's directives. And because the plant operators considered the cost system to be more important, they organized the work flow to minimize downtime for the new machine. In addition, the cost system showed that the new machine could recover its overhead fully only on long runs. Therefore, the operators used the machine for long runs and continued to use the older machines for the shorter runs: the opposite of the original purpose. Naturally, the experiment failed, and managers concluded that the new investment was a bad idea! They never gave the project a chance, because they failed to understand their own control system and did not bother to find out what was actually happening. Had senior managers spent time trying to understand the systems in the organization, they could have discovered what was taking place and saved the experiment.

Accounting systems are not the only culprits in mature organizations. Many other systems, such as scheduling and quality measurement, may also need scrapping or substantial modification. In one business, scheduling rules caused many problems. After much effort, a production system was developed to allow goods to be made to order. The new system involved substantial investments in training and operating systems. Managers were surprised when customers continued to complain that goods were not arriving promptly. Further investigation revealed that the trouble occurred in the delivery unit. Although the unit's managers had heard about the program, they were still required to operate through an old system that told them to maximize truck usage. This could be achieved only by storing customers' goods until a full truckload was on hand. Goods therefore piled up in the delivery area. As no one had adjusted the rules in the shipping department, the company did not reap the value of its expensive change in production.

In another company, quality was measured as the average of the number of days it took goods to reach a customer after they arrived in the shipping office; everyone believed that a smaller number indicated better performance. The system had several unintended consequences. The shipping department often sent goods early to improve their measures of quality. This practice upset those customers who worked on just-in-time schedules and specified exact delivery dates. Another problem was that many items were sent to customers very late. But because the quality measure was an average, overall measures of quality could rise while complaints from customers also rose. There was no internal signal to trigger corrective action.

Personnel systems can pose other problems. Many organizations have job-grading and pay structures that set out what is expected of each employee. These systems may interfere with what the organization is trying to do by making it difficult to move people between functions or to broaden the scope of what they do. Such interference can impede change most severely in places where staff is rigidly categorized, often at union insistence. It becomes almost impossible to persuade staff in one category to undertake work normally done by staff in another category. The categorization, whether on the shop floor or at more senior levels, acts as an effective barrier to certain kinds of experiments and change. These problems are magnified when rewards are made wholly individualistic, impeding the development of cross-functional teams and the building of organizational skills.

All these examples of data and system problems have a common thread. They are manifestations of the confusion caused when measures influence people to take actions that are contrary to the competitive purpose. They are indicators that systems work to limit people's sights and prevent them from seeing the whole picture. For example, when the budget clashes with the strategy, the budget almost always wins, frustrating new purposes. A business that has been hacked about in its product and market scope, but has still to tackle the internal systems, is not ready to begin the building process.

Managing Stakeholders

Simplification of both external scope and internal systems acts as an important signal to everyone concerned that something is happening. It marks a clear break for many organizations from a previous era of partial moves, inadequate actions, or paralysis and hemorrhage. Owners, unions, suppliers, distributors, banks, and other stakeholders may have grown cynical about the willingness of top management to take remedial action. They may fear that inertia and resistance will destroy the organization. It is vital to enlist the active support of middle and junior managers or workers who can revolt by means of strikes and sit-ins. Even dumb acquiescence can be damaging. Though the early actions of simplification do not persuade intelligent stakeholders that nirvana has been reached, the indications of a new purpose may at least incline them to give the organization some space in which to maneuver.

Whether a parent company or outsiders, owners are especially important, as they have direct power to give or withhold the space to maneuver. We found striking instances where the process of rejuvenation had come to a complete halt because of pressure from parent company boards of directors who did not realize what was going on. Investors can stem the flow of cash into a business, or demand to take out more cash than the business can afford. They may force a change of direction or go as far as to remove the top team and thus endanger the whole rejuvenation. Outside shareholders need equally careful attention, which is better understood in the United States because of the frequency and intensity of analysts' meetings. In Europe there have been numerous incidents of major firms mistakenly feeling it unnecessary to woo their stockholders and neglecting the role of corporate communication. Successful rejuvenators are clearly among the former group: they make a virtue of their sense of purpose and seek to tell everyone who will listen.

One example of the costs of failure to attend to external stakeholders makes the point. Zanussi's divisional managers wanted to rejuvenate their business, but top management failed to simplify the overall firm, which had many unprofitable distractions such as house-building and television factories as well as appliance factories outside Italy. Top management failures caused the firm's bankers to lose faith in the organization and precipitate bankruptcy. When Electrolux's management team arrived, it constructed a plan of simplifying and properly rejuvenating the business. First it divested or closed many of the company's noncore businesses; next, many old bureaucratic procedures were dropped, much work was subcontracted, and the main work force was slimmed down. This revealed that much of the core appliance business was generating profits. From this position, the management redefined the scope, shifting the focus of attention to improving Zanussi's position in its core Italian market. While it did not go as far as Hotpoint in reshaping scope, the change of emphasis was in line with economic and technical imperatives. Perhaps surprisingly, the plan was implemented and later much extended by existing managers. It had taken the shock of a change of owner to cure entrenched bad habits.

Many top managers are understandably concerned about the ethical dimension of cutting, in particular the future of those affected by cuts. Individuals whose jobs are to be eliminated may feel that they are being offered a Faustian bargain: eternal vitality for the enterprise and damnation for them. Experience has shown that the bargain need not be so stark. British Steel, for example, found that its investment in creating a company to manage the exit process for individuals, providing retraining and placement help, paid a double dividend. Not only did most of those discharged find alternative and sometimes superior employment, but the message of care also greatly encouraged those remaining in the corporation to take the personal risks involved in managing their own changed circumstances. Top managers are also concerned about the future of businesses they sell. Our kind of simplification need not necessarily mean termination for those involved: it is sensible that the eliminated operations be sold as a going concern to another, perhaps more viable organization. It is often possible to find new owners who will nurture the business. Where it is part of a larger diversified concern, the business may be transferred to other parts of the group or offered as a management buyout on favorable terms. Where neither of these courses is possible, the pain is harder, but no less necessary, for without the pruning the whole organization may die and its jobs go to other firms, perhaps in other countries.

CLARIFYING PURPOSE

We have said that it is premature and quite undesirable in these early stages to promulgate a set of detailed plans. Even when they are sure of the need for particular cuts and system simplification, most top managers do not have an adequately clear perception about the market and their organization's future, or about operational details. Even so, they must provide a clear rationale for what they are beginning to do if they are to have a chance of engaging the support of those who will be affected. Providing a rationale is not the same as relying on rationality to make their case. Indeed, the rationale is often more powerfully couched in emotive language, spelling out hope and emphasizing the values as well as the disciplines of behavior that will carry the business forward. Managers must, of course, be exceptionally careful at this stage in the kinds of statements they use. Rash promises about the speed of the upturn invite cynicism, or, worse are noted and used against the top team if the results are not "on schedule."

We found many instances where the CEO and his top team spent a good deal of time working out just what that rationale should be. Indeed, this was frequently a central part of the galvanizing process. The CEO had to be convinced that the company was pointing in the right direction and that senior colleagues shared the same sense of purpose. Together, they then had to find a way to articulate their conclusions to the organization as a whole. This had to meet at least three basic tests to be effective. First, the message had to be capable of raising morale: one of the most depressing features of a mature organization is the low level of aspiration individuals set for their own work. Second, it had to be sufficiently simple to be readily communicated and understood by people at all levels. Third, it had to frame or specify clear and measurable goals for improvement. A fourth test was that of durability. Individuals in a mature organization are used to hearing messages from the top that change with the seasons. To overcome the mistrust that such inconstancy breeds, the new message must be seen to define higher-order values and standards of behavior that can last long into the future. It does not seem to matter if the vision for the direction of future progress is oral or written, provided it poses ambition for greater achievement as a challenge. Remember Richardson's homespun message, which we cited in Chapter 3: "Answer every telephone in seconds; answer every telex in minutes; send every sample within forty-eight hours." This important message still exists, but the firm's ambition is to send samples within twenty-four hours!

To an outsider, this may seem a rather trivial exhortation. Yet everyone in the organization knew it and saw it as a significant statement to distinguish the firm from most rivals, whose customers remained subservient to available production. The value behind the message was clear: speed was vital and the customer was king. Customers got what they wanted, when they wanted it—provided, of course, the price was right. The message went beyond the sales department: production had to play its part, too, by providing samples quickly.

Richardson's management ensured that the message could be seen as more than an exhortation. They made sure their actions signaled that it was part of their new beliefs. An example is their reaction to a German customer that wanted an order processed quickly. After the sales staff had negotiated a good price, the company received a contract almost as big as a book—in German. The order seemed to be in jeopardy. "No one could understand what the legal jargon meant except that it had lots of fierce-looking clauses. Most organizations would have stalled, or else reached for a lawyer: both actions would have meant a missed opportunity to serve a customer and make some money."

Management decided that the customer really needed the order quickly and that by fulfilling the sales staff's promise with a top-quality product it could make the contract clauses irrelevant. So the managers signed the contract before knowing the full import of what they were doing: they relied on their own quality.

As with Richardson's, the best messages define an informal system of standards and include tests to help people. Without these, the much publicized motto attributed to Siemens: "Quality is when your customers come back and your products don't" can go wrong. The motto offers no guide to cost, and slavish adherence to an idea can risk overspecification of a product. Despite such risks, many U.S. corporations find much value in simple slogans, just as we observed. For example, Paul Allaire, the Xerox CEO, says that "focus on the customer" retains its power to grab attention. An incident from a few years ago shows how the informal values embodied in the message can lead to productive solutions to problems. Xerox prided itself on shipping copiers faster than its competitors could. But customers were not interested in that. They wanted to know when their copier would arrive, to have it installed in full working order on schedule, and to be presented with an accurate bill. Allaire was embarrassed to discover that the standard sales answer to queries was "two weeks": no better information was available. To solve that problem, he assigned a manager to pull together a team from distribution, accounting, and sales. The team found a way to simplify the process and to provide accurate information where and when the copier and the bill were needed. Customer satisfaction rose from 70 to 90 percent. Allaire's conclusion was "You can't get people to focus only on the bottom line. You have to give them an objective like 'satisfy the customer' that everyone can relate to. It's the only way to break down those barriers and get people from different functions working together."[10]

Schreiber held the same view. Soon after his arrival at Hotpoint, he promulgated several messages throughout the company. One was the importance of the independent retailer. As noted in Chapter 4, this message helped focus everyone's minds on the fact that *all* customers mattered, not just one group (a mass market symbolized by the chains) at the expense of another (the niches). Other messages included attention to quality and innovation, both vital in giving Hotpoint a competitive edge. Taken together, they added up to a workable vision that emphasized customer-centered innovation.

In Courtelle, the vision of "serve the customer" helped transform the fortunes of the company. As noted in Chapter 4, its changed strategy rested on an understanding of a possibility of new service to industrial customers. The consequences of turning that understanding into action were radical. For a long time, the firm had split its business into two parts: a basic low-cost, low-price product (undyed fiber and standards) and a high-cost, high-price niche (dyed fibers and specials, delivered in small lots). This split had little relation to customer needs and was symbolic of lingering industry traditions. The change meant reorganizing into a single business, where undyed fiber and standards were treated like specials. The focus was to produce the variety that customers wanted at an *acceptable* cost.

Targets for Improvement

Richardson promoted another value: constant improvement in production, efficiency, and quality. Instead of a single target, such as a 50 percent improvement over five years, the company chose an endless goal, similar to that espoused by many Japanese firms. Over a decade, machine productivity rose five times and labor productivity almost thirty-five times. To achieve this, the production managers focused on taking time out of each stage of the process. Long before The Boston Consulting Group did, those managers realized the importance of time-based competition.[11]

Our rejuvenating firms believed that if the basics were right, profits would follow. It was striking that among them only Hotpoint used profit as a central part of the vision—or mission, as some people like to call the idea for the future. But Hotpoint constantly emphasized more tangible activities. When questioned, people in every organization gave similar responses: financial objectives, such as a 25 percent return on capital, may be appropriate messages to give to senior managers, but they cannot be part of an effective mission directed at the whole organization. Some felt that financial objectives were dangerous. They might be powerful when a firm is showing losses, for they put across the message of survival, but they fail to command attention once profitability is restored. Profit objectives can erode the values attached to

190

continuous improvement and do not provide employees with a clear strategic direction; no shop-floor worker is likely to go to work each day saying, "I can't wait to make more money for the shareholders."

From the perspective of those at lower echelons, nonfinancial slogans made sense, and when properly understood and valued could be used to resolve organizational problems. Slogans can illuminate the way forward and justified efforts to try out new ideas. They also acted as a bridge between lower and upper levels of the hierarchy, a feature that proved important later on when problems of maintaining the momentum were frequently encountered.

The central point about communicating targets for improvement is that it must touch a chord of responsiveness in the work force. If the targets are vague and quite different from how subordinates see their superiors behaving, the message is ineffective. If, however, the challenge is anchored in day-to-day reality, it can inspire enthusiasm and effort. Besides, people everywhere need to feel they are part of an ennobling mission to give dignity to their efforts.[12]

Without clarity, any attempt to develop a way forward is apt to be an expensive waste of time. Consider, for example, what happened at Shell some years ago when its U.K. refining operation set out to create an atmosphere of mutual trust and confidence to alleviate industrial relations and staffing problems. Management chose to mount an expensive exercise involving outside experts from the Tavistock Institute and designed to create "a new philosophy of management."[13] Yet when later the work was carefully assessed, few signs of the hoped-for changes in behavior could be detected. Many factors seemed to have impeded change: most recipients did not understand the message; they did not really trust it, because it was so different from management's preceding actions; and top management support waned rapidly as the difficulty of achieving tangible results became apparent.[14]

The same sense of inertia was implied by Roger Smith, past chairman of General Motors, when he said, "I sure wish I'd done a better job of communicating with GM people . . . then they would have known why I was tearing the whole place up . . . I never got this across. There we were, charging up the hill right on schedule and I looked behind me and saw that many people were still at the bottom, trying to decide whether to come along."[15]

Just as the chief executive has to set the "climate" of communication to help galvanize the top team in the initial stages, so the top team in turn must work to relay the messages of the new climate to a broader audience. In this respect, the firms we studied differed sharply from many others, where senior managers had not sufficiently appreciated the need for communicating the purposes of their new initiatives.

191

"Skunkworks," where small groups pursue their own initiatives outside the mainstream of the collective purpose, can help break the mold of past rigidities in behavior. But taken too far, they can lead to severe dislocations and impede progress for firms as a whole. Consider what happened to the group that developed the Macintosh computer. In the early 1980s, the team broke away from the rest of Apple, where the main thrust of developmental effort was on the humdrum Apple II. Though the new group developed further innovative products, its actions fractured the business and led eventually to John Sculley's decision to go for a conventional, functional organization.[16]

Our successful firms ran this risk, but, perhaps because many of them were small, managed to avoid severe dislocation. Their efforts to build initiatives within the functions had many of the characteristics of skunkworks, and were allowed to run for a time. However, when the firms turned to linking functions—putting the roof on the house emerging behind the scaffolding, to pursue the analogy we used earlier—they turned attention to keeping everyone focused on common values.

To last, these values must evolve. Visions can wither if people feel they must read tablets of stone passed down from above. Allowing people some say in developing initial statements can help maintain energy and enthusiasm, and engagement in purpose is essential if a firm is to get the most out of its scarce resources. This provides the emotional glue that binds the various parts of the organization and provides counterpoint to the rational choices of strategy.

These ideas have been put forward in various forms by many others. For example, Tom Peters and Robert Waterman stressed the importance of values and of work on all seven dimensions of the McKinsey 7-S model. They did not, however, deal with the essential requirement for adaptation.[17] In Chapter 9 we develop the theme of the adaptive capability of the firm: the dynamics of markets must be reflected in the dynamics of organizations.

NEW INITIATIVES

All too often organizations stop dead when a new management takes over or cuts activities. Middle managers are waiting for signals as to what is acceptable, and what the new mission is. Perhaps used to vacillating leaders who are swift to blame and slow to praise, they respond to change by being as risk averse as they can. Contrary to what is sometimes believed, the early stage of rejuvenation is not the moment for grand new strategies; it is the time for exploration.

Top management must harness the energy of its organization and stir it into action. Top-down initiatives can produce only a limited result; lasting success needs corporate entrepreneurship. Fortunately, this can on occasion be relatively simple provided top management gives the appropriate signals. In many mature organizations there are individuals who have wanted change but have been frustrated by the traditional beliefs, culture, and systems which have prevented the pursuit of new directions. There may also be groups of people who are keen to see change and are willing to work hard together to make it happen. The problem facing top managers is to identify such people and give them support.

Some parts of the organization will have taken action even before the top team has galvanized itself. This is most likely in departments away from the mainstream: perhaps in a distant location or in a largely autonomous function. Such groups have an important role to play in the rejuvenation process. It is the job of the top team to foster the work of these groups and to make them examples to encourage others more resistant to change and immune to the excitement of exploration.

In the remainder of this chapter, we examine the kinds of initiatives rejuvenators take to build new strengths within functions and to start the process of communication across the functions and across levels in the hierarchy. We look at how the organization adapts its structure. We first examine how new investments of limited scope can be used to build new strengths and create new data that help to improve managers' appreciation of the challenges that lie ahead.

New Investments
First and most important, managers must realize that investments during an initial rejuvenation phase may be short lived. The scaffolding analogy may again be helpful. When an old building is renovated or restored, builders put scaffolding around the edifice so that they can scrutinize it carefully, so that workers may do their restoration with greater ease and safety, and so that the building can be physically supported. When the building is finished, the scaffolding is removed. No one in the building trade views it as a waste of money on any major project, even though the price of the scaffolding may be a substantial proportion of the overall cost. To try to work without scaffolding would make the project more risky, probably take longer, be less well done, and perhaps cost a great deal more. Eliminating scaffolding does not save money.

Thus it is with rejuvenation. During the process of renewal, one must erect temporary systems and structures to replace the old ones, which must be torn down and thrown away. The temporary structures may subsequently be replaced by better ones. Investments in physical assets, skills for the work force, and even human capital may also acquire a "scaffolding." Machines may be required to produce goods that subsequently lead the way to an even better and newer process. People may be hired for relatively short periods to teach the organization new skills.

Our evidence shows that, at this stage of rejuvenation, the bulk of the initial investment expenditure is for small items: new equipment, new software, new systems, and the like. The time for larger, more complex investments is the second phase of rejuvenation, described in Chapter 8. Fact-finding missions, acquisition of data bases, getting out to meet customers and suppliers, are also crucial activities which yield immediate value. Such data can open the eyes of everyone in the organization.

Most organizations have complicated investment appraisal rules and procedures that are inappropriate for the early stages of rejuvenation. If an experimental culture is to be fostered, cumbersome committees, complicated appraisals, and the like must be scrapped. Although large investments can be justified only if the analytical homework has been meticulously prepared, simple guidelines are all that a firm needs for its small, path-finding explorations.

Building within Functions

In the initial stages it is often obvious that some of functions need considerable strengthening, and require urgent work. At Richardson, the factory was in dreadful shape. Because the firm was short of cash, it bought secondhand machines from bankrupt competitors and adapted them to improve its existing capital stock. Benetton was so short of capital in its early years that it, too, was obliged to buy used machines from other manufacturers.

In many organizations the marketing and sales functions are adrift, for the firm has lost sight of its customers. Investments may be needed in rebuilding image and quality by running advertising campaigns and focusing on getting editorial coverage. Functions can be augmented by importing people from other areas who are perceived to be excellent and who, despite lack of specific knowledge, can bring enthusiasm to a weak and beleaguered team.

For example, Schreiber found Hotpoint's marketing in dismal disorder, largely because the focus was on industry statistics alone. He found that he knew more than its personnel about the products and their distributors—knowledge he had gleaned from a few days in stores. For him, improvement meant immediately eliminating the department

194

and hiring new people whose approaches were grounded in the realities of the trade.

Accounting and information systems also require reconstruction to avoid repetition of the earlier mistakes described. Here, too, initial moves can be temporary. For instance, Edwards invested much time and a great deal of money in a factory information system that it soon discarded. This system, however, pointed the way forward by providing interim information that helped define the larger and more comprehensive systems introduced a few years later.

Building within functions often means recruiting new people, a paradox when existing staff are being laid off. But newcomers may supply the fresh perspective and talent needed to pull along those who remain. As with many other moves at this stage, one can see a process of simultaneous cutting and building.

Starting Communications Across Boundaries

Getting those in various functions and territories to talk about their problems is vital from the earliest stages. Such discussions are intended to provoke initiatives to resolve issues by changing perspectives. They are not meant to develop grand investment projects: those come later.

Just as Schreiber had made tremendous progress at a very early stage by forcing the service department to talk to production, so a knitwear company found it could advance rapidly once it got its agents to talk directly to production—and got production to listen. Here, the importance of not delaying certain shipments was explained, and production found new ways of resolving difficulties. The necessary investment was minimal, involving merely new procedures for order processing and the shipping functions.

At a leading service firm, the accounts department had not been aware that the professional department always rewrote reports, charge sheets, and bills before sending them to the customer. Accounting had not realized how confusing its format was. At a stroke, it changed its systems to make the reports more customer friendly, a step that cost little money, speeded up the sending of information to customers, and eliminated a significant amount of wasted time in the professional department.

These initiatives are but a few of the many we observed and heard about. They eliminated waste, provided better service, excited employees, and generated spectacular improvements in profitability. In addition, almost all required little or no new resources. Later, sustained moves to turn these experiments into standard ways of daily operation required greater investment and more time.

Similar developments are needed to initiate vertical communication across layers of the hierarchy. To rebuild confidence in a work force and the lower echelons of management takes time and effort: skepticism and mistrust cannot be eliminated overnight. There are few quick fixes. However, some moves appear to be powerful in releasing energy and the flow of information. Ordinarily, these steps involve reframing the nature of the hierarchy and power relationships.

The most obvious way to proceed when there are many tiers of management is to flatten the organization by removing unnecessary layers. Unless top management is close to the problem solvers and doers, and unless all are willing to interact on a one-to-one basis with the core of the organization, rejuvenation will be compromised. Some initiatives have to be deferred until simpler ways of building closer communication have been put in place.

Often these early moves, like abolishing the executive dining room and insisting that managers eat with workers in a single canteen, were symbolic. Equally often, they went further to start reducing the psychological "distance" between managers and workers. For example, Schreiber abolished many of the privileges of management and established basic workers' rights over such decisions as allowing workers to take breaks as they wished, leaving each person responsible for ensuring no disruption to production. He also abolished the infamous time clock. These changes gave the workers a sense of dignity and increased their self-confidence and status. It is important to note that Schreiber also made workers more responsible for their actions: quality charts were posted in the plant; targets were set; changes in the organizational climate and context were matched by communication initiatives that fostered a better interchange of ideas and suggestions among levels.

New Systems

Throwing out existing systems often revealed enormous gaps. Many found it urgent to build new systems to create new measurements. Some were to reinforce new desired behavior, such as getting close to customers, or improving quality. They typically started off as simple systems, gradually becoming more sophisticated and adaptive. Some new systems were created to measure costs in a way more appropriate to the new tasks. Top management must select the building of new systems with care and avoid attempting to fix everything at once—the organizational equivalent of the dangerous strategic big hit.

One initiative that was common to all was gathering new data to change people's perceptions of what is possible. The absence of correct data may be a powerful disincentive for change, but the lack of necessary data to make informed choices in the early stages of rejuvenation permits old ways to persist by default. Early stages of rejuvenation are therefore greatly helped by actions to collect *new* data to help frame problems in novel ways and indicate new solutions. The need for new data should not be confused with the large volume of data routinely collected in all businesses. Managers who try to figure out their firm's emerging strategy realize that they have only a limited grasp of some fundamentals. In the firms we studied, the extent of this ignorance was large. As one manager noted, "The problem with ignorance is that you don't know you've got it."

We found many gaps in the understanding of critical internal issues, such as the true costs of a product or how changes in product mix affect overall costs. In some cases the gaps of understanding external factors went as far as ignorance of the firm's ultimate customers; one industrial goods firm had only a list of those who purchased their products. Market research, if it existed at all, was often based on the wrong customers or the wrong questions, as well as being out of date. Data on competitors, especially foreign firms, was hopelessly inaccurate or missing altogether. New systems may be required to create the new data that help an organization progress.

Even a firm that has invested in competitor data can belatedly discover crucial gaps in its armory of intelligence. In one case, we discovered how a misdefinition of the strategic market distorted a manager's aspirations. At the opening of a new factory, in, let us say Spain, to disguise the incident and spare the company blushes, the CEO praised the investment as setting new standards of productivity. When it was pointed out to him that another facility elsewhere in Europe had been in operation for several years with nearly twice the productivity, he replied, "But that is irrelevant, we are a Spanish company." He had defined his horizon so narrowly that he failed to recognize how others outside his peripheral vision posed an important potential threat to his own business.

The same problem plagued a major automobile-component company. Top management had defined the competition as other component makers supplying major European car companies. For many years, European assemblers had dominated the European scene and sourced only from European component producers. Then Japanese assemblers made inroads into the European finished car market, capturing more than 30 percent of many national markets not closed by protectionist trade policies. Top managers still considered European component producers as the only serious competition: their data told them that the Japanese firms were not supplying European assemblers. Slowly it dawned on some executives that they might have defined the problem incorrectly: perhaps the Japanese component makers were serious indirect competitors. At a high-level meeting, top management asked for a report on the Japanese producers: none could be found in the company. A quick survey revealed that most people in the company could not name even one major Japanese component manufacturer. A team was given the task of examining the competition, but its members did not know where to start and after a month had made little progress. They had no budget to travel to Japan or to commission expert consultants. Because their report was thin, top management reputedly concluded that the Japanese were not competitors! Several months later, however, top management commissioned a secret report from consultants, apparently to cover up its own lack of awareness. While all this was going on, top management felt paralyzed and unable to initiate firmwide action. Fortunately, lower-level managers were experimenting—but the learning was limited.

Procrastination is the thief of time. The managers in this organization were probably unaware of the extent to which their traditional routines had prevented them from collecting relevant and useful data on the Japanese. Where there is an absence of data, the temptation is to maintain the status quo until the right data can be found and analyzed. But it is better to make a decision to experiment simultaneously with the collection of better data so that less time is lost and momentum is maintained.

Adapting Organizational Structures

One of the most common ways by which managers force change is to redesign both the *formal* and *informal* organizational structures of their business. Merely redrawing the lines of formal responsibility on the organization chart does not bring about change. Other moves to reduce complexity and build mechanisms that support the chosen direction of change are needed. The process can be in cycles, for a business that has had its scope reduced and unnecessary control systems removed often requires a further change in formal structure.

We found many different types of organizational solutions to the problems created by moves away from the stasis of maturity. The danger of overdomination by functional and inward thinking has to be averted so that managers are motivated to look outward, across functions, and to the market. Old functions may have served objectives to seek excellence along dimensions which relate to past, not future needs. Unduly dominant functions may also cause difficulties in communication within an organization.

There are no standard solutions to such problems: each case has its own specific needs. Some rejuvenators have swept away large, monolithic functions and replaced them with small business units focused on market rather than internal logic. While this change can fail to deal with important complexities right away, it has the virtue of allowing people to see the business more clearly, and a general freeing up can put new life into an organization. In other cases, rejuvenators have suffered from too many independent small units, which created chaos, or complex matrix structures, which failed to work and caused confusion. We found, however, most firms adopting a temporary structure as a way of alleviating the most pressing difficulties and providing a vehicle for testing alternatives.

Consider the difficulties commonly encountered in a matrix structure. Some firms have imposed a matrix as a way to recognize the complex interdependencies of business. Unless the firm is vibrant and forward looking in its procedures, matrices can be dangerously stultifying. Even a large, sophisticated organization like Hewlett-Packard has found that matrices can impede its business and have had to move to more simple structures to get initiatives going. Eliminating matrix structures can also reduce costs, for most are accompanied by many committees, complicated control systems, and the like, that do not always add value. Removing these can often cause costs to fall fast and more than make up for the loss of synergy. Interdependencies can sometimes be handled adequately by modest structures, provided the systems are simplified and redundant controls removed. A move to a simpler structure often forces managers to think again and compete on a simpler basis; it can also empower them to take action.

In all the cases we reviewed, we found that firms altered formal and informal systems. Some changed the formal structure first, then moved to adapt the informal mechanisms; others changed the informal structures first, then legitimated those shifts in a later formal change. In both cases we saw the step-by-step building discussed earlier. Equally consistent was the later behavior to readapt both the formal structures and the systems to new requirements. As we show in later chapters, most successful rejuvenators have found it imperative to build upon the simple core of activities they created; this in turn has forced more structural changes. Strategy and structure have to evolve together.

PROGRESS ON THE ROAD TO ENTREPRENEURSHIP

In Chapter 5 we highlighted five features of the entrepreneurial organization: teamwork, aspirations, experimental behavior, learning, and dilemma resolution. At the early stages of rejuvenation, none of these features can be highly developed. Instead, the task is to begin to develop them all, but in varying proportions, depending on the circumstances that caused the original problems.

Effective teamwork at the top is essential from the start, but lower down it tends to be halting and sporadic. It needs to be encouraged by initiatives from the top. Aspirations also need to be altered, but this is never the work of a moment. Cynical, bemused, and generally exhausted by past failures, most middle and lower levels of an organization need to be coaxed to raise their sights. Cutting activities and collecting new data, along with good communication from the top and a willingness to listen, are the first steps.

Experiments must be encouraged. Ideally these should be small, to avoid excessive risk. They should usually, but not always, be confined to a single function, even though they may have been initiated by information from another group. Learning, one of the most difficult behaviors to induce, is helped by good communication and the publicizing of successes. The careful but efficient handling of failure also helps. The effective organization learns from both. Finally, in this stage the ability to perceive and resolve dilemmas is in its infancy. People see progress, but it is usually impossible to identify with precision what must be the first target, and there is sure to be uncertainty about the order in which to build advantages that can later be combined.

Above all, top managers must be self-aware during this first phase. All employees will watch to see if their behavior is consistent with their words. It is essential to preserve proper leadership, but it must avoid the style of constantly telling others what to do. Cutting costs at operating levels without cutting expenditure at the board level justly raises cynicism. An organization becomes energized only if it is encouraged and given space. A proper foundation provides great opportunities for businesses to enter the next phase and build an effective, dynamic organization. But to build it requires the courage, determination, and, above all, the personal involvement of those at the top.

NOTES

[1] For more details see M.R.S. Green, *The Hotpoint Story: A Study in Excellence*, London Business School, 1987.

[2] For one assessment see J.M. Stopford and C.W.F. Baden-Fuller, "Flexible Strategies—The Key to Success in Knitwear," *Long Range Planning* 23, no. 6, December 1990: 56–62.

[3] Paul Strehel, *Breakpoints: How Managers Exploit Radical Business Change* (Boston: Harvard Business School Press, 1993).

[4] Daniel J. Eisenberg, "How Senior Managers Think," *Harvard Business Review*, November–December, 1984: 87.

[5] Warren Bennis, *Why Leaders Can't Lead* (San Francisco: Jossey-Bass, 1989), p. 119.

[6] Rosabeth Moss Kanter, "Thinking Across Boundaries," *Harvard Business Review,* November–December 1990: 9.

[7] See, for instance, S. Slatter, *Corporate Recovery* (Harmondsworth: Penguin, 1984), P.H. Grinyer, D.G. Mayes, and P. McKiernan, *Sharpbenders: The Secrets of Unleashing Corporate Potential* (Oxford: Basil Blackwell, 1988), and D.K. Robbins and J.A. Pearce, "Turnaround: Retrenchment and Recovery," *Strategic Management Journal* 13, no. 4, 1992: 287–309.

[8] R.M. Cyert and J.G. March pointed out many years ago that organizations do not change their behavior easily and that inertia is often a greater obstacle than overt resistance. See Cyert and March, *A Behaviorial Theory of the Firm* (Englewood Cliffs, N.J.: Prentice-Hall, 1963). In the same vein, Herbert A. Simon's notions of "bounded rationality" and "satisfying" behavior raise questions about the nature of the obstacles to be removed. For an excellent collection of his Nobel Prize–winning work, see Simon, *Models of Thought* (New Haven: Yale University Press, 1979).

[9] See, for example, C. Argyris, *Overcoming Organizational Defenses: Facilitating Organizational Learning* (Boston: Allyn & Bacon, 1990).

[10] Quoted in *Fortune,* June 17, 1991: 30.

[11] G. Stalk, "Time—The Next Source of Competitive Advantage," *Harvard Business Review,* July–August 1988: 41–51, and J.L. Bower and T.M. Hout, "Fast-cycle Capability for Competitive Power," *Harvard Business Review,* November–December 1988: 110–118.

[12] In many Japanese firms, this approach has been raised to a high art and is symbolized in many company creeds and songs. At Matsushita, employees' recitation of the creed of recognizing responsibilities, promoting the welfare of society, and so on, reinforces the firm's *purpose*. When singing the song about "sending our goods to the peoples of the world, endlessly and continuously, like water gushing from a fountain," they espouse the corporate *vision*. And when they go to internal training sessions about such topics as "courtesy and humility" and "struggle for betterment," they learn about the firm's carefully crafted *values*, which Matsushita calls spiritual values. For details, see M. Moskowitz, *The Global Marketplace* (New York: Macmillan, 1987).

[13] For details see C.P. Hill, *Towards a New Philosophy of Management* (London: Gower, 1971).

[14] For details see F.H.M. Blacker and C.A. Brown, *Whatever Happened to Shell's New Philosophy of Management?* (Aldershot: Saxon House, 1980).

[15] Cited in *Strategic Direction,* May 1990: 9.

[16] D. Schon, *The Reflective Practitioner: How Professionals Think in Action* (New York: Basic Books, 1983).

[17] Thomas J. Peters and Robert H. Waterman, Jr., *In Search of Excellence* (New York: Harper & Row, 1982); see also A. Campbell, M. Devine, and D. Young, *A Sense of Mission* (London: Hutchinson, 1990).

Shape the Collective Effort

Without pausing or even allowing time to worry about incipient fatigue, a galvanized top team has to broaden the scope of its work; it has to orchestrate and link many small initiatives set into motion at the start of rejuvenation. Some of the starting points for this task will already have been made in a myriad of minor ways, as we saw in Chapter 7. Now the top team has to work hard toward making much larger investments to create new competitive advantages in the marketplace. These initiatives have to be larger because they involve more people, cut across functions in new forms, require perhaps significant capital expenditures, and certainly require substantial investment of human effort.

We label these larger investments "frame-breaking" to symbolize the distance an organization has traveled from its earliest moves in creating corporate entrepreneurship. They represent a congruence between what top managers want and what those in the middle are capable of delivering. Whereas any big-hit investment is dangerous at the start of rejuvenation, sizable investments become appropriate because the firm has built new skills, better understood its economic challenges, and started building corporate entrepreneurship. These investments consolidate past advances and help to set managers' sights on new and higher goals for the whole firm, not just one department.

FRAME-BREAKING ORGANIZATIONS

Edwards and the Japanese Market

The entry of Edwards into the Japanese market was a radical move both in the context of the company's history and of the international market structure. Edwards made this move some years after its first halting moves to rejuvenate. Historically, most of the vacuum pump industry had been bound within countries or regions. The Americans dominated North America, the Europeans dominated in their respective home countries, and the Japanese dominated in the Far East. In 1972, Sargent Welch had over 60 percent of the U.S. market, and the combined U.S. share of Leybold (Germany's number one producer), Edwards (number one in the United Kingdom), and Alcatel (number one in France) was less than 5 percent. The push by Edwards for Japan could be seen as radical, especially in a firm that had only recently emerged from trouble. Although Edwards had some help from its parent company, BOC, which had established good local relationships with Nippon Sanso for its industrial gas products, many hurdles remained. The Japanese had their own pump industry and for them to purchase from Britain was a major break with tradition.

Although Edwards had to struggle for some years before it broke into the market, the Japanese investment proved successful. It provided tangible evidence to those inside the organization, as well as customers and suppliers, that the chosen strategy, globalizing the capability to make and deliver primary pumps, had come to fruition. As explained in Chapter 4, this strategy was a shift away from that of the competitors, a novel reading of the market. Edwards was at the stage of the rejuvenation when it was necessary to make the strategy, which was originally more accidental than thought out, a deliberate play. The strategy was not just an idea; it permitted Edwards to participate in a lucrative growing market, proving that the global niche was profitable. This move would have been impossible some years earlier.

The move to Japan had additional closely related advantages in providing a listening post to monitor Japanese activities. There were weak signals that some Japanese were planning an invasion outside their territory and that they had built considerable strengths. By going to Japan, the organization would be better placed to assess, and possibly reduce, these threats.

The presence of Edwards in Japan also demonstrated to everyone that the organization still had some way to go. Edwards's standards were still below those of the world's most demanding market—standards the firm had to meet if it was to hold on to sales elsewhere in the world. These standards, once gained, helped Edwards deploy its efforts in other countries. The success of the Japanese move can be gauged by the fact that by 1990, Japanese sales had risen to over 20 percent of Edwards's business, making it one of the market leaders there, and that Edwards continued to grow its business elsewhere.

Richardson and the Fashion Market

After the invention and success of the Laser knife, Richardson made another bold move to break the rules of the game. It explored and put considerable effort behind making its knives a fashion item, breaking the traditions of the industry. One tradition in the United Kingdom, is that knives are not given as gifts. Convention had it that the giver offers bad luck: the knife may cut the friendship. Richardson changed all that by packing sets of knives in boxes, in packets, and on blocks of wood specifically designed for presents. Richardson made the knife an acceptable gift—modern, fashionable, but inexpensive. Within a few years it had changed consumer perceptions and beliefs. It also exploited the idea of disposability, which, paradoxically, it promoted side by side with the five-year or longer guarantee offered on all Stay-sharp products. The consumer bought an image of quality and fashion at relatively low prices.

How novel was Richardson's approach? It could be argued that Richardson was doing only what any reputable consumer-product company ought to do. However, few large, sophisticated consumer goods-firms are equally proactive, and none in the cutlery trade shared Richardson's approach. One need only look at the lack of progress of other U.K. cutlery firms to realize how much Richardson broke the rules. As noted in an earlier chapter, conventional wisdom—as expounded by government agencies such as the National Economic Development Office and the trade association—suggested that the future of the U.K. cutlery firms lay in concentrating on the classic look: silver and silver-plated products capturing value through high margins at low volumes, the antithesis of Richardson's focus on trendy, fashionable, mass-market products.[1]

Hotpoint's New Production

In 1982, eight years after Chaim Schreiber took over, Hotpoint rebuilt its washing machine factory at Kinmel. This plant differed from generally perceived European best practice. It was only about half the size of the accepted optimum size of one million units a year found in the plants of the leaders in Germany (Bosch-Siemens), Italy (Zanussi and Philips), the United States (GE and Whirlpool), and Japan. The new factory was designed to exploit numerous small process innovations that had been overlooked by rivals, including the elimination of the paint shop we discussed earlier. The new facility gave a triple benefit: lower labor and capital costs, partially offset by more expensive raw material; better quality of output (fewer rejects); and a greater flexibility in production, particularly the ability to make small batches of machines in a selection of colors.

Because the company broke many industry norms, it must have seemed to be taking a leap in the dark, when viewed from outside. Conventional competitor analysis would have indicated that Hotpoint's move was both bold and foolish. Three factors would have predicted failure: demand growth had slowed, there was excess capacity in the industry, and rivals would probably retaliate. To insiders, however, the move was not a leap but a pulling together of ideas tested over the previous few years in the older factories.

Up to the late 1970s, much of the demand for appliances was from first-time buyers, and replacement demand was just emerging. By the mid-1980s, replacement demand for washing machines and refrigerators had become dominant, as overall sales growth had slowed.[2] Conventional analysis suggested that these segments were mature and, because customers would replace machines only when their old ones broke down, forecasters predicted lower margins and excess capacity. The only sources of growth were seen to be in dishwashers and freezers. Yet Hotpoint's new facility was to provide attractive, fashionable new models of mature products.

Hotpoint's managers, although well aware that they were adding to already severe excess capacity and running risks, were confident that they could do better than competitors. Their confidence stemmed from the knowledge gleaned from their purchases from Zanussi, Europe's largest producer at the time. The investment could be justified only as a strategic innovation, based on the belief—justified only in hindsight—that Hotpoint's production capability would be somehow different and better, a crucial first step in building further advantages for the business. Subsequent events showed that Hotpoint's products were more attractive and created fresh demand in an apparently mature market.

Conventional wisdom would also have predicted that its rivals would retaliate against Hotpoint. The rivals had depreciated plant whose cash costs of operation should have been low, but reality was different. Most of their plants, bloated by inefficient practices, were producing high-cost, poor-quality machines and allowed their managers little maneuverability for retaliation. Tangential evidence suggests that they did not even try, perceiving Hotpoint's investment as a gamble doomed to fail.

Risk was reduced to acceptable proportions by two factors, neither obvious to competitors. One was the role of earlier initiatives improving the core capabilities and competencies of the firm; the other was a structural shift in the market. Hotpoint's ability to supply good products of increasing variety allowed the firm to attack many niches without incurring excessive costs. The resurgence of the sales and distribution functions also provided customer value at acceptable cost. Hotpoint could combine the *push* factors of excellent supply management with the *pull* factors of consumer preference. Rivals, whose strength lay only in either push or pull, found themselves squeezed.

Hotpoint's actions were consistent with a belief that the market was continuously changing; Hotpoint's rivals acted as if the market was essentially stable. When introducing new models, Hotpoint's managers anticipated continuous modifications. Rivals' failures to be flexible cost them dearly. For example, Thomson, a major French producer, had invested $20 million in a new model, the BD40. Supposedly at the forefront of design, it was expected to remain unchanged for many years, but it became apparent within a year of the launch that changes were urgently needed. Such changes were unanticipated, and as production and other systems could not cope easily, further large investments were necessary.

FRAME-BREAKING INVESTMENTS

The frame-breaking moves we have described had the important symbolic purpose of establishing a new era (see Exhibit 8.1). It seems that earlier moves of cutting and starting new initiatives had indicated only that change was on the way, and it took these frame-breaking steps to push the message home to all concerned. Those who work with organizations know that actions speak louder than words. More effective than mission statements, corporate training programs, or a company tour, these big initiatives demonstrated that conditions were really different from those of the past. People could see tangible results.

Rather than substituting for the many small initiatives started in the earlier stages of rejuvenation, frame-breaking moves helped orchestrate those which were available to create new opportunities. Hotpoint's factory gave a new focus to the efforts of the marketing and design depart-

----

EXHIBIT 8.1   FRAME-BREAKING INVESTMENTS

Symbolic purpose	Prove to the stakeholders, especially those working in the organization, that a new era has arrived and that a new direction has been established.
Keep up the pace of progress	Provide a mechanism for exploiting existing initiatives and maintain the stimulus for starting new ones.
Change the economic rules	Build new steps on the strategic staircase by orchestrating disparate innovations and combining them into something economically powerful.

----

ments and encouraged them to introduce many more models as well as improve the speed of introduction. This in turn set up challenges for other parts of the organization. Richardson's emphasis on fashion demanded a wider range of products, new work for designers, and a whole new set of tasks for marketing, production, accounting, and the other functions. Far from slowing down the pace, it speeded it up for everyone in the business. At Edwards, the move to Japan also spurred its initiatives for better quality in production. It forced logistics to adopt new policies and provided challenges for marketing, sales, and accounting.

The purpose of the frame-breaking investments went beyond the organizational agenda, helping to cement economic progress. In the language of the strategic staircase, it helped ensure that activities of each business were orchestrated to build sequential steps. It ensured that an initiative in one area of each firm was coordinated with a matching effort elsewhere. The importance of orchestrating initiatives should not be underestimated. Whereas in the first stages of rejuvenation such orientation could (and arguably should) be overlooked, it can no longer be ignored.

The need for collaboration is illustrated by one Italian appliance manufacturer that found itself unable to achieve European leadership. Though its factories were among the most flexible and most automated in Europe, combining speed, efficiency, and low cost, customer and retailer needs were constantly being frustrated by the inability of the organization to link its factories to the market. Finished goods were delayed in shipping and logistics, eroding the benefits of flexibility, speed, and lower costs in production. Service to customers was constantly falling short of the achievable, because one department's progress was hindered by lack of comprehension elsewhere. This left gaps in the value chain, and the competitive impact of the customer-oriented initiative was not felt by the retail customer. By contrast, the ability of Hotpoint to be first to the U.K. market and its responsiveness to changes in market demands reflected its ability to integrate its organization and earned it admiration from competitors across Europe.

Although total quality management (TQM) and process reengineering were not yet in the management vocabulary of our organizations at this stage of their work, several instituted TQM and process reengineering types of programs to orchestrate their efforts. Hotpoint's new factory was a form of process reengineering, which, although it lacked computers, involved much of the organization. Richardson's initiatives on the Laser knife, as much a frame-breaking move as the shift to fashion, was clearly an application of sophisticated TQM involving principles of *kaisen*, "continuous improvement benefiting the customer." Just as TQM advocates, that project involved many functions.

As noted in Chapter 6, our firms shunned programmatic changes only in the first stages of rejuvenation because they were inappropriate when skills had not been built, capabilities did not exist, and strategy was unclear.

Our firms discovered the seemingly obvious, that it is impossible to change an industry's economics without large initiatives which cover all the functions and involve substantial investments. But when such moves and investments were successful, there was significant payoff. These investments were designed to create *multiple* advantages simultaneously and required extensive operational collaboration among departments. They reflect what is now common knowledge, namely, that it is not the invention of a new product or process which is critical, but its application and full dissemination. Each of our frame-breaking moves represented an attempt to break the bounds of industry tradition by transforming earlier small initiatives into larger ones.

Richardson's moves to the Laser knife and fashion items altered the industry's economics and put Richardson in the position of driving change in the industry rather than being driven by it. Hotpoint's initiatives, first with distribution, then with a novel factory, secured the firm as the innovator not just in the U.K. market but also in Europe. Rivals that tried to attack Hotpoint in the United Kingdom found not a minor niche player but an alarmingly efficient and effective organization. Edwards, in its achievements in global expansion, has outpaced its European and American rivals to sit among the best in the world. It has forced new methods of pricing and delivery on its competitors.

Linking organizational and economic agendas to achieve frame breaks requires much work. We identified a number of our rejuvenators' activities that appear to be critical in shaping collective efforts and highlight them in Exhibit 8.2. They can be grouped under three headings: *orchestrate efforts* is the linking of functions and parts of an organization with one another and with the rest of the value chain; *filling gaps* refers to the efforts of the top team to ensure that skills and capabilities are continually built to support the initiatives under way and contemplated, and that the learning culture is continually reinforced; last, but by no means least, we touch on the need to *mobilize middle management*, a vital body representing the core of the organization.

ORCHESTRATING EFFORTS

Competitive battles are not won by gifted individuals; they are won by effective teams, none of whose members may be individually bril-

---

EXHIBIT 8.2 STEPS REQUIRED PRIOR TO FRAME-BREAKING INVESTMENTS

Orchestrate efforts Link functions	Ensure that initiatives in one area are not frustrated by contradictory priorities elsewhere.
Rebalance functions	Ensure that functions which have a critical role in the creation of steps on the staircase have a proper say in the power structure.
Create new functions	Match the economic imperative with resources and the way they are deployed.
Filling gaps New skills	Bring in new skills to complement those which exist, and build the skills of those already in an organization.
Detailed analysis and assessment	Raise the level of organizational awareness and learning about strategizing.
Invest in information	Information is a critical resource for developing an organization.
Mobilize middle management Mobilize all levels of middle management	Recognize that the key resource of an organization is its people.

---

liant. To be able to design and achieve the full potential of frame-breaking investments, functional departments have to collaborate intensively, sharing their specialist skills and knowledge. Individuals and departmental teams have to become accustomed to thinking in terms of their firm as a whole, not just of their own patch. The qualities of "systems thinking" and *team* learning, emphasized by Peter Senge in *The Fifth Discipline*,[3] assume heightened importance.

In the process of rejuvenation, these frame-breaking investments are the first really significant test of whether the organization is making substantial progress toward the goal of the entrepreneurial organization we sketched in Chapter 5. Not only do the teams have to work in new ways, but there are more teams whose work has to be coordinated. Even more testing are the demands of learning from success and failure. Some of the experiments made earlier will have met the initial objectives; others will have failed. One critical task in the new arena is to ensure that the worth of the resources revealed by the experiments can be fully assessed and harnessed at larger scale. Even from failure can some learning usually be salvaged. Conversely, success at small scale may not work at larger scale. The investments are therefore inherently speculative. Moreover, because they are also innovative in their competitive markets, conventional financial appraisal techniques may give misleading signals.

Top managers are thus more than usually dependent upon the quality of the teams at middle levels to reduce the risk to acceptable proportion. Whereas they could tolerate failure in the small-scale investments with relative comfort, the stakes now have risen. A frame-breaking investment necessarily represents a commitment to the future, based on a firm belief that the surest resource was the quality of the teams leading the way.

We found many times that our successful firms had long understood these messages. As one chief executive said, "I am only as good as the team I am supposed to lead. Sometimes, the team is way ahead of my thinking. I have had to learn to listen." He was quite clear that his role was that of orchestrator. Of course, there are times when different approaches are needed,[4] but the values of orchestration are most evident at this stage of moving toward sustainable collective action.

We saw in Chapter 7 how a top team initiated moves to start people talking across traditional boundaries. Orchestrating the effort carries that further to link the functions more closely in their daily operating behavior. Teams in the form of groups, task forces, committees, "skunkworks," and corridor lobbies exist in all organizations, good and bad. A notable feature of rejuvenating firms was their ability to emphasize the good and limit the bad.

Linking and Rebalancing Functions

All our rejuvenating firms found that departments had to change the way they worked together in their daily operations; groups that were at arm's length became closer. At the prerejuvenation stage, most of the manufacturing businesses we studied allowed the production department to dominate operations. The sales department sold what production had manufactured (or what was in stock), and the purchasing department ordered what production required to meet its schedules. Product-design functions were in the wings, as were consumer demands. The absence of customer awareness always has adverse consequences. For example, logistical delays in one firm meant that televisions that were supposed to be in the shops before Christmas were not produced until January. The organization did not cancel its work plan, as it probably would have done had anyone contacted the sales department or the retailers to ask if late delivery was acceptable; the Christmas order was delivered in February. Because the price cuts necessary to clear the stock meant substantial losses, it would have been cheaper to have abandoned that order and found more productive ways of pacifying an irate customer.

211

The old method of production was neatly summed up by the senior manager of one of the largest domestic appliance plants in Germany: "We used to produce relatively long runs of items, with infrequent changeovers; now all that has changed. The short runs cause havoc. I have tried to explain to the sales department, but they do not understand. If we could only have less variety, we could run our plant efficiently."

This German firm earned profits in spite of itself, but it was not as successful as some of its smaller rivals that had adopted the new philosophy and rebalanced departmental relationships. The experience of a smaller, but much more profitable U.K. firm shows the difference: "Right from the start, marketing was charged with developing the product range based on the supposed requirements of the consumer. Marketing was also responsible for loading the factory—on a week-by-week basis. We still do this . . . On this site we make 370 different products. Yes, [sales] tells them what to make."

One can link the changing relationships among functions to changing economic rules in the marketplace. In earlier chapters we spoke of the problems faced by mature firms that had become out of step with the market. In our organizations, the old rules of producing a high volume of standardized products had given way to the new rules of producing variety or high quality or both at low cost. In the past, new products had long lead times and arrived infrequently. The new rules required more product innovation, shorter lead times in development, and shorter life expectancy in the market.

When production can lower its unit costs and provide greater variety, marketing can discover the means to probe markets more deeply. Consider, for example, the Miata, Mazda's small sports car. What distinguishes Mazda from American producers is that it can make a profit on low volume—40,000 units. The key was not greater perception of the market opportunity, but the ability to link supply know-how to that opportunity.[5]

Paradoxically, the problem in our firms was that in the past, the dominance of production in operations was not reflected in its role in determining strategy. It often had no voice in shaping choices about how to serve markets. Many U.S. studies have depicted production as the "good soldier" mutely implementing the strategies that top management periodically decided.[6] Its concerns were predominantly with efficiency and rationality in the execution of commands, not with the creation of new options for the enterprise as a whole. The lost opportunities were legion. To make the new way effective, all departments, including production, had to learn more about the markets and competition, and top managers had to listen and learn.

212

Production was not the only function in need of reshaping and creating new linkages. Research departments, like engineering, usually found that they had to change their position in the organization. Research, which at one time may have focused on increasing productivity and reducing cost within a constraint of little change in variety and limited responsiveness, found the rules altered. Cost reduction was critically important, but had to be balanced by equally stringent challenges such as ensuring greater quality or speed of response to fashion. This entails fresh programs, new time frames, new masters, and new relationships. So too with other functions, as one manager explained: "We found that to improve productivity and continue growing we had to cut down the interfaces within and between the divisions, particularly in staff areas. This was needed particularly among sales, contracts, technical, and purchasing."

Our firms found that rebalancing often involved bringing to center stage some "Cinderella" functions. At Hotpoint the role of the service department was altered operationally and strategically; it shrank in size but increased in importance. In the past it was a Cinderella that existed merely to rectify production's mistakes. Although a large department, and a significant profit center, it was ancillary to the strategy. When the quality drive was instituted, the service department moved to a more central position close to production, providing information so that mistakes were not repeated. But this role was taken over by marketing, and service took on an even more central position as provider of valuable information on customers' desires for new product variations, moving close to the center of thinking for the whole organization.

Many of our other rejuvenators also found that the integration of service was a specific source of competitive advantage. They invested in building new capabilities to transform what used to be a minor function. At Edwards the changing balance in the new relationship is symbolized by the fact that factory managers have explicit responsibility for customer service, which is measured by what happens to the firm's output after installation.

Creating New Functions

In rebalancing traditional functions, our firms found that they had to create new ones as well. Sometimes this entails bringing in-house previously subcontracted activities or creating new functional skills in an existing activity. We use the example of design to illustrate some of our points.

Before rejuvenation, U.K. knitwear firms had only weak links among design, sales, and production. As recently as the early 1980s, there were few design departments and design was perceived by many as of secondary importance. As one buyer commented on one supplier, "The perception of the role of design was terrible. When we asked to see this season's ideas, the supplier merely ripped off the sheets from the last season's list."

While this supplier may have been the very worst of the pack, designers were generally a forgotten group. They worked on the fringe of the organization, were subcontracted on poor terms, or were doing the job part time between other activities. Worse yet, many part-time, in-house designers had not been properly trained. There was the appearance of a resource, but no strength. The problems were exacerbated by the small size of the teams and weak links with production, with the result that many new items could not easily be produced, and feedback was slow or nonexistent.

For collective action to be enhanced, these relationships had to be changed. Design increased in importance and began to influence strategy. Part of the change came from new CAD-CAM—computer-aided design–computer-aided manufacturing—technology that allowed designers to work directly with production, but the major changes came from top managers' fully appreciating the changes in consumer tastes. Every firm was forced to go outside for new talent to build a new corpus of knowledge and skills. Each then had to find ways of adjusting other functions to use its new skills to the full.

Better design requires intimate communication among all the functions and has shifted the location of critical bodies of knowledge. For some, "design," considered broadly, takes the lead role in defining customer requirements, present and future—a far cry from the days when designers were regarded by senior managers as effete products of art colleges.

For Benetton, design has always been critical. It has linked design, production, and sales in a revolutionary manner. In the first place, it adopted the industry tradition of making up samples, showing them to customers, and taking orders. But for Benetton there was a difference: the designs came from a group which offered coordinated ranges that were tested with production and modified in the light of customers' initial reactions. Unpopular items were dropped, and rush or specials—*pronto moda*—were inserted as the season progressed. The retailing information system allowed the firm to monitor sales during a given season so that designers and production could respond to subtle changes in selling patterns and competition. Benetton believed that if it produced to retailers' orders, the buffer between it and the consumer would be less than ideally flexible. Consequently, it produced what had sold in the previous week, responding directly to final consumption. Waste was kept to a minimum and flexibility to a maximum.

Our point is not that design is important to all organizations—this is surely not true—but that Cinderella functions have to be enhanced. As Benetton's success shows, altering departmental relations is not achieved by talk but by actions that change the way decisions are made. The relationships among Benetton's functional departments stood in sharp contrast to those in most traditional garment firms. The differences reflected the varying ways in which the firms operated to capture competitive advantage. Benetton aggressively altered its internal rules to give itself market advantage and capture new trends. It has flourished while those that ignored trends and refused to rebalance their functions have failed.

Linking Suppliers and Buyers

Just as internal coordination and a rebalancing of functions helps a firm to gain leverage from scarce resources, so the same approach applies to relationships with suppliers and buyers. Besides, closer links across legal boundaries of the firm allow more sources of innovation to be tapped. To some extent we are merely reinforcing the messages offered in Chapters 3 and 4 when we assert that to add value, a firm must mobilize its whole value chain. Although there are risks involved, if they are contained and controlled, the payoffs can be high.

Ford's Team Taurus program exemplifies the value of change in approach to a rejuvenating organization and shows that risks need not be out of control. As the program changed the balance among the functions during the 1980s, it also altered Ford's relationships with suppliers.[7] Ford had realized that its survival rested on its ability to speed up new product development, at lower cost, to catch the innovative Japanese.[8] The need for speed altered the traditional methods by which Ford planned its new product range. Previously, it had designed the product and then put the components out for bid by suppliers. The resulting delay between design completion and initial production was exacerbated by modifications introduced by suppliers. With Team Taurus, Ford collaborated with suppliers early in the design process and asked them to anticipate opportunities and problems. This helped reduce the overall cycle time from design to production and lowered costs through the team's ability to anticipate faults. The new system, so obviously essential in the new era, would have been unsuitable earlier, when product changes were less frequent.

Many other rejuvenating organizations have been making similar moves that emulate what the Japanese have long practiced in their keiretsu groups. The objective is to create commitment among loyal supporters who can identify with the long-term aim of the firm.[9] The use of "preferred supplier" relationships has been spreading rapidly where managers have begun to see that the benefits are real. A careful study of changing practices in the textile industry recently concluded:

> Garment makers feel they can improve their ability to respond to their customers' demands for variety and short lead times through managing a supplier strategy around a primary supplier to whom they show considerable loyalty . . . That some price premium is paid is part of the implicit bargain . . . and controllable by maintaining relationships with secondary suppliers.[10]

To help improve responsiveness further, some have harnessed the power of electronic data interchange with customers and suppliers. But as with all changes, there has been trouble. One manager explained: "At the moment the relationship is all one way, and to make the system work properly it will have to be two way. We shall need to know what their inventories are and these issues touch on confidentiality. We shall have to break down barriers not only between the functions within our own firm, but also between different organizations."

Most rejuvenators wish they had more resources, and close external relations can also allow firms to tap sources of innovation that would otherwise be denied them. Compaq overcame its limited resources during the 1980s by collaborating with suppliers and buyers to enhance its focused attack on the much larger IBM. It did not compete against its dealers as some other computer manufacturers do, but insisted that *all* sales were to be made through them. The dealers rewarded Compaq's trust by working hard to provide an effective series of local networks of service and support and so ensure success for "their" ally. Compaq has also collaborated with its component suppliers. It was able to launch a 32-bit, IBM-compatible PC before IBM did. For this, it relied on a close relationship with Intel, the developer of the microprocessor at the heart of the machine. Intel, in which IBM has a financial stake, was willing to give Compaq preferential treatment, because Compaq could develop an end product faster than others, including IBM itself. This was one of the best ways for Intel to ensure that its chip would work on non-IBM machines and establish it as the industry standard.

Linking with suppliers and buyers provides no guarantee of lasting advantage. Indeed, Compaq is being seriously challenged by others that seem to be playing the same game. But linkage can help accelerate progress when resources are in short supply. To get even some gain, however, it would seem that firms must first build better internal, interfunctional linkage.

PLUGGING GAPS

All our rejuvenating firms estimate that they have invested as much in hiring people with new skills and training staff as they have in buying physical assets. Frequently, investments in human assets and skills could not be justified in traditional investment appraisal terms, as it was unclear exactly what the new skills would bring. However, in many cases the investment was paid back many times over comparatively quickly. The focus on new skills proved to be one of the catalysts that changed departmental relationships and developed essential learning processes.

Why are new skills necessary? Think of the new rules of competition that require previously separated functions to be combined. To be managed effectively, new combinations typically need new capabilities that cannot be created out of existing functions and knowledge bases. In almost all cases, the firms had to hire from outside their industry new staff whose skills augmented those in the firm to develop these capabilities. Some were alluded to earlier, but we develop the idea further.

In Richardson, one starting point for radical change was combining electronics with existing mechanical skills. The company had long allowed a single skill—mechanical engineering—to dominate on the production floor. Bryan Upton realized early on that "there had to be a better way," so he experimented by hiring electronic engineers unfamiliar with cutlery. The newcomers worked in the production department and, with fresh eyes, were able to perceive solutions to known but unresolved problems. They developed optical instead of mechanical checks to solve the problem of ensuring that the knife edge was ground at the correct angle. At a cost of only a few thousand dollars, the new system proved far more accurate at detecting rejects. Through this, Richardson doubled machine efficiency and quadrupled labor productivity.

Richardson has as a central philosophy continued to hire skills that were not standard to the industry and thereby achieved novel solutions to traditional problems. But for that to happen, top management had to learn to listen to the newcomers and to adapt behavior in production and elsewhere.

Hotpoint also brought in staff with new skills. We have already alluded to the early development of capabilities in customer research, consumer testing, and other areas of market information gathering. Like Upton, Geoff Samson also brought in new electronic skills. He could see that Hotpoint engineers "had little conception of what electronics could do for both the product and the production process" and

217

set about developing the capability needed to provide fresh product advantages.

Courtelle also found that it had little idea of what the final consumer wanted: traditionally it had focused on the role of the immediate customer, the spinner of fiber. But it came to realize that if it understood the final consumer, the product could be "pulled through." Again, this meant investing in new skills and new people to upgrade and adapt many functions.

A complementary policy of job rotation at all levels was one of the means used in these firms to foster the mobility of information and skills. For example, many senior Edwards managers had worked in more than one function, and it was considered quite acceptable to make sideway career moves. We found similar evidence of lateral moves within the other firms. In some cases, the approach was extended to temporary postings to buyers and suppliers. These moves allowed managers to take a wider perspective on problems and draw on a multiplicity of experiences. By contrast, many managers in stagnating firms had experience of only a single function and found it hard to broaden their perspectives.

Detailed Analysis and Assessment

All good business ideas require thorough reconnaissance.[11] If an organization is to go forward and reshape its environment, everyone has to appreciate the distinction between a general vision that lacks specific detail and the analysis needed to underpin target-setting and investment decisions. Attachment to value- and performance-driven visions for collective purpose should not detract from the need to use data to help calculate the value of specific strategic moves and of interdepartmental cooperation. The analysis we are talking of is not just financial thinking, although the finance department should be involved early on to help define the options properly. We mean a proper assessment of all major investments on the workings of the firm and its competitive surroundings.[12] Moreover, in our organizations the analysis and thinking did not stop when projects were approved; the thinking had to extend to how the projects grew.

In teaching organizations about strategizing, there is an important role for top managers to act as coaches, teaching others how to codify their instincts and become more systematic than they have been. For example, Samson taught his managers the critical need for careful, detailed market research to help judge what consumers would want. But he also taught them not to use numbers as a rigid budget, but as a guide for new product development. Sometimes, of course, the analysis was wrong: but again it is instructive to see how the organization coped with errors. The mistakes in planning one product launch provided the company with a valuable spur to improve its learning and adaptive capacity, as one manager explained:

> When we launched the washer-drier in March 1985, our market research showed that we would sell 375 units a week, or about 20 percent of the market we could identify. We thought this was a good place to start: we had the exhibition and said that we would start deliveries in October. I allocated new capacity of up to 500 a week. A week after the exhibition it looked as if we would have to make 1,000 a week and we adjusted accordingly. Sixteen months later we are up to 4,000 a week. There are not many companies that can grow their capacity for a new product this fast.

When others in the industry heard the story, they said that they too had underestimated the washer-drier market. They did not, however, respond to the unexpected demand and allowed Hotpoint to sweep up much of the market. They were stuck with unalterable "plans." When sales exceeded the budget forecast, effort stopped; they sat back and did nothing to exploit the new opportunity. Their plans and budgets were a constraint to action, not targets to be exceeded.

Flexibility in the use of targets, plans, and budgets was a value we heard many times. In one engineering firm, the spirit was described as "Targets, *not* plans, are critical in driving our business forward. These targets must change as competition shifts. The shifts, though, are *additive.*"

At Edwards, Danny Rosenkranz regarded formal strategic planning as inappropriate, for "our business is fast moving and volatile." Yet he emphasized the need for analysis. Shortly after he arrived, he forced his managers to justify an approximately $4 million investment proposal in great detail. Given that the parent company's turnover was more than $2 billion and that results rather than forecasts were the usual justification for investment, Rosenkranz seemed to be using overkill. His view, however, was that "the main board did not need it, but [the managers] did." He wanted his managers to understand properly what they were proposing to do. One who worked on the plans said, "It was a revelation—he gave us a horrendous task, he drove us hard—but in the end we understood much better the risks and challenges."

Detailed analysis is evident everywhere in firms that progress beyond the stage of nascent experimentation. Meticulousness does not have to become pedantic fussiness. All our rejuvenators shared an attention to detail unmatched in many rival organizations, and still retained

219

lithe flexibility. They all realized that if learning was to take place, the role of information systems had to be expanded.

New Information Systems

"Information is power: share it" seems to have become an implicit slogan in many of our firms. But before they reached this point, they had to overcome severe handicaps. At the early stages of rejuvenation, most had poor or failing systems, many of which had to be scrapped or dismantled. As we showed earlier, many worked with inadequate data and were essentially feeling their way in the dark.

Moving toward collective action makes the development of permanent and sophisticated information systems a priority. As a strategy becomes clearer and tasks more fully defined, the benefits of investing to turn data into intelligence become more obvious. Besides, the emerging styles of new behavior demand not only different types of information about internal and external conditions, but also new ways of disseminating and sharing data among departments in two-way communication.

After Rosenkranz arrived, Edwards's top managers realized that they needed a system which could *integrate* product-costing data with market information. Until then, the two sets of information had been run separately. The effect had been to provide wrong signals so that, for example, prices were computed haphazardly. A senior manager was assigned the task of building a system to handle world market data, differing currencies, different costs, and a wide product range. The resulting computer-based system identified ultimate users as well as intermediate users and permitted the organization to price precisely for each product and customer segment. The consequence of the new system was dramatic: "We added [about $4] million to profits in the first six months. For the first time we had a handle on our costs and revenues. It transformed the fortunes of the organization and allowed us to reap the benefits of all the hard work we had been doing in the past years."

Turning data into intelligence that can be used effectively requires more than an information system: users have to become closely involved in networked systems. Benetton's real-time, retailer information system makes the point. For fashion goods, understanding the exact situation in the market is one of the keys to profitability. Overproduction can cause losses from markdown sales; underproduction is almost as costly, for profit opportunities are missed and customers may not return. Though many in the fashion trade have copied the Benetton systems, relatively few can make full use of them, because the consequential internal functional connections are hard to emulate.

220

Investment in information systems extends beyond those linking functions. Almost all of organizations developed market information systems to track new developments, customers, and competitors. But it has proved easier to develop internal systems than external ones. Most of the information managers we met regarded the creation of systems capable of linking a firm more closely to its market as one of the great contemporary challenges. Perhaps the most telling comment we heard on the need to improve the intelligence base of the whole enterprise was: "We are looking for continuous learning. We need more information to create more ideas."

Structures

Where does the information department lie in the new organization, and how did our firms redraw the structure to reflect rebalancing of functions? Without exception, our successful firms regarded the *formal* structure of organization as a *complement* to other initiatives. None attempted to use structural geometry as the sole means of provoking adaptation and providing support. A few introduced new structures as a means of forcing the pace of change and reinforced them with matching changes in systems and measures. Many changed the formal structure only *after* numerous other moves affecting the informal structure had been well established.

The latter approach is illustrated by Edwards's actions. The company abandoned its rigid, functional structure around 1984, after work to build new capabilities had shown that alternatives were workable and effective. Some of the early work was in the production department, started after two new managers had been recruited in 1980. One of them explained what happened. "We were being asked to be functional. The brief was 'Sort out production: it is in a mess.' But that wasn't totally the case, and we could have wasted a lot of time if we'd just kept the blinkers on. We were very concerned about building the infrastructure of the commercial enterprise and started building bridges back from sales to manufacturing right away."

Their personal initiatives showed not only what could be accomplished without changing the formal structure, but also the limits. To capture more benefits the company adopted a flexible, quasi-matrix structure that could cope with the multiplicity of simultaneous demands placed on it across all departments. In effect, the change was a legitimation and extension of what had already been put in place.[13]

Building informal links combats organizational arthritis and helps in sharing values and norms of behavior across departmental boundaries. To provide the momentum, all departments have to become used to the idea that a purely blinkered and parochial view of the enterprise is insufficient. Besides, an entrepreneurial organization must be capable of rapid action, free from the familiar "not-invented-here" barriers. One manager at Mather & Platt, now part of the Weir Group, said, "We are very much a multidisciplined work force and have the advantage of being under one roof. We don't send memos a lot. If we have to talk to somebody else, we just go—we get off our bottoms . . . Yes, we do break the rules at times, but it works."[14]

MOBILIZING MIDDLE MANAGERS

Middle managers are the people who make or break an organization. Not only are they the key to the "doing of management" but they are also vital to new thinking. As we indicated in earlier chapters, the ideas that informed the choice of strategy in the first place came from many sources in firms, not just from the top. Moreover, those in the middle have to take ideas from all quarters, including the top, and make them work in daily operations. The common distinctions made among top-down, bottom-up, and lateral processes of communication blur in practice: all have to be operative in entrepreneurial organizations. Unless middle managers are clear about their central role in companywide affairs, they inhibit progress.

The critical role of middle managers has been extensively examined by Rosabeth Moss Kanter, and many of our points echo what she has put forcefully.[15] Our purpose here is to stress that in this stage of rejuvenation, middle management can unwittingly be overlooked. Some top teams seem to have had such a crowded agenda that they thought the issue of involving some subordinates could be put off.

This mistake was made by the chief executive of one of our less successful firms; he had trouble relaying information during the first stage of rejuvenation and confessed that he had worked only with his top team of six people and had not "got much further down." He, like many others, once believed that his firm's strategy was so commercially sensitive that it could not be shared. Like others, he saw his mistake: "We were initially afraid our competitors would get hold of the plan. But we then discovered they had it already and our employees were the only ones in the dark before our presentations."

All too often middle managers wait until a corporate plan has been unveiled before they act. Top management must mobilize those people to look upward, sideways, and downward as an essential part of their role in a complex network of relationships. Only then will they espouse the values of becoming more proactive, more questioning, and not wait either for external events or instructions from above to trigger change

(See Exhibit 8.3). But to get to that state, considerable resistance has to be overcome.

One common source of resistance is that of initial enthusiasm giving way to fear. In pyramidal organizations, whole layers of middle managers can exist merely to pass on, and often distort, information. They make no decisions of competitive consequence. In the pre-information age they had a purpose in the control structure, but today they have become an endangered species. An example from one of our firms shows a way forward. Reflecting on a controversial proposal to cut jobs at a time of business expansion, one chief executive recalled,

> I set a man to the task of finding out what could be done. His evidence was so overwhelming that now everyone agrees that the cuts were necessary and "obvious." Even the work force agrees, though not the unions. Putting people on such projects releases ideas and adds further information and options. We aim to build consensus by discussion, where parochial feelings are eroded. Even when the functions of several directors were threatened, I heard no cries of "it can't be done."

In other words, he had been careful to co-opt middle management in the process of seeking a solution. But he had done more. He had earlier built a climate in which it was possible for the evidence to be credible and become a force for action. He had set the target, but had not imposed a solution. As he added, "The solution we finally adopted went far beyond what I originally had in mind."

Perhaps even more important, he had reduced the personal risks to acceptable proportions for all involved. In another company we heard, "You don't get fired for making mistakes; not learning from them is a sin." Even when individuals fall by the wayside, the climate of progress can be retained. One chief executive said, "My dilemma is that too

---

EXHIBIT 8.3 MOBILIZING MIDDLE MANAGERS

In mature firms	In rejuvenated organizations
Message carriers, controllers, and even spectators	Doers, thinkers, and implementors
Isolated specialists	Specialists *and* integrators
One-way filtering	Two-way communications
Inward focus	Outward focus

---

many of the team have fixed "achievement ceilings." We have to find homes for these people somewhere in the firm, for I do not believe in hire-and-fire."

Such approaches place a high premium on frank and honest communication. The necessary climate for progress cannot be created when managers obfuscate. All too often, "managers who are skilled communicators may also be good at covering up real problems."[16] Defensive routines and perhaps reluctance to risk personal friendships that grew during earlier, less stressful periods can undermine the drive for progress and continuous change.

Learning organizations have to confront the persistent problem that many middle managers feel their status rests heavily on their power to tell others what to do. This is especially so in large organizations with long traditions of powerful specialist functions such as engineering. Comfortable in a world of specific plans and actions, managers can find it acutely uncomfortable to ask themselves or their juniors to think through what the goals ought to be. This problem has been tackled head-on in Exxon Chemicals. Though progress has been rated painfully slow, one corporate vice president stated:

We're steadily improving performance. What we have done . . . is to drop plan reviews at the company level and replace them with strategy discussions. After all, if the top of the organization isn't thinking in strategic terms, who is? . . . When objectives and strategies are clear and understood, planning is no problem, and the reviews of plans at lower levels assume a different and more positive character.[17]

Emphasizing the positive makes obvious sense, especially when confronting moving targets. One chief executive stressed, "We build confidence in a winning team and this reinforces individuals' desires to play on the team." Pushing the team onto the upward spiral of achievement pays off and helps to link the strategy with new values. It also allows individuals freedom to take personal responsibility for experimentation.

Repeating the Process Lower Down
The effort to build a climate for continuous improvement has to extend beyond middle management if it is to create durable vitality. People at low levels have to be able to "buy in" to new values in terms that affect the reality of their own work. In places where unions are acceptable or a way of life, union structures have to be harnessed to support efforts.

Many others have investigated this important question in greater detail than we. Revealing studies have been done of the transformations wrought by the Japanese in rejuvenating automobile plant workers in their joint ventures.[18] In all cases, intensive effort was made to repeat, even at the lowest levels, the kinds of positive developments among mid-level teams of managers we have discussed above. For example, at NUMMI, the GM-Toyota joint venture in Freemont, California, the dramatic improvements in productivity and quality required fundamental shifts in shop-floor behavior. Gary Convis, who took over the manufacturing function, explained the importance of new pay procedures in the context of other critical changes as:

> Our team members are ready and willing to change as long as they feel they are being treated fairly and equitably. We've tried to avoid favoritism and to level out the harder jobs. A single pay level is as fundamental to the success of this company as is security of employment. We have learned from the Japanese the importance of tying the company's success, and the success of the individual, to things they can control.[19]

Peter Wickens, the personnel director of Nissan's U.K. manufacturing company, places equal emphasis on the same set of issues as one of the fundamental platforms on which the success of the subsidiary is based.[20] Wickens goes on, however, to explore how difficult it has been in the United Kingdom to resolve a classic dilemma. Far from being based solely on commitment of the work force, the results are also dependent on the maintenance of tight control. Management should not choose between commitment or control as Richard Walton seemed to suggest some years ago.[21] What Nissan and others have been trying to achieve is the combination of commitment *and* control—and do so without seemingly exploiting the worker and destroying the base of trust.

Precisely the same challenges faced our rejuvenators. Like their counterparts at NUMMI and Nissan, managers had to work hard to establish two-way communications right down to the bottom levels. One observed that "for some years the communications down to the shop floor were all one way. People did not really believe what we [top management] were saying and they did not wholly trust us. It took some years before we could start a two-way dialogue." This firm, like so many of the Japanese, learned that workers' ideas were a source of profits, which were released not by limited efforts such as a suggestion-box scheme, but by a far-reaching program of building upon trust and enthusiasm.

The full development of horizontal and vertical collaboration right down to the shop floor requires close cooperation and mutual understanding among all levels in a hierarchy. Consider what happened in a company that put in place a quality improvement program on a consultant's recommendation. Later checks revealed that defects were still pervasive in the output. Why? "We were improving the quality on the assembly line, but pressure from sales meant that we encouraged staff to send out goods that were *almost* right." In other words, a sensible policy of great strategic importance was defeated by the functions at low levels being unable to share the same sense of purpose.

In a similar vein, Northern Telecom concluded that "our ability to network resources, technologies, reward systems, supplies, markets, and customer demands to ensure continuous improvement to the product delivery process is the key to future success." New learning came from a major revamping of the entire production process at the company's Santa Clara plant and resembled much of what we saw in other rejuvenating organizations. Middle managers were the most resistant to new developments, for they feared a loss of status. They and lower-level supervisors required extensive retraining before they could recognize and accept the benefits of the new approach. Not until everyone could feel important and involved could a climate of sufficient mutual trust be built to allow the full plan to be undertaken.[22]

The same sense that progress had to be made in stages of eroding resistance at progressively lower levels and that the real payoff had to wait until after (often reluctant) middle managers had been co-opted into the process marked the experience of Lucas, a major British maker of auto components. Lucas faced severe competition in the supply of brakes and recognized that the performance of their brake factories across Europe was far from uniform. In particular, the factory in Wales faced extinction unless it could match, and preferably exceed, the performance of the German factory. The challenge had been clear for some time, but little was achieved until a sustained program of selling the ideas of possibility and hope was initiated. Looking back on what became a most successful rejuvenation, managers and workers alike attributed much of the success to the *combination* of many familiar factors: training, "cell" production rather than specialization modeled on Taylorist principles, fewer supervisory levels, quality targets, improved industrial labor relations, and so on.[23] Senior managers first had to overcome resistance from middle managers fearful that the new patterns of work would diminish their status. Similar resistance was encountered on the shop floor, where skilled workers disliked the idea that they had to retrain to stay at top pay scales. They were, however, persuaded to adapt, largely at the urging of their union representatives, who had themselves become converts to the new approach. As one said, "I told my toolmakers that they were in danger of going the same way as the skilled blacksmith."[24]

At Richardson, top managers symbolized their new values by their willingness to load boxes when rush orders demanded such customer care at late hours. In other firms we found piecework being abandoned in favor of team measures. In all firms we found the attention to training managers being extended to all workers. But these efforts also introduced new dilemmas. How many skills do team players really need? In what order should they be introduced? Middle managers had to rethink the basics before they could communicate essential needs. As one said, "Our greatest progress has come from developing simple tools, not complex ones." Moreover, we found quite different views about how training should be managed. Some invested in crash programs, and others told us, "We found massive training before the event a waste of money. We now concentrate on training people as they begin to use their new skills."

This brings us back to the central point of our chapter, the need to build an entrepreneurial organization. Success has come to those firms which have invested in all dimensions of their task and have understood that partial efforts are wasteful. They value the importance of creating an exciting but tangible vision, capable of building a durable sense of collective purpose and value. To reinforce the abandonment of old ways of working and thinking, they have made frame-breaking investments that signaled their seriousness of purpose and provided the organization an economic setting for further progress.

NOTES

[1] From the earliest days of its rejuvenation, Richardson bucked convention. When Bryan Upton arrived, many were arguing that the South Koreans had an invincible advantage in their low labor costs. Economists would have recommended that Richardson focus on marketing and distribution, subcontracting production to overseas firms. A major U.K. rival, Kitchen Devil (now owned by Swedish Match), also believed that knives could be produced locally at a profit. Both prospered while many others disappeared.

[2] Household penetration (percentages) of domestic appliances in the United Kingdom, 1970–1982 and 1990

Product	1970	1974	1978	1982	1990
Refrigerator	63	80	91	100	100
Washing machine	64	70	76	81	89
Freezer	—	10	24	35	38
Dishwasher	1	2	3	4	13

Sources: AMDEA and AGB statistics.

[3] Peter M. Senge, *The Fifth Discipline: The Art and Practice of the Learning Organization* (New York: Doubleday Currency, 1990). The other three disciplines that Senge stresses are

"building shared vision," "personal mastery," and "mental models," all issues that we stress elsewhere in this book.

[4] The roles of the chief executive of a diversified portfolio are somewhat different. See M. Goold and A. Campbell, *Strategies and Styles: The Role of the Centre in Managing Diversified Corporations* (Oxford: Basil Blackwell, 1987), and M. Goold with J.J. Quinn, *Strategic Control: Milestones for Long-term Performance* (London: The Economist Books/ Hutchinson, 1990).

[5] K.B. Clark, "What Strategy Can Do for Technology," *Harvard Business Review,* November–December 1989: 93–98.

[6] W. Skinner, *Manufacturing: The Formidable Competitive Weapon* (New York: Wiley, 1985). See also R.H. Hayes and S.C. Wheelwright, *Dynamic Manufacturing* (New York: Free Press, 1988).

[7] For details see R.L. Shook, *Turnaround: The New Ford Motor Company* (New York: Prentice Hall Press, 1990).

[8] See J.P. Womak, D.T., Jones and D. Roos, *The Machine That Changed the World* (New York: Rawson Associates, 1990).

[9] Marks and Spencer, which has long understood this message, is justly famous for its buying practices from U.K. textile suppliers. It offers technical and design support for its chosen suppliers. Provided they meet stringent performance criteria, suppliers are given time to develop new capabilities and so avoid the fate that has overtaken many in the much diminished U.K. industry.

[10] P. Williamson, "Supplier Strategy and Customer Responsiveness: Managing the Links," *Business Strategy Review,* Summer 1991: 75–90.

[11] The need for exploration of new possibilities to increase understanding was well put by T.S. Eliot, who wrote: "We shall not cease from exploration and the end of all our exploration will be to arrive where we started and know the place for the first time" ("Little Gidding," *Four Quartets* [New York: Harcourt, Brace, 1943]).

[12] In this respect, the firms acted, as have others, to link strategy and finance. See, for example, P. Barwise, P.R. Marsh, and R. Wensley, "Must Finance and Strategy clash?" *Harvard Business Review,* September–October 1989: 85–90.

[13] This structural change was followed by another at the end of the decade to adjust to the greater demands of its growing global success.

[14] Weir acquired Mather & Platt, a rival U.K. pump producer, and transferred to it many of the systems it had developed in its own rejuvenation.

[15] R.M. Kanter, *The Change Masters: Innovation for Productivity in the American Corporation* (London: Allen & Unwin, 1985), and R.M. Kanter, *When Giants Learn to Dance* (New York: Simon & Schuster, 1989).

[16] C. Argyris, "Skilled Incompetence," *Harvard Business Review,* September–October 1986: 74–79.

[17] Cited in *Strategic Direction,* June 1990: 8.

[18] For an analysis of the changes in work practice at the GM-Toyota joint venture in California, the New United Motor Manufacturing, Inc. (NUMMI) see, Wellford W. Wilms and Deone M. Zell, "Reinventing Organizational Culture across Boundaries," a California Worksite Research Committee working paper presented at the Carnegie-Bosch Institute symposium, Stuttgart, Germany, May 1993. See also, C. Brown and M. Reich, "When Does Cooperation Work? A Look at NUMMI and GM-Van Nuys," *California Management Review* vol. 31, no. 4 (1989): 26–37. For a critical assessment of Mazda's work practices, see Joseph Fucini and Suzy Fucini, *Working for the Japanese: Inside Mazda's American Auto Plant* (New York: Free Press, 1990).

[19] Wilms and Zell, "Reinventing Organizational Culture across Boundaries," p. 19.

[20] Peter D. Wickens, "Lean, People Centred, Mass Production," in *Lean Production and Beyond: Labour Aspects of a New Production Concept* (Geneva: International Institute for Labour Studies, Occasional Paper No. 2, 1993), Chapter 3.

[21] Richard E. Walton "From Commitment to Control in the Workplace," *Harvard Business Review,* March–April 1985: 76–84.

[22] These observations are from a study by Richard Allison and Stu Wimby for the American Productivity and Quality Center, cited in *Strategic Direction*, August 1989.

[23] The story is well told by David Bowen, "How Lucas Learned to Live with the Rest of the World," *The Independent* on Sunday, July 8, 1990.

[24] Much of the U.K. program was led from the top by the manufacturing director. By contrast, in Germany, where "we did it all before him," understanding of the necessity of constant change had been deeply engrained for years. "Everybody is aware that stop means down," said a member of the Works Council. The culture in Wales is as yet shallow and needs constant fostering. The international comparison illustrates both how widely progress can differ from one unit to another.

Chapter Nine

Maintaining Momentum

It is risky and difficult to be an industry leader, and the risks are no less for a rejuvenated business that has reached a position of technical or market supremacy. Only a few of the businesses we studied achieved that rare characteristic of Schumpeterian entrepreneurship: the ability to change the competitive rules of an industry. None of these was complacent. One considered excluding its name from this book saying, "We do not want any reader to give us the label of excellence: we are frightened of falling." In another organization, a senior manager echoed the feeling of his colleagues with a quotation from Alice in *Through the Looking Glass*, "We have to run faster just to stand still." Everywhere we went there was a sense that the success was fragile. Remembering the words of Shelley in his sonnet about the great king Ozymandias, they knew how the mighty could fall.[1]

The sense of fragility prevailing among our most successful organizations was not felt because their success was an illusion. They had built substantial enterprises with secure foundations, and their achievements were not marginal. On the contrary, in every case they have attracted the envy or admiration of their rivals. Our leaders were not so much pessimistic as realistic. Maintaining vitality and leadership is a never-ending battle that has to be won many times with will and skill.

Popular wisdom suggests that large market share, large absolute size, and a strong brand image insulate an organization from competition and allow it to reap, effortlessly, high profits and other rewards. This is misguided. As we explained in Chapter 2, many high-share firms have slipped from their position, large size is no guarantee of profitability and value creation, and popular strong brands can be weakened if competitors innovate more exciting and better quality products or services.

Consider first the dangers from competition. We have argued, with examples, that it is possible for businesses to rejuvenate on limited resources and challenge their leaders. We have described the logic of renewal and explored possible routes, especially those centered on creativity and innovation. If our findings are valid, the leaders face serious risks from other rejuvenators. In addition, they can be challenged by new entrants and strong competitors. They can stay ahead only by being better and more creative. Like the hare being chased by the hounds, it is necessary for the leaders to run a constant race against a pack of aspiring competitors. The leaders must escape all if they are to avoid a grisly fate.

To stay ahead, organizations have to deepen their existing capabilities, ensuring that they do not lapse or crumble, and they have to create new steps for the strategic staircase. We call this activity *stretch*, and in this chapter we detail three different kinds of activities that help stretch: incremental improvements, substantial projects, and blue-sky programs. We suggest that as firms become more successful, the process of building becomes harder, not easier.[2]

Reaping profits from the existing capabilities that have been so carefully built also makes demands on the organizations. We call this activity *leverage*. Without these rewards, stakeholders may be disappointed, and, as we pointed out in Chapter 1, the task of the firm is to satisfy all its stakeholders. Failure to leverage can result in loss of effort, disaffection, or even the loss of skilled staff and the threat of takeover by other firms.

Leveraging requires many different kinds of activities, including organic expansion, acquisitions, and the use of alliances. Each has a different risk profile. Leverage also requires constant attention to the proper choice of strategic territory, an issue highlighted in Chapter 4. The organization must be continually alert to changes taking place in the environment, harnessing and controlling them.

According to researchers, the most common cause of slippage from a leading position is when organizations lose the sense of vitality and excitement, becoming complacent, bored, or exhausted.[3] In such circumstances, the efforts at maintaining stretch and the desire to leverage are lost and fall out of balance. The firm can revert to maturity. Several of our sample firms admit to being perilously close to falling into this trap. We describe a wide variety of initiatives for maintaining *vitality* aimed at avoiding this danger, most of which do not demand large financial resources, but rather top management time and effort.

Vitality, stretch, and *leverage* are activities that can be in harmony, but they can also be in conflict. Harmony comes when building a new capability such as flexibility can help the leverage into new territories, or when taking over a firm to leverage advantages in a new territory reveals an unexpected set of competencies that can be used elsewhere in the organization. But conflicts also occur, for instance, when leveraging existing competencies demands resources and attention that are not in harmony with building a new capability, such as coping with a potentially dangerous emerging trend.

Successful rejuvenators maintain a judicious and delicate balance among these potentially competing priorities. They look for growth as a fundamental means of leveraging the benefits of what they have achieved, but they guard against the dash for growth in a blind belief that bigger is better. They invest in enhancing capabilities to provide strategic innovations that complement and build on those already achieved, as well as exploring blue-sky possibilities.

Maintaining organizational vitality helps balance competing priorities, but it is not the solution to all of them. Moreover, greater vitality can bring raised expectations, which then have to be fulfilled. For these reasons, we set these three agendas as being in tension (see Exhibit 9.1).

Our firms had to confront dilemmas akin to those facing the European Community in the 1990s. For the EC to prosper and grow, it needs to maintain a sense of vitality and diminish the boredom and frustration created by the burgeoning bureaucracy in Brussels, which has some of

EXHIBIT 9.1 A DELICATE SENSE OF BALANCE TO MAINTAIN MOMENTUM

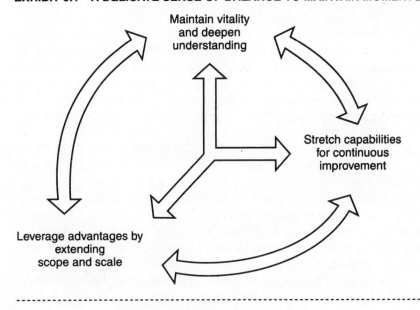

the worst features of a federal government. It has to balance the competing pressures to widen its scope and deepen the integration. Widening the scope means adding more member states from such diverse places as Scandinavia, Eastern Europe, and possibly Turkey, each of which will bring problems and demands as well as opportunities. Deepening the integration among the existing twelve members means working together more closely in the political and economic spheres and staving off the threats from other trading blocs, such as NAFTA. Each of these agendas has to maintain a sense of individual freedoms within each state and recognize the legitimate demands of small, indigenous ethnic groups. As those who live in Europe know, these agendas are both exciting and threatening. Failure of the whole system can occur if there is excessive emphasis on one dimension of the task at the expense of progress on others.

We begin by examining each of these issues in turn: that of maintaining vitality, stretching resources, and leveraging benefits. Finally we turn to some difficult questions of the structure and shape of an enterprise, and how top management can work to ensure continual progress.

MAINTAINING VITALITY

"Compete with yourself, before others do so first" is a thought that spurs many in positions of industry leadership. "Innovate or evaporate," a slogan that captures this thought, is widely used in GE, and is also gaining currency in other firms. Such threats are powerful weapons that may have to be used. Far better than a threat are a sense of excitement and a sense of challenge. Our rejuvenators were aware of the threats, but they wisely tried to give the task a positive note. The top teams in our firms recognized that they had to build a climate for *continuous improvement*. Without innovation or continuous improvement, there is a serious danger that organizations will slide back to maturity. The obstacles are real, and in Exhibit 9.2 we list those which we consider most likely. Senior managers we talked to were creative and persistent in finding ways to overcome them.

In Chapter 5 we dwelt at length on the features of the corporately entrepreneurial organization, stressing the role of teams, aspirations, experiments, learning, and dilemma resolution. All these features have to be built, and the building has to be careful, but there are ever present obstacles to their continuance.

There is a serious danger that the organization will relax and stop trying. In the quest for leadership, many organizations establish explicit

---

EXHIBIT 9.2   OBSTACLES TO MAINTAINING VITALITY

Boredom	The goal has been reached; no further challenges of interest.
Exhaustion	The rewards to the efforts are not being captured and distributed, so why make extra effort?
Repetition	Difficulty in keeping a focus on priorities, dangers of creeping overhead and rising costs.
Loss of speed	Difficulty in making people see the dangers from rivals and keeping up the pace of progress.

---

targets for profitability, market share, or some such goal; attaining the leadership position often means that these targets have been met. Many we talked to told us of the tensions this created among members of a once cohesive organization. Some wanted to relax when the prize had been won, while others wanted to push on and saw dangers ahead. Unless new targets are constructed, the organization may well slow down or, worse, be precipitated into a minor crisis, as Avis the number two car rental company with the slogan "We try harder" discovered when it reached the premier position.

There is an urgent need for tangible rewards, else employees and other supporters feel exhausted and demoralized, particularly if there is a continual resetting of targets without rewards. In the quest for leadership, many stakeholders, particularly employees, will have given up sustained time and effort over a long period. If they are not rewarded by anything besides another target, they become disgruntled. The rewards do not have to be exclusively monetary. Many organizations have found that well-publicized recognition within the "family" can have as much effect, or even more, as money. All this costs senior management is the time to learn who is doing what and to show that it cares. Sometimes the quest for public prizes, such as the Baldrige Award or the Deming Prize, can act as powerful additional spurs to foster greater team efforts.[4]

Choosing what particular activities to reward is an especially important task for managers who lead the efforts to climb the staircase of adding capabilities. The need is to reward both general success and the achievement of specific nonfinancial "milestone" targets that may not have shown up in the bottom-line performance. In earlier chapters we have discussed the problems that accrue to organizations that fail to maintain a sense of consistency in the direction and purpose of the climb. How to maintain consistency when many of the details are unknown in advance of the necessary experiments is a constant puzzle.

Although there no general answers, we have found successful firms paying particular attention to tailoring the reward system to changing strategic priorities. As many of the details are discovered at low levels in the hierarchy, these firms seem to be adding to the old slogan of "What gets measured gets done" an additional clause: "what gets measured and rewarded gets done first." Where people have a choice of how to spend their time and energies, rewards have a direct influence on that choice. In phases of building, the details of the reward system can assume power in setting what is only later rationalized as strategy.

Even when highly rewarded, initial enthusiasm can give way to boredom and complacency. One manager explained: "The problem is that success brings repetition; repetition brings efficiency and growth; and more orders bring more repetition. How to make people go on being challenged remains a priority issue for the firm." To add to this problem, new recruits may not share the same sense of urgency and enthusiasm that, for a time, marked their more experienced colleagues.

A common indicator of boredom and complacency is trouble maintaining focus on priorities and allowing a "creep" in indirect factory labor costs and overhead generally. Keeping things "lean" is hard, and with growth come the inevitable demands for more overhead and more staff functions. Just as the middle-aged have to work hard to keep slim and fit, so the creep in indirect costs is insidious and hard to combat. One chief executive felt that he had an important role in creating a climate of communication in which it became "obvious" to the team that adding overhead was not the way to grow. In another firm, where cost targets were set for a decline in real terms, we heard that "there is a creep in total costs as marketing is constantly saying, 'You must supply more for a given level of sale.' "

Closely related to boredom and complacency is the loss of urgency. Managers in leading organization are easily lulled into a sense that there is plenty of time to take steps because the opposition is far behind. This is rarely the case, for the seeming distance between followers and leaders is always a dangerous illusion. While the chosen strategic territory for operations may be small, the potential competition comes from a wider arena. Some go as far as to assert that all firms with similar customers or similar processes are in some way a potential threat. As the Banc One executives said, "It is of little concern to us that we are much better than [almost] every other bank in the United States. There is plenty of other serious competition out there which we need to beat." They explained that against the benchmarks of the best service companies, they were not first.

The task of top managers is to turn a challenge into one that inspires people. In some organizations they find it useful to talk about fun.

"Make it fun" was a slogan that we heard senior managers using to help maintain enthusiasm. Part of the sense of fun has been fostered by efforts to create challenges in ways that breed excitement. Without a sense of pervasive excitement, people become bored and exhausted and cannot justify continuous effort, given the other tensions that exist in their lives.

Actions to Improve Vitality

When rejuvenators become leaders, benchmarking assumes a new importance. Leaders never hold a monopoly on wisdom; they need to augment their capabilities so as to be able to respond quickly to new challenges. Close followers are often performing well, and some are doing much better. Thus, leaders must find out how others are innovating as they come up from behind.

For some firms we studied, the challenge was to benchmark every business in their sector in the world and to understand how much progress they had made in resolving a wide variety of individual issues (see Exhibit 9.3). One chief executive explained that such extensive benchmarking had proved most revealing. "We thought we were world class in many areas, but found that this was not so. For example, there was a small producer outperforming us by a large margin in some aspects of our processes. We heard how [it] had adapted its product designs to achieve a significant reduction in manufacturing costs. We could not believe at first that [it] had solved a problem we had struggled with for years. But when we reverse-engineered the product, we saw what [it] had done." This process of benchmarking showed the organiza-

---

EXHIBIT 9.3 ACTIONS TAKEN TO MAINTAIN VITALITY

Benchmark	Benchmark all aspects of competitors' operations. Benchmark the best companies in the world in all related sectors.
Targets	Set targets against the benchmarks. Set targets for a continuous rate of improvement. Set targets for teams as well as individuals.
Prizes and races	Use outside awards or prizes. Set up achievement and learning races for teams inside the organization. Create races between the firm and its partners, or among its partners.
Crises	Create quasi-crises to induce action.

---

tion that, although highly profitable and a leader, it still had progress to make.

One organization subscribed to Komatsu's detailed procedures for benchmarking world leaders across a wide range of industries. Its top team wanted to see how different organizations with different mind-sets resolved similar problems. This helped reframe the challenge to give explicit targets, which could be used and justified in the organization. Another used benchmarking in a different, rather provocative manner: "We have turned competitor assessment into a hate complex. We set up a procedure to define the threat in specific terms and also showed the workers their products. Everyone knew that we had to win, otherwise 'these people are going to eat our lunch.' "

It seems obvious that benchmarking leads to targets for improvement and that the more detailed the benchmarks, the easier it is to create specific targets. That logic, however, presupposes that the organization conducting the benchmark knows what it really needs to look for. We found repeated evidence that successful rejuvenators did not rely on benchmarking at the early stages, except to gain a very general sense of external threat. As one director explained:

> When we started out ten years ago, though we did not admit this at the time, we lacked a proper understanding of our cost functions across the firm. We simply could not use any information about competitors' costs to help guide the choices of strategy and operations we had to make. It is only now, when we believe we have our costs under control and continuously declining in real terms, that we can use benchmarking. Today, we have detailed procedures to find out what is going on around the world. We see relatively little of the data at the board, for the teams have learned to turn the data into intelligence for themselves so they can gauge what they must do to stay ahead.

In other words, benchmarking without internal discipline and understanding can be an expensive waste of time.

Organizations do not have to rely solely on benchmarks of other firms' behavior for the inspiration needed to set stretching targets. They can look to general, external factors, for example, remaining competitive on export pricing within an exchange-rate goal. Such a benchmark has to be achieved if organizations are to continue to do well in international markets. Some Japanese export-oriented enterprises have used this mechanism to compensate for the rising real exchange rate of the yen against the dollar. Instead of using a forecast that can all too easily be ignored by operating managers, they use a target that cannot be ignored. Suppose management is concerned that the yen might rise to Y100 = $1, then the target is the definition of specific courses of action that will ensure export competitiveness at that exchange rate. If the yen fails to rise so far, the export margins can be correspondingly greater. And if there are specific rewards attached to the achievement of those actions, the chances that the organization will truly remain competitive are enhanced. A Ph.D. in economics is not required to understand what is at stake.

Some organizations prefer to set goals against a continuous rate of improvement within the context of benchmarks. Such a target has the merit of providing a firm with a stable rather than an uncertain goal. It is a particularly important mechanism when benchmarks reveal fuzzy or uncertain signals, or when it is impossible to obtain good data. The target is set in the light of known and possible rates of improvement. Since benchmarking reveals only what has taken place among competitors, not what may be about to happen, the absolute rate of improvement has the advantage of dealing with possible future rates of progress rather than past events.

The result of benchmarking and target setting may produce multiple goals. To avoid potential confusion, some have tied multiple goals and targets to teamwork. One explained:

> We have explicitly examined each function to create specific
> priority achievement targets and action programs. All of them
> require interfunctional collaboration to be effective. But it is
> taking time to get the thinking into the fabric of the organization.
> We set up factory teams in 1988, helped by the fact that we had
> done a good job in the core products. Now we are [using teams
> elsewhere and] working on more ambitious targets and finding
> them helpful in generating ideas for further change.

Targets can be given unusual labels such as service excellence or "customer delight" as one firm termed it. They can spur individuals both to be at the leading edge of specific skills and to be team players. "We found that a new perception of 'true' customer needs led us to revise our approach to new product development and to emphasize reliability as a fundamental value in quality."

Some have experimented with learning races among various parts of the organization. A far-reaching goal is set, and a prize is offered to the winners. The 3M Corporation uses such systems to stimulate development, its prizes including the funds and time off to develop an innovation. Such races help maintain the spirit of corporate entrepreneurship, because the winner has to share the discovery with others.

The prize is often quite modest in comparison with the benefit. Such a system of races and prizes, which can also be used with partners, exists in leading computer companies and such consumer organizations as Benetton and Nike.

STRETCH

While benchmarking, target setting, races, and prizes can create a sense of vitality, the challenge to an organization is to turn these into the reality of strengthening existing capabilities and building new ones. All our rejuvenators made haste to enlarge each step of the strategic staircase they had built and to build new stairs of advantage. In their battle against seen and unseen competition, they had a sense of urgency. It seems that all of them knew that competitors were close behind, diminishing the value of each competency. Threats come from all quarters—new entrants, other rejuvenators, and sleepy big competitors. As Percy Barnevik, chairman of the Swedish-Swiss combine ABB said, "The winners will be the fast ones, not necessarily the big ones. However, when the big ones become fast, watch out."

In the quest to stretch resources and build still more capabilities, managers need to realize that being in front makes many investments bigger and riskier. The leader has no unique advantages in smaller projects, except that of a better starting base. But its position is better in respect to the more risky large big-hit investments, especially those we advised the rejuvenator to avoid in the early stages. Such investments are typically systems approaches to building multiple advantages that exploit current possibilities.

To appreciate the significance of what we are saying, it is sensible to consider how the investments of rejuvenators have been historically structured. As we explained in earlier chapters, at the start of the rejuvenation process, many small initiatives are undertaken, the majority of which have modest self-contained risks. At this stage the organization is typically so far behind the leaders that the payoffs can be high for little outlay. As rejuvenation proceeds, the characteristics of investments change. While many small initiatives continue, more substantial ones emerge; we labeled them frame-breaking. These moves involve more complex and longer-term projects whose risks are greater than the small initiatives, yet they are not unmanageable because the initiatives build on the strengths created by previous experiments.

In the final phase, maintaining momentum, the organization must continue to evolve, adapt, and gain new sources of strength. At this time, larger investments usually become more necessary. Provided they are predicated on exploiting existing capabilities and competencies, rather than rash leaps in the dark where the organization lacks expertise, they represent a competitive way forward.

Of course, large investments complement many small investments. They also complement blue-sky projects that examine new possibilities. The latter may threaten existing systems but hold out scope for even larger profits. (See Exhibit 9.4.)

All big leaps run two major risks. The first is obvious—the project may fail—and understandable. The second is less well appreciated— the project will be highly successful and attract emulators that quickly duplicate the innovation. These emulators, learning from the leader's moves, may imitate at lower cost. Such emulation may not be preventable, but its adverse consequences can be minimized providing the time between first innovation and subsequent copy is used to effect, with exploitation and market preemption. With effective exploitation, the time between discovery and duplication can be spent reaping the gains from the innovation and setting out a strategic position that controls if not prevents the copying. These points are touched on in the section on leverage.[5]

Readers should note that making much larger risky investments is consistent with the ideas of corporate entrepreneurship explored in Chapter 5. We can identify five key features in particular. *Aspiring* to lead their sectors, the big moves are the best kinds of *experiments* for retaining leadership. Risks are minimized if the leader ensures that the large projects are firmly embedded, *exploiting* the skills and knowledge base of the organization learning from experience. And last, the projects that should take precedence are those which seek to resolve the com-

---

EXHIBIT 9.4 PROFILES OF INVESTMENT AND RISK IN REJUVENATION STAGES

Galvanizing	Small investments with low perceived corporate risk. Potential payoff high owing to great distance between leader and follower.
Building	Medium-size investments complementing many small investments. Payoff greatest from frame breaks that alter the rules of the game by capitalizing on previous moves.
Stretching to maintain momentum	Blue-sky projects and large radical investments complemented by many incremental small moves. High risks to these investments compensated by the capabilities of the leader to carry off the projects.

---

plex *dilemmas* the organization faces; in other words, it builds new steps on the staircase.

Stretching through Incremental Investment

In Exhibit 9.5 we identify and illustrate three kinds of actions taken to stretch an organization. The first requires only modest investment resources yet is vital to ensuring that best practice is everywhere identified and attained. The second is to take a systems approach to building new advantage, which seeks to exploit existing capabilities and build more sustainable positions by degrees. Such investments are potentially large in size, long in gestation, and highest in risk. Blue-sky approaches, which can potentially cannibalize the firm's previous approaches, represent the third area of investment, in which the firm sets itself the goal of re-creating its own industry.

When Richardson bought a special new grinding machine from a leading machine manufacturer, the first thing its managers did was take the machine apart to see how it solved the technical challenges they had laid out in the specification. They were impressed by their supplier's ingenuity and identified several features that were transferable at relatively low cost to other machines in the factory. Richardson's managers viewed such an activity as routine, essential reverse engineering and extended it to all parts of the organization, not only production. Richardson had established a policy of deliberately buying from the best in the world so that it could learn from them and then go on to evolve a personalized and improved machine.

Benetton's approach is similar and extends to the way it manages its partner-suppliers and distributor-retailers. Benetton buys its way into their knowledge bases, seeking to understand how they resolve the dilemmas they face. When it finds that a partner has worked out a problem in an unusually creative manner, such as finding a novel

----

EXHIBIT 9.5   ACTIONS TO STRETCH THE CAPABILITIES

Incremental actions to deepen current capabilities	Reengineer the latest technology from outside suppliers.
	Transfer technology between suppliers and distributors to other suppliers and distributors to keep the leading edge.
Substantial investments to build new capabilities	Systems approach to building multiple advantages
Blue-sky investments	Looking for breakthroughs that redefine the products, the markets, and even the industry

----

promotion plan or a new way of solving a production challenge, Benetton congratulates the partner and ensures that all its other partners benefit from the innovation. Benetton also incorporates this piece of learning into its own knowledge base. Partners are willing to let Benetton undertake this unusual activity because they know that the firm has high standards for its partners and that each of them in turn will benefit from the innovations of others. In addition, they appreciate that Benetton views itself as a teacher and coach of the system, always investing to improve.[6]

These examples provide a sample of the ways in which leaders maintain and deepen their current advantages by incremental actions, which are typically low cost and easy to implement, providing the climate is right. Arguably, leaders need to invest more in these activities than their followers do if they are to stay ahead. With higher rates of investment, the follower can be disadvantaged: followers typically lack the knowledge base to undertake such effective reverse engineering. It takes a high level of skills to appreciate the quality work of others. Supplier and distributor learning is also difficult, for suppliers are keen to share best practice with proven leaders, but reluctant to share with those which are less successful. As one major firm not of the leading class informed us, "We do not command respect from our partners; they are unwilling to give us their hard-won secrets."

Stretching through a Systems Approach

Constantly stretching existing capabilities through incremental investment is a basic necessity for leaders, but that is not sufficient for staying in front. Deepening the understanding of existing steps on the staircase must be complemented by more ambitious programs designed to create new steps. This is the novel combining or creating of multiple skills, different kinds of knowledge, and various resources.[7]

Creating a systems approach that pervades an entire organization is one way to achieve the goal of devising new steps on the strategic staircase. First, specific skills are created within territorial units, functions, or even small teams to solve particular problems. These skills provide a platform or step that can be extended in combination with others in a system of linked development. As we examined the record of firms that have climbed far up their own particular staircase, we were impressed by the frequency with which building linking systems was efficiently managed in an iterative manner.

The record of Edwards illustrates how iteration can work. By recapping some of the evidence discussed in earlier chapters, we can summarize the process in simple terms. Its start on the path of rejuvenation was the decision by Edwards to focus its business, on a core product, the primary—vacuum—pump. A robust design of a new range of these pumps provided the main strength of the firm in the mid-1970s; weakness characterized almost all other parts of the operation. The first issue to be addressed was production costs. Aided by the installation of the IBM system for manufacturing control, MAAPICS, to replace earlier systems, the factories developed much better understanding of the cost drivers, which led to lowering costs. Work within the production function was extended to the sales and pricing functions by the installation of another IBM system, OSACS, that allowed prices to be more accurately related to cost across the whole product range. Equally important, factory loadings could be tied closely to fluctuating and shifting demand. Improved mastery of both dynamic effects helped push total costs even lower and widen margins. Considerable internal development work was undertaken to link these partial systems to financial controls and information. All this happened in the late 1970s and early 1980s within the U.K. operation. (The systems and benefits were later transferred to the overseas units.) About this time, Edwards chose to reorganize its top team and adopt a form of matrix structure that was an extension of the one already in place between sales and production. The top team was greatly assisted by an expanded information system, managed by the planning director, which allowed reasonably accurate, multiple measures of performance to be deployed to help develop the business.

These new capabilities were exploited as Edwards caught the wave of accelerating demand growth in a new application for vacuum pumps for semiconductor manufacturing. Edwards expanded its scope to the United States and Japan and faced new challenges in learning to manage an international matrix effectively. It also had to contend with the complexities of keeping total costs low as the product range was expanded with the introduction of a stream of new products. Production costs in the United Kingdom were reduced further in real terms and lead times shrank as new methods of work, including the Yamazaki system,[8] were introduced.

A major advance was made in the early 1990s when the entire basis of the worldwide distribution system was set on its head. The earlier information systems were combined with the newfound production flexibilities in a "smart logistics" system. The shrinkage of total lead time from market assessment through production planning to delivery was remarkable. In 1990, the whole cycle took 23 weeks. By 1992, the cycle took just 5 weeks for most products. There were variations in the manufacturing lead times for some products, because of technical obstacles that remained, but the "thinking time" had uniformly been slashed by over two months. For some of the product range, this permitted Edwards to produce near-commodity items to order. It was by these means that Edwards built the capabilities it needed if it were to achieve the reductions in inventory we alluded to earlier. The time gains and cost reductions were matched by service gains. The effect was remarkable. Even in a depressed 1992 market, when most of its competitors were showing significant losses, Edwards was profitable and growing.

Though our simplified version of events omits many important details and glosses over many mistakes and blind alleys, Edwards's experience points to two lessons we saw elsewhere. First, the role of the information function is key, as is correctly highlighted in the currently fashionable literature on process reengineering cited earlier. It acts as an enabler for other work to be done. Properly used, the information helps enlarge perspectives so that managers can build a mental map which allows them to understand the whole. Information technology by itself is of limited use: it must be supported by changes elsewhere.

Our second and more important point is that, unlike those who believe that process reengineering allows dramatic progress in a quick period of time, our example condenses the long-drawn-out steps required for improvement. If one looked at Edwards only between 1990 and 1992, one would conclude that a dramatic transformation had taken place. But, in truth, the key actions that led to its rapid shift in performance had been started more than ten years earlier.[9]

We argue that the leader needs to think about systems approaches in the context of its capabilities. Its importance in rewriting the rule book of strategy can be seen vividly in the difference between Honda's Acura organization, set up in 1984, and GM's matching move in its Saturn project, set up in Tennessee in 1985. The Acura division, designed as an extension of the worldwide system, was intimately linked to existing capabilities. Saturn was developed as a separate division, effectively divorced from Detroit to allow it to write its own rule book, uncontaminated by bad habits elsewhere. The Acura Legend was launched in 1985 and rapidly developed exports through the Honda system. By 1991 Acura had created three models and eight model variants. Meanwhile, Saturn had a prolonged gestation period and did not launch its first model until 1990. Though the Saturn organization has developed many procedures and developed close union cooperation to make a fundamental break from the rest of the corporation, it did not benefit from other GM capabilities that might have accelerated progress. The Saturn project was more akin to the blue-sky ideas we discuss in the next section.

Stretching through Blue-Sky Projects

Charles Handy discusses the need for upside-down thinking, as he tells us how to cope with the stresses of the current world; it seems that our leaders had long before taken his advice.[10] Entrepreneurial organizations rewrite the rules of their industries not just once but many times over. Rethinking the basis of the organization, its products, its processes, its assumptions, and its purpose was a theme that pervaded many of our firms. They indulged in blue-sky projects that examined wholly new approaches. Some were complementary to existing efforts, but some were threatening, for if they came to fruition, current activities might have to be curtailed. Blue-sky projects may have risky outcomes, so they are not for the fainthearted, but the challenge is to draw out the best in the entrepreneurial firm.

Richardson explained to us that it invested considerable resources in developing the "cutting edge of the future," involving nontraditional materials and nontraditional methods of production. Building partnerships between people inside and others outside the organization had allowed the core skills in Richardson to be joined with those of others. It also ensured that existing prejudices are not uppermost: the outsiders can borrow ideas from inside the organization but have nothing to lose by suggesting something radically different. Bryan Upton described the task of the team as doing "blue-sky research." He admitted that any innovation in this sphere was likely to make most of the existing investments worthless, for it would alter "the whole basis of our existence." But, as Upton stressed, "We must be on the leading edge, for if we do not do it, others will."

Sun has no doubts on this score. Each generation of the Sun workstation reduces the profits of the previous one. Sun's policy of guaranteeing users that they have access to upgrades at a price no greater than the difference between the original price of their machine and the new one assures a loyal customer base and destruction of sales of the old model.[11] Managers who constantly reframe their businesses, like those at Sun, view the path of progress as both creative and destructive. The creativity is in finding new sources of value, the destruction in cannibalizing existing sources of profit.

Benetton has also cannibalized its processes by its development. One of Benetton's key success factors was offering solid-color sweaters, which were made of undyed yarn by subcontractors and subsequently dyed in Benetton's own dye house. This system, called late dyeing, is one of the ways in which the organization was able to offer flexibility to its retailers. However, fashion trends changed, and it became evident that multicolor clothes would become much more popular. It was originally considered impossible to late-dye multicolor garments. Benetton did not hold back; it went the route of pressing for such garments, simultaneously seeking ways to produce them by a late-dyeing

246

process. This decision threatened much of the investment of Benetton and of some of its partners, for the organization had decided to introduce multicolor garments even if it meant using new subcontractors and jeopardizing the entire dye-house investment. (Some of this investment was subsequently recovered because the organization found ways to late-dye garments of more than one color.) The principle of the organization was to stay ahead regardless of cost.

GROWTH TO LEVERAGE ADVANTAGES

"Grow or die" is an often repeated phrase that captures the essence of one of the major tensions facing organizations in maintaining momentum. Rapid and profitable growth is needed to exploit the advantages an organization has already built, to "fund" the necessary investments required to sustain vitality, and to reward those who have made sacrifices. Without rapid and profitable growth, the organization will find its credibility diminishing among its stakeholders, and resentment will creep in. More serious, some of the best and most talented people may leave. Their knowledge and the success of the organization, makes them highly marketable. Also, suppliers and distributors may sign up with others, owners may ask searching questions, or takeover threats may emerge. Loss of support will undermine the organization's capabilities, especially those which are based on such intangible factors as people skills and relationships.

By profitable growth we mean that which adds value and can be distributed among the many stakeholders. Managers, especially chief executives, can easily fall into the seductive trap of believing that great size is a desirable end in itself. Large size brings greater status for managers, and often greater salaries, but it can also bring with it the seeds of its own destruction. Size does not necessarily bring advantages, especially if it is not building on existing capabilities and competencies. One manager told us, "We are not setting out to be a billion-dollar business, for scale does not earn profits in this business—some of our much larger competitors are highly unprofitable—but we need scale in service activities to provide the standards our customers are increasingly demanding."

In this case, the firm had created a service division that grew rapidly by offering service for all makers' products, not just its own. Building scale in some parts of an organization usually lead to greater scale for the whole. But adding scale should be a means to achieve specific ends, not an end in itself.

247

If an organization has found a way to secure a 20 percent cost advantage over its rivals, and can do it on a large scale, the incentive to grow is clear, and the rewards can be identified. If, however, the organization has not secured any clear advantage, and assumes that size will assure lower costs, it is treading a risky path. As we noted in Chapters 2 and 5, size rarely brings substantially lower costs. In most markets, size or market share should be seen as a way of exploiting advantages, not creating them.

Growing to exploit competitive advantages must be done speedily. The flight of disgruntled employees can occur remarkably swiftly, takeover threats are rarely preceded by polite warnings, and disaffected suppliers and distributors can cause much damage quickly. In addition, the pace of change facing a leader means that all capabilities and steps on the staircase are threatened. The advantages may evaporate because of the competition. Patents can be circumvented, new services duplicated, new products reverse-engineered, new processes imitated. The threats come from direct competitors, indirect competitors, and from the inventive activities of the firm itself.

How Should an Organization Grow?

How should a firm grow, especially if some advantages are temporary? Many believe that only organic growth is certain. With it the firm can control the quality of the people it hires, the machines it buys, and the systems and processes it uses. While organic growth may take time, it may allow more complete control than acquisitions or alliances do. Organic growth may be attractive if the competitors are temporarily weak, for it may send strong signals of commitment to customers, suppliers, and the industry generally. However, as many writers on competitor analysis have pointed out, organic growth may be difficult if the competitors are strong, or possess strong exit barriers that resist attacks on their market share.

Some have argued in favor of acquisition, especially if suitable candidates are available. They allow the firm to buy access to markets and supply channels that may otherwise be blocked. They may remove competitors from the market. Acquisitions have the great benefit of allowing the organization to grow its sales rapidly in new areas and territories. But acquisitions create value only if the leader transfers its capabilities and routines to the acquired enterprise. This may take considerable effort, and, more important, time. Full transfer of capability can take years, not months.[12]

Both acquisitions and organic growth commit the firm's resources to particular markets, processes, and courses of action. Such commitment can be a two-edged sword. On the positive side, it may deter competition and allow better exploitation of the existing staircase of capabilities. But it may become a liability if rivals catch up and the organization finds a new direction imposed by its blue-sky investment, which makes expensively purchased assets worthless. For this reason, several experts have argued in favor of alliances, which permit the firm to exploit its newfound advantages without making risky investments. The alliance route is the most exciting, yet potentially the most difficult to manage, for it requires a special relationship between the partners to retain flexibility without destroying the income stream.[13]

The experience of our successful leading organizations suggests that each route to growth has its merits, the choice depending on particular circumstances. One of our pump makers has been most successful in acquisitions, buying ailing organizations that have been turned around. In addition, it has purchased small firms whose success made them attractive. It has transformed them by transferring its core skills and capabilities across organizational boundaries. Because the pump maker has undertaken many acquisitions and devoted much time and effort to improving the process of transfer, it has become skilled at the task, cutting down on the time and costs of transfers.

Richardson has combined organic growth with a single large acquisition to achieve world leadership. The acquired resources gave Richardson access to new world markets, new products, and new brands that complemented its existing activities, leveraging its previously hard-won capabilities. The added resources also provided a platform from which Richardson could develop further capabilities.[14]

By contrast, Edwards has focused on internal growth, partly by design and partly of necessity. It tried to acquire a significant firm, Varian, in the United States, but was blocked by the Federal Trade Commission. It admitted that even the negotiations were distracting. The lack of suitable acquisition partners in its sector has been frustrating, but by organic means Edwards has become a truly global company, selling in most countries and producing pumps and parts in six. It has exploited its innovative capability to serve the diverse needs of many different and demanding customers in new markets. Benetton has taken a still different approach. Judged by its total sales of $3 billion, it seems to be much larger than most of the businesses we studied, but the central firm remains small, with fewer than 4,000 employees. Benetton has used closely knit subcontractors and retailers to leverage its resources and capabilities. It believes that its partnership approach allows it to move quickly and gives it greater flexibility to adjust in times of crisis.

Where Should an Organization Grow?

At the end of Chapter 4, concerning the choice of strategic territory, we emphasized that organizations need continually to rethink where they compete. We also gave examples of the alterations in strategic territory of our firms. Whereas a rejuvenating organization, in its first steps, has some excuse not to undertake a careful analysis because it lacks good data, no such excuse can be accepted from leaders. They need to reassess their strategic choices on the basis of careful analysis of market trends and competitor moves.

In considering where to go, an organization must take account of tastes, technology, and competitors. For most of those we studied, the pressures from international competition have been the most pressing. They have forced the alteration of geographic or product scope, or both.

In the domestic appliance business, although much of the economics confirms the value of alternative national positions, it is clear that such positions are becoming increasingly hard to defend as competitors find ways to exploit advantages across borders. Players have found themselves reassessing *where* to invest, whether in new products, new territories, new sources of supply, or combinations of all three. Learning about the complexity of international markets and the differences among territories outside the firm's current sphere of activities has become a necessity. Hotpoint's use of an alliance among Europe's strongest national players—Thomson of France, Hotpoint in the United Kingdom, GE in the United States, and Fagor of Spain—is creative in this regard.

Fearful of competitors invading their chosen core segments, Edwards and Weir have responded by adding products. Always global in outlook, Edwards is finding itself forced to expand its business even further. One manager reported, "We deliberately invest ahead of demand and risk overcapacity. But we are doing this to allow ourselves to build the infrastructure necessary for the late 1990s. We are in effect setting out our stall for the decade."

Several firms have adopted an aggressive attitude to expansion. They have taken the view that their core capabilities in one area have permitted them to expand into others. While this was not evident in any of our leaders, it is in leaders elsewhere. We have already spoken of Marks and Spencer and its move into fresh prepared foods: an example of taking existing competencies and building new ones in related sectors. So too in Honda, which developed a core competence in engines and power trains that it first exploited motorcycles, then automobiles, before moving on to conquer related markets of outboard motors, lawnmowers, and other machines. In undertaking these extensions, Honda also transferred such capabilities as the

250

management of dealer networks and skills in building new market-related competencies.

MAINTAINING CORPORATE ENTREPRENEURSHIP

Balancing the forces between leverage and stretch requires that new skills be incorporated in the top team, making its members, like jugglers at a circus, able to keep several balls in the air while running forward. This requires attention to new agendas to complement the old. Some agenda items affect the top team composition, and its actions and aspirations; others affect those further down (see Exhibit 9.6). To examine and unravel these changes would require further research and probably another book. However, some significant insights can be revealed from even our limited interviews. We pick up a few of these balls in the brief discussion below, where we touch on the top team agenda, the need to give clear messages, the need to continually reduce overhead costs and adapt control systems.

In some of the organizations we studied, the existing team was able to adjust and rise to the challenge of maintaining momentum; others had to make changes in membership, even in CEO. In all the businesses, the shape of the organization has changed, new structures have been tried, new control systems introduced, and new measurements of performance agreed upon. When revisiting our research sites to follow events and check whether managers' visions for progress had been turned into reality, we were struck by the frequency with which the discussion reverted to issues, raised in Chapter 5, concerning corporate entrepreneurship.

First, it is clear that unity of purpose does *not* mean consensus. We were struck by the extent of disagreement among members of the top

----

EXHIBIT 9.6 A JUGGLER'S AGENDA FOR TOP MANAGEMENT

Top team agenda	Maintain principles of corporate entrepreneurship.
Clarity of messages to middle managers	Avoid giving mixed messages when discussing tensions.
Flatten the organization	Continue pressure to reduce costs while building new steps on the staircase.
Adapt the control and measurement systems	Ensure that information systems are constantly informing and encouraging.

----

teams, something we regard as most significant, for it strongly suggests that winning companies have avoided the dangers of groupthink. There is always someone on a team ready to challenge received wisdom and current policy. That seems to us to be important if progress is to be maintained and the dangers of refreezing avoided. Everyone needs a burr under the saddle to stay alert.

The second is that, no matter how successful a firm had been, there was continual dissatisfaction with the extent of the achievement. All the businesses were clear that they had high aspirations and were investing in the necessary capabilities. We regard this as confirmation of our earlier surmise that entrepreneurial firms really have to behave in the ways we outlined in Chapter 5. Limiting strategy choices to today's resources denies much of the potential for building. Dissatisfaction coupled with high aspiration seems to be a force that leads firms to continue reaching out to climb new hills, respond to competitors' moves, and "stretch" capabilities.

Although all rejuvenators had developed a sense of common purpose, even the most successful admitted that they still had a distance to travel before everyone in the organization understood the messages about where the business was heading. They also believed that they could enjoy more experimentation—a key feature of entrepreneurial organizations—because of the strength of their shared purpose. Partly stimulated by the current pace of change in IT and partly for other reasons, everyone stressed the importance of information systems and internal and external data. It was notable that all chief executives were particularly insistent on the need to improve both, perhaps because, as one commented, "I keep on finding that people confuse information with understanding about what is really going on."

All believed that they had become more adept at learning from past mistakes and that learning was necessary for progress. Several managers commented that the idea of learning was obvious, for how could anyone deny the value of learning? Yet, when challenged, several admitted that they had only recently started thinking in such terms for their organizations. We suspect that many much less capable organizations would provide quite different answers and value efficiency and logic above learning.

Finally, in this catalogue of perspectives about capabilities and attitudes, we heard a good deal about managing dilemmas—a repetitive theme in this book. It is here that the rejuvenators really stand out. They consider the management of dilemmas a matter for creative resolution. In contrast, many other organizations tended to oscillate between extremes and had not found effective ways of managing them. Yet, revealingly, no one denied that dilemmas were a fact of managerial life.

Mixed Messages

It is not just what happens in a top team that is important; the message must be passed down with clarity. Vitality, stretch, and leverage are potentially conflicting messages that can cause confusion and resentment among middle managers. Some of the mixed messages we heard are aptly described by Rosabeth Moss Kanter and summarized in Exhibit 9.7. We take, for example, the common instruction "Grow the business but do not overextend." All successful firms need to grow to exploit their capabilities and defend their territories, yet growing too fast, in the wrong way and in the wrong territories, can be dangerous or even fatal. Unless there is understanding of the underlying reasons for the paradoxical message, and the necessary data and support systems in the organization to help a manager work out how to go forward, he or she will be hopelessly confused. The command will seem ridiculous and threatening.

A team-building meeting for middle managers in a long-established international firm provided a vivid example of a mixed message. The meeting was opened by the planning director, who stated that, despite predatory attacks on the unit's business by a price-cutting competitor, the team had to retain its market share as specified in the strategy. The regional director followed and emphasized the importance of delivering the numbers in the budget. The goal was seemingly impossible: maintain both margin and share in the face of new competition. Neither director explained how the paradox should be resolved. To compound the problem, after some rather confused discussion each director spoke in turn to emphasize the original priority of the other. As might be expected, the meeting closed in uproar. Immediately afterward, when

---

EXHIBIT 9.7   SEEMINGLY MIXED MESSAGES

Grow the business *but* do not overextend.

Invest for the future *and* deliver profits today.

Be entrepreneurial and take risks *but* do not fail.

Know your business in detail *and* delegate more responsibility.

Be a leader *and* a team player.

Improve on what you have been doing well *and* spend more time communicating with others, serving on teams, launching new initiatives.

Source: Adapted from: R.M. Kanter, *When Giants Learn to Dance* (New York: Simon & Schuster, 1989).

---

asked why they had been so inconsistent, both were puzzled by the question. "We have no trouble at the board in deciding that both objectives are vital." Neither appreciated how easy it was for the board to take that position when their necks were not on the block. They failed to provide any guidance about how the conflicting targets might be resolved and did not appreciate that the necessary systems and support were absent. They had inadvertently sown such seeds of confusion that progress in building an adaptive organization—the original purpose of the meeting—was set back.

Avoiding such confusion requires making careful choices over timing, recognizing that even successful organizations cannot always do everything. Problems arise when sequences are rushed through in ways that lead subordinates to view them as no more than passing fads or "flavors of the month." Many of the new slogans for effective management developed since the early 1980s have been embraced enthusiastically by top managers, only to be soon discarded in disillusion when results are slow to materialize. For example, surveys have shown that total quality management programs had improved competitiveness in only one-third of 500 U.S. firms and a mere one-fifth of 100 U.K. firms, and many had given up the effort. The same reactions greeted the advent of other programs—total customer satisfaction, time-based competition, managing for shareholder value, empowerment, and the like.

As noted earlier, each of these programs can, in the appropriate setting, add great value, but even in successful dynamic enterprises, each can take years to make a significant impact. It is unrealistic to expect instant results from instituting such programs. If a top team passes rapidly from one initiative to another, middle managers are likely to greet each one with cynicism and wait-and-see attitudes. The consequence is that the firm, far from climbing the strategic staircase, maintains the illusion of progress by bumping along at the bottom, losing vitality and ultimately its skills.

Flattening the Organization

All our successful organizations competed in international markets where the drive to reduce costs was ever present owing to the advances of foreign competition. As production and operations became more and more efficient, there was a need to examine overhead cost most carefully. As the chairman of Swatch noted, when factory labor costs represent only a small percentage of the overall price, administration and supporting functions become the areas for attention.

In the continual search for progress, many of the organizations stressed the need for flatter hierarchies. Progress in building both horizontal and vertical teams can be assisted by moves to flatten the organization: delayering, as it is sometimes called. As Jack Welch of GE once observed, "Layers of management mask mediocrity." All our rejuvenators either took out layers or worked hard to stop more layers from creeping back in as the complexity of the operations increased. They pursued the logic of the earlier actions to shorten the organizational "distance." Most of the firms removed layers relatively late in the process of rejuvenation. Rather than rushing at the problem and risking severe demoralization, our successful firms worked first on building the climate of trust.

A flatter organization necessarily involves broader spans of control. For example, the behavior of one managing director, who has fifteen direct reports,[15] challenges much conventional thinking about the limits to effective spans of control. In his view,

> The minimum number is ten, but I do not know what the maximum is. The limits are really set by teamwork and the expertise in the team. I allocate my time in three groups. First, I delegate to experts and see them seldom. Second, I have close contact with people involved in areas of my personal expertise. Third, I have very close contact with those responsible for the high-risk and experimental activities. The task of the 1990s is to find out about managing organizations differently.

Middle managers in flatter organizations have to find their own ways to make such adjustments work effectively for their relationships with their own subordinates. Flattening is seen as an evolutionary process. Much learning is involved and different people in different parts of the firm run at different speeds, which means that progress is best undertaken with the grain of organizational change.

To make its flatter organization work effectively, one firm employs the rhetoric "make everyone participants, not spectators." It uses an organization chart (Exhibit 9.8) to make the point that it must move away from the past when people at lower levels were treated as though they had no heads and were nothing more than machines. To do this, the top team is building a high degree of commitment to group goals and providing the necessary skill training for all.

To support team efforts in a flatter organization and reinforce the drive to increase effectiveness, Weir has developed two systems. One is the "mob meeting," which it borrowed from Boeing, to foster lateral links at the top. Every week, between twenty and twenty-five people, excluding sales, meet to discuss contract issues and problems. The two-hour discussions lead to solutions and feedback to sales. The mob

EXHIBIT 9.8   MAKING A FLATTER ORGANIZATION WORK

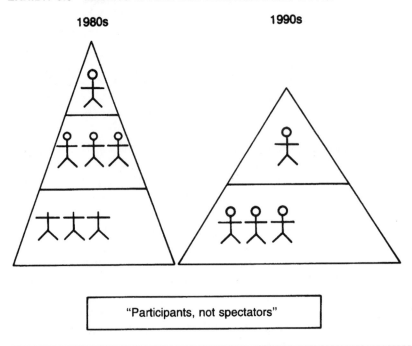

1980s   1990s

"Participants, not spectators"

meeting provides a forum that focuses on priorities for the business as a whole. It fosters team learning, for each department's performance on each contract is rigorously measured, and managers are expected to learn from their mistakes. The second is the cost-control meeting, which extends the mob meeting to include sales. Learning about cost control has proved to be critical in bettering pricing decisions and bidding performance. The two meetings plus the cost records are, in effect, a form of class notebook that records performance as well as experiments and new initiatives.

Adapting Control and Measurement Systems

When a firm is seeking to build momentum, control systems need to be adapted to excite and empower the middle and lower levels of the organization. All too often controls are merely for the benefit of those at the top. Earlier we stressed the need for firms to tailor their control systems to emphasize strategic priorities and avoid confusing messages blurring the focus of the effort. Our firms added new measures compatible with new, interrelated tasks. The beginnings of the trend to add back complexity shed earlier were foreshadowed in Chapter 7; now the pace of addition has to be accelerated.

We found many examples of changes in how factories were controlled and monitored. In one firm, we heard,

> Our factories are achievement oriented now. We have provided the vision and the enabling systems. We also provide the information on what happens to what they produce in terms of customer levels, stock levels, and competitor actions. We give specific targets for continuous improvements on all the key ratios. Where we used to measure performance quarterly on variance against forecast, now we measure many dimensions of meeting customer expectations of delivery; the level of output for uniformity of product range; and quality both in the factory and later in the field.

In this firm, quality targets had been refined to include small items such as loose screws and scratches. The attention to detail that we found being introduced earlier had been augmented to great effect. Faltering rivals had made much less progress in altering their systems.

We found that the changing nature of the organizations and their technology meant that control and measurement systems had to change as well. For example, with much less direct labor, activity-based costing systems substituted for less appropriate systems. As H. Thomas Johnson and Robert Kaplan, and others, point out, standard systems can be most unhelpful in this situation.[16] But the changes were not just in accounting systems; there were many others, too. Market intelligence, customer satisfaction, technological tracking, were all important aspects of the organization's needing systems. It seems that all our organizations had progressed a great distance from the early stages of their rejuvenation when their measures were primarily internally focused.

The growing multiplicity of measures introduced the risk that the signal would once again be drowned out by noise, especially at low levels in the hierarchy. This time, however, we found many firms paying attention to receiving input from the teams and individuals at all levels. In this way they aimed to avoid the mistakes of earlier behavior when the measures were, often blindly, imposed from above.

THE NEED FOR CONTINUOUS REJUVENATION

Success provokes new challenges and new questions. One pressing question is whether leaders must repeat the full cycle of the crescendo model to maintain their vitality. Is it possible to learn from the experience of the first full "loop" of progress and put in place actions that preserve momentum and remove the need for wholesale galvanization, simplification, and rebuilding? We believe that this new challenge can be mastered, even though we heard some who were more pessimistic.

To explain our optimism, we must recap the territory we have covered. By the time firms have reached the last stage of rejuvenation, most of the managers and even many in the work force are clear that changes in the "rules" of competition are a fact of life. They know that they cannot forecast with any confidence the form of future shifts and have prepared themselves to adapt as need or opportunity arises. They know that they must continue to invest in building capabilities and go on improving their ability to innovate through greater variety, higher quality, and the like, all at lower cost. They know that they face a stream of choices about where to concentrate their strategic market focus. Their growing sense of "winning" can create greater confidence in their ability to escape the trap, described in Chapter 2, of believing that industry economics determines their future.

Their progress, it would seem, has come from an ability to combine four factors: a collective sense of shared purpose and "stretching" goals; knowledge and the perception of possibilities; willingness to go on innovating and experimenting; and meticulous attention to the details of the stream of hard strategy choices. These virtues may seem a far cry from those of rational strategy beloved of the textbooks, but our evidence convinces us that they are the basis of effective and adaptive strategic management.

It was clear to the managers of our successful firms that the detailed elements of strategy had changed over time. What worked at one stage may not have worked at another. Thus it was that action at the beginning of rejuvenation was quite different from that required later on. As time passed, it became a more subtle art to determine *where* and *how* to compete. The ability to find ever more sources of organizational leverage, to husband scarce resources and still meet stretching goals, sorted out the winners from the losers.

In this evolution, the top team of a business plays a decisive role at all stages. Unlike many who advocate the benefits of passive decentralization, we espouse the values of personal involvement by business unit leaders. By this we do not suggest that in large, complex organizations such as Royal Dutch Shell the very top should be intimately involved in all the units of the group; that would be physically impossible for the executives. But rather, at the business level, effective leadership is vital and involves many facets, including the judicious exercise of power.[17] Learning how to exercise leadership is possibly one of the greatest benefits to arise from the toil of managing the crescendo. When introducing the crescendo model, we implied that the whole organization moves together between each stage of progress. Yet as the text has illustrated many times, reality was different. Parts of the organizations moved at different speeds, and many temporary structures and systems had been put in place along the way. These were, in effect, a series of small loops of learning complicating the larger loop of the crescendo.

To master that variable geometry of continuous progress, some of our firms managed to remove many of the hindrances to learning. By developing systems thinking and two-way communication across organizational boundaries, they made continuous progress. Their moves suggest that successful rejuvenators need never revisit the first steps. Extending the earlier crescendo model (see Exhibit 9.9), they showed that it is possible to achieve a rising and beneficial spiral of

---

EXHIBIT 9.9   MAINTAINING CONTINUOUS RENEWAL

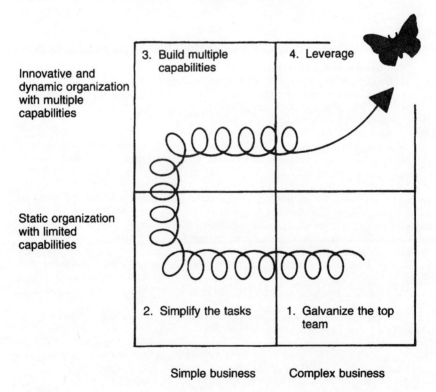

---

greater competitiveness by constant attention to small and large matters and escape the trap of limiting strategy to current resources.

When all is said and done, it is up to managers to create their own futures, choosing from among four alternatives. At one extreme, believing their firms are mature and trapped by low growth, they can fail to invest in new capabilities that provide routes of escape from the trap. These managers and their firms have no hope. Alternatively, they can hold high ambition for market dominance of their firms but fail to make the necessary internal investments in capability. These managers will sleep but have vivid dreams. As a third possibility, they can seek to build new capabilities for their firms, but have only modest ambition for themselves and their firms. The progress these managers achieve will be modest and notable for its unrealized potential. Finally, they can strive for continual improvement of their firms and commit themselves to building their future. They will be adaptable people who are best suited to gain success and to survive unforeseen market "shocks." These managers are the winners, the ones for whom we wrote this book; they exist in all industries and provide the hope for all our futures.

NOTES

[1] "My name is Ozymandias, king of kings:
Look on my works, ye Mighty, and despair!"
Nothing beside remains. Round the decay
Of that colossal wreck, boundless and bare,
The lone and level sands stretch far away.
—Percy Bysshe Shelley, "Ozymandias."

[2] We note that contemporary to the European edition of this book examining this issue, our colleague Gary Hamel has published an article discussing stretch; see G. Hamel and C.K. Prahalad, "Strategy as Stretch and Leverage," *Harvard Business Review*, March–April 1993: 75–84.

[3] There is a voluminous literature on this subject, but a neat synthesis of some of the issues is contained in P. Lorange and R.T. Nelson, "Organisational Momentum," in Charles Baden-Fuller, ed., *Managing Excess Capacity* (Oxford: Basil Blackwell, 1990).

[4] Although the Baldrige Prize has been criticized for many failings, it has acted as a powerful spur to internal efforts. For a thoughtful assessment, see David A. Garvin, "How the Baldrige Award Really Works," *Harvard Business Review*, November–December 1991: 80–95.

[5] See also P. Ghemawat, *Commitment: The Dynamic of Strategy* (New York: Free Press, 1991).

[6] G. Lorenzoni and C.W.F. Baden-Fuller, *The Strategic Centre: A Way of Managing Partners*, Working Paper, University of Bath, 1993.

[7] See G. Hamel and C.K. Prahalad, "The Core Competence of the Corporation," *Harvard Business Review*, May–June 1990: 79–91, and G. Stalk, P. Evans, and L.E. Shulman, "Competing on Capabilities: The New Rules of Corporate Strategy," *Harvard Business Review*, March—April 1992: 57–69.

[8] This system was originally developed in Japan by Yamazaki as a means of improving

speed and control over complex, large-scale projects. Later developments allowed the basic ideas to be adapted to smaller scale projects and to assembly operations. Rather than requiring specialized labor to perform single tasks on a moving assembly line, the system is based on the idea that teams of workers can follow the assembly process—literally moving along the line with the growing product—and ensure that quality is built in from the start, mistakes rectified immediately, and so on. This is one of the many variations of what is often called "cell production" and requires that workers have multiple skills as well as high levels of dedication and pride in what they produce. Yamazaki now licenses its system around the world to noncompeting enterprises.

[9] We have similar feelings about quality assurance and TQM programs. Quality assurance requires a firmwide approach to capture the multiple benefits, such as service to the customer, lower costs, and added product quality. Their value, as we said earlier, lies in extended effort and in their complementary effects. As Canon reminds us, "When pure water flows from the upper stream, there is no need to purify it farther downstream." Yet Canon knows that it "will have to redouble [its] efforts as European and American companies wake up to the issue of quality." (Hiroto Kagami, senior general manager, quality assurance at Canon, cited in *World Link*, November–December, 1989: 15).

[10] Charles Handy, *The Age of Unreason* (London: Hutchinson, and Boston: Harvard Business School Press, 1989).

[11] More details are provided in R. Garud and A. Kumaraswamy, "Changing Competitive Dynamics in Network Industries: An Exploration of Sun Microsystems' Open Systems Strategy," *Strategic Management Journal* 14, no. 5, July 1993: 351–370.

[12] See, for instance, P. Haspeslagh and D.B. Jemison, *Managing Acquisitions: Creating Value Through Corporate Renewal* (New York: Free Press, 1991).

[13] See, for instance, Lorange and Roos, "Organisational Management," and Lorenzoni and Baden-Fuller, *The Strategic Centre*.

[14] The acquisition, mentioned earlier, was unusual. Richardson's new parent, McPherson's turned over to them the operations of its existing knife-making empire. McPherson's recognized that its newfound affiliate had a far better chance of improving the whole division than it did itself.

[15] As one of our reviewers noted, this contradicts some rather old-fashioned notions.

[16] H.T. Johnson and R.S. Kaplan, *Relevance Lost: The Rise and Fall of Management Accounting* (Boston: Harvard Business School Press, 1987).

[17] Although it seems contradictory to talk about power in "caring" organizations, power can and should be exercised at times. See J. Pfeffer, *Managing with Power: Politics and Influence in Organizations* (Boston: Harvard Business School Press, 1992).

Bibliography

Abernathy, W.J., K.B. Clark, and A.M. Kantrow (1981). "The New Industrial Competition." *Harvard Business Review*, September–October: 68–81.

Abernathy, W.J., and R.H. Hayes (1980). "Managing Our Way to Economic Decline." *Harvard Business Review*, July–August: 67–77.

Argyris, C. (1986). "Skilled Incompetence." *Harvard Business Review*, September–October: 74–79.

———(1990). *Overcoming Organizational Defenses: Facilitating Organizational Learning*. Boston: Allyn & Bacon.

Baden-Fuller, C.W.F. (ed.) (1990). *Managing Excess Capacity*. Oxford: Basil Blackwell.

Baden-Fuller, C.W.F., and J.M. Stopford (1991). "Globalisation Frustrated." *Strategic Management Journal*, 12, 7: 493–507.

Bain, J. (1951). "Relation of Profit Rate to Industry Concentration: American Manufacturing 1936–1940." *Quarterly Journal of Economics*, 65: 293–324.

Bartlett, C.A., and S. Ehrlich (1990). "Caterpillar Inc.: George Schafer Takes Charge." Case # 9-390-036. Boston: Harvard Business School.

Bartlett, C.A., and U. Srinivasa Rangan (1985a). "Caterpillar Tractor Co." Case # 9-385-276. Boston: Harvard Business School.

———(1985b). "Komatsu Limited." Case # 9-385-277. Boston: Harvard Business School.

Barwise, P., P.R. Marsh, and R. Wensley (1989). "Must Finance and Strategy Clash?" *Harvard Business Review*, September–October: 85–90.

Beer, M., R. Eisenstat, and B. Spector (1990). *The Critical Path to Corporate Renewal*. Boston: Harvard Business School Press.

Bennis, W. (1989). *Why Leaders Can't Lead*. San Francisco: Jossey-Bass.

Beres, M.E., and S.J. Musser (1988). "Avenues and Impediments to

Transformation." In R.H. Kilmann and T.J. Covin (eds.), *Corporate Transformation: Revitalizing Organizations for a Competitive World.* San Francisco: Jossey-Bass, pp. 152–182.

Blacker, F.H.M., and C.A. Brown (1980). *Whatever Happened to Shell's New Philosophy of Management?.* Aldershot: Saxon House.

Bleeke, J., and D. Ernst (1991). "The Way to Win in Cross-Border Alliances." *Harvard Business Review,* November–December: 127–135.

Block, Z., and Ian MacMillan (1993). *Corporate Venturing: Creating New Businesses Within the Firm.* Boston: Harvard Business School Press.

Bodrug, D., and J. Wilson (1988). "Wolsey Knitwear." London: London Business School.

The Boston Consulting Group (1968). *Perspectives on Experience.* Boston: The Boston Consulting Group.

Bowen, D. (1990). "How Lucas Learned to Live with the Rest of the World." *The Independent* on Sunday, July 8.

Bower, J.L. (1986). *When Markets Quake.* Boston: Harvard Business School Press.

————(1990). "Management Revolution: The Response to Global Glut." In C.W.F. Baden-Fuller (ed.), *Managing Excess Capacity.* Oxford: Basil Blackwell, pp. 19-39.

Bower, J.L., and T.M. Hout (1988). "Fast-Cycle Capability for Competitive Power." *Harvard Business Review,* November–December: 110–118.

Brandes, O., and S. Brege (1993). "Strategic Turnaround and Top Management Involvement: The Case of ASEA and ABB." In P. Lorange et al., *Implementing Strategic Processes: Change, Learning and Co-operation.* Oxford: Basil Blackwell, pp. 91–114.

Brown, C., and M. Reich (1989). "When Does Cooperation Work? A Look at NUMMI and GM-Van Nuys." *California Management Review,* 31, 4: 26–37.

Buzzell, R.D., and B.T. Gale (1987). *The PIMS Principles.* New York: Free Press.

Campbell, A., M. Devine, and D. Young (1990). *A Sense of Mission.* London: Hutchinson.

Chandler, A.D. (1962). *Strategy and Structure: Chapters in the History of the American Industrial Enterprise.* Cambridge, Mass.: MIT Press.

Clark, K.B. (1989). "What Strategy Can Do for Technology." *Harvard Business Review,* November–December: 94–98.

Colchester, N., and D. Buchan (1990). *Europe Relaunched.* London: The Economist Books/Hutchinson.

Cubbin, J. (1988). "Is It Better to Be a Weak Firm in a Strong Industry,

Or a Strong Firm in a Weak Industry?" London: London Business School, Centre for Business Strategy, no. 49.

Cyert, R.M., and J.G. March (1963). *A Behaviorial Theory of the Firm.* Englewood Cliffs, N.J.: Prentice-Hall.

Davenport, T.H. (1993). *Process Innovation.* Boston: Harvard Business School Press.

De Geus, A. (1988). "Planning As Learning." *Harvard Business Review,* March–April: 70–74.

——— (1990). "Strategy As Learning." Stockton Lecture, London Business School, May.

Deming, W.E. (1982). *Out of the Crisis.* Cambridge, Mass.: MIT Press.

Dixit, A.K., and B.J. Nalebuff (1991). *Thinking Strategically.* New York: W.W. Norton.

Eisenberg, D.J. (1984). "How Senior Managers Think." *Harvard Business Review,* November–December: 81–90.

Eliot, T.S. (1943). "Little Gidding," *Four Quartets.* New York: Harcourt, Brace.

Feneuille, S. (1990). "A Network Organisation to Meet the Challenges of Complexity." *European Management Journal,* 8, 3: 296–301.

Fucini J., and S. Fucini (1990). *Working for the Japanese: Inside Mazda's American Auto Plant.* New York: Free Press.

Gabor, A. (1990). *The Man Who Discovered Quality.* New York: Times Books.

Garud, R., and A. Kumaraswamy (1993). "Changing Competitive Dynamics in Network Industries: An Exploration of Sun Microsystems' Open Systems Strategy." *Strategic Management Journal,* 14, 5: 351–370.

Garvin, D. (1991). "How the Baldrige Award Really Works." *Harvard Business Review,* November–December: 80–95.

Ghemawat, P. (1991). *Commitment: The Dynamic of Strategy.* New York: Free Press.

———, and B. Nalebuff (1985). "Exit." *Rand Journal of Economics,* 16, 1: 184–194.

Goold, M., and A. Campbell (1987). *Strategies and Styles: The Role of the Centre in Managing Diversified Corporations.* Oxford: Basil Blackwell.

———with J.J. Quinn (1990). *Strategic Control: Milestones for Long-term Performance.* London: The Economist Books/Hutchinson.

Grant, R. (1991). "The Resource-based Theory of Competitive Advantage." *California Management Review,* 33, 3: 114–134.

———, and C.W.F. Baden-Fuller (1987). *The Richardson Sheffield Story.* London: London Business School Case Series, 2.

———, and S. Downing (1985). "The UK Cutlery Industry 1974–1982:

A Study of Structural Adjustment, Business Strategies and Firm Performance." Working Paper, London Business School, Centre for Business Strategy.

Green, M.R.S. (1987). "Beliefs, Actions and Strategic Change: A Study of Paradigms in UK Domestic Appliances Industry." In *Papers and Proceedings of Academy of Management Conference*, New Orleans, August.

———(1987). *The Hotpoint Story: A Study in Excellence*. London: London Business School.

Grinyer, P.H., D.G. Mayes, and P. McKiernan (1988). *Sharpbenders: The Secrets of Unleashing Corporate Potential*. Oxford: Basil Blackwell.

Hall, W.K. (1980). "Survival Strategies in a Hostile Environment." *Harvard Business Review*, September–October: 75–85.

Hamel, G. (1991). "Learning in International Alliances." *Strategic Management Journal*, 12, special summer issue: 83–103.

Hamel, G., and C.K. Prahalad (1985). "Do You Really Have a Global Strategy?" *Harvard Business Review*, July–August: 139–148.

———(1990). "The Core Competence of the Corporation." *Harvard Business Review*, May–June: 79–91.

———(1993). "Strategy as Stretch and Leverage." *Harvard Business Review*, March–April: 75–84.

Hampden-Turner, C. (1990). *Charting the Corporate Mind*. New York: Free Press.

Hampden-Turner, C., and C.W.F. Baden-Fuller (1988). "Strategic Choice and the Management of Dilemma: Lessons from the Domestic Appliance Industry." London: London Business School, Centre for Business Strategy, Working Paper, no. 51.

Handy, C. (1989). *The Age of Unreason*. London: Hutchinson and Boston: Harvard Business School Press.

Hannan, M.T., and J. Freeman (1988). "Structural Inertia and Organisational Change." In K.S. Cameron, R.I. Sutton, and D.A. Whetten (eds.), *Readings in Organisational Decline*. Cambridge, Mass.: Ballinger.

Harrigan, K. (1980). *Strategies for Declining Business*. Lexington, Mass.: Lexington Books.

Haspeslagh, P., and D.B. Jemison (1991). *Managing Acquisitions: Creating Value Through Corporate Renewal*. New York: Free Press.

Hatch, J. (1970). *Competition in the British White Goods Industry 1954–1964*. Ph.D. diss., Cambridge, Cambridge England.

Hayes, R.H., and S.C. Wheelwright (1988). *Dynamic Manufacturing*. New York: Free Press.

Hill, C.P. (1971). *Towards a New Philosophy of Management*. London: Gower.

Hounshell, D. (1984). *From the American System to Mass Production.* Baltimore: Johns Hopkins University Press.

Itami, H. (1987). *Mobilizing Invisible Assets.* Cambridge, Mass.: Harvard University Press.

Johansson, H.J., P. McHugh, A.J. Pendlebury, and W.A. Wheeler (1993). *Business Process Reengineering.* New York and Chichester: Wiley.

Johnson, H.T., and Kaplan, R.S. (1987). *Relevance Lost: The Rise and Fall of Management Accounting.* Boston: Harvard Business School Press.

Kagami, Hiroto (1989). Cited in *World Link,* November–December, p. 15.

Kanter, R.M. (1985). *The Change Masters: Innovation for Productivity in the American Corporation.* New York: Simon & Schuster.

———(1989a). *The Change Masters: Innovation and Entrepreneurship in the American Corporation.* New York: Simon & Schuster.

———(1989b). *When Giants Learn to Dance.* New York: Simon & Schuster.

———(1991). "Transcending Business Boundaries." *Harvard Business Review,* May–June 1991, pp. 151–164.

Katzenbach, J.R., and D.K. Smith (1993). *The Wisdom of Teams: Creating the High-Performance Organization.* Boston: Harvard Business School Press.

Lamming, R. (1993). *Beyond Partnership: Strategies for Innovation and Lean Supply.* Hemel Hempstead: Prentice Hall.

Levitt, T. (1983). "The Globalization of Markets." *Harvard Business Review,* May–June: 92–12.

Lorange, P., and R. Nelson (1990). "Organizational Momentum." In C.W.F. Baden-Fuller (ed.), *Managing Excess Capacity.* Oxford: Basil Blackwell, pp. 165–192.

Lorenzoni, G. (1988). *The Benetton Case.* London: London Business School Case Series, 4.

———, and C.W.F. Baden-Fuller (1993). "The Strategic Centre: A Way of Managing Partners." Working Paper, University of Bath.

Love, J. (1986). *McDonald's: Behind the Arches.* New York: Bantam Books.

Mangham, I.L. (1986). *Power and Performance in Organizations: An Exploration of Executive Process.* Oxford: Basil Blackwell.

Marshall, Alfred (1890). *Principles of Economics.* London: Macmillan.

———(1919). *Industry and Trade: A Study of Industrial Technique and Business Organization, and of Their Influences on the Conditions of Various Classes and Nations.* London: Macmillan.

Matsushita, K. (1988). "The Secret Is Shared." *Manufacturing Engineering,* March.

Mintzberg, H. (1990). "The Design School: Reconsidering the Basic

Premises of Strategic Management." *Strategic Management Journal*, 11, 3: 171–196.

Mintzberg, H., and J.A. Waters (1985). "Of Strategies Deliberate and Emergent." *Strategic Management Journal*, 6, 3: 257–272.

Morgan, G. (1986). *Images of Organization*. Beverly Hills, Calif.: Sage.

Morita, A. (1992). "The Innovation Lecture." London, February.

Moskowitz, M. (1987). *The Global Marketplace*. New York: Macmillan.

Nonaka, I. (1991). "The Knowledge-Creating Company." *Harvard Business Review*, November–December: 96–104.

Ohmae, K. (1982). *The Mind of the Strategist*. New York: McGraw-Hill.

———(1985). *Triad Power: The Coming Shape of Global Competition*. New York: Free Press.

Pascale, R.T. (1990). *Managing on the Edge*. New York: Touchstone, Simon & Schuster.

Peters, T.J., and R.H. Waterman, Jr. (1982). *In Search of Excellence*. New York: Harper & Row.

Pfeffer, J. (1992). *Managing with Power: Politics and Influence in Organizations*. Boston: Harvard Business School Press.

Pine, B.J. II (1993). *Mass Customization*. Boston: Harvard Business School Press.

Piore, M., and C. Sabel (1984). *The Second Industrial Divide: Possibilities for Prosperity*. New York: Basic Books.

Porter, M.E. (1980). *Competitive Strategy*. New York: Free Press.

Prahalad, C.K., and Y.L. Doz (1987). *Multinational Mission*. New York: Free Press.

Prahalad, C.K., and G. Hamel (1978). "The Core Competence of the Corporation." *Harvard Business Review*, May–June: 79–91.

Quinn, J.B. (1980). *Strategies for Change: Logical Incrementalism*. Homewood, Ill.: Richard Irwin.

Reich, R.B., and E.D. Mankin (1986). "Joint Ventures with Japan Give Away Our Future." *Harvard Business Review*, March–April: 78–86.

Robbins, D.K., and J.A. Pearce (1992). "Turnaround: Retrenchment and Recovery." *Strategic Management Journal*, 13, 4: 287–309.

Rumelt, R. (1991). "How Much Does Industry Matter?" *Strategic Management Journal*, 12, 3: 167–186.

Rumelt, R., and R. Wensley (1981). *In Search of the Market Share Effect*. Proceedings of the Academy of Management, August, pp. 1–5.

Sabel, C. (1992). "Studied Trust." In T. Romo, and R. Swedberg (eds.), *Human Relations and Readings in Economic Sociology*. New York: Russell Sage, pp. 104–144.

Schaffer, R., and H. Thomson (1992). "Successful Change Programs

Begin with Results." *Harvard Business Review*, January–February: 80–89.

Schaie, K.W., and J. Geiwitz (1982). *Adult Developing and Aging*. New York: Harper & Row. 1982

Schein, E.H. (1985). *Organizational Culture and Leadership*. San Francisco: Jossey-Bass.

Scherer, F.M. (1973). *Industrial Market Structure and Economic Performance*. Skokie, Ill.; Rand MacNally.

Schon, D. (1983). *The Reflective Practitioner: How Professionals Think in Action*. New York: Basic Books.

Schmalensee, R. (1985). "Do Markets Differ Much?" *American Economic Review*, 75: 341–351.

Schumpeter, J. (1934). *The Theory of Economic Development*. Cambridge, Mass.: Harvard University Press.

Senge, P.M. (1990). *The Fifth Discipline: The Art and Practice of the Learning Organization*. New York: Doubleday Currency.

Shaw, R.W., and P. Simpson (1990). "Rationalisation within an International Oligopoly: Increase of the West European Synthetic Fibre industry." In C.W.F. Baden-Fuller (ed.), *Managing Excess Capacity*. Oxford: Basil Blackwell, pp. 75–94.

Shook, R.L. (1990). *Turnaround: The New Ford Motor Company*. New York: Prentice Hall.

Simon, H.A. (1979). *Models of Thought*. New Haven: Yale University Press.

Skinner, W. (1985). *Manufacturing: The Formidable Competitive Weapon*. New York: Wiley.

Slatter, S. (1984). *Corporate Recovery*. London: Penguin.

Spence, A.M. (1977). "Entry Capacity, Investment and Oligopolistic Pricing." *Bell Journal of Economics*, 8: 534–544.

Stalk, G. (1988). "Time—The Next Source of Competitive Advantage." *Harvard Business Review*, July–August: 41–51.

Stalk, G., P. Evans, and L.E. Shulman (1992). "Competing on Capabilities: The New Rules of Corporate Strategy." *Harvard Business Review*, March–April: 57–69.

Stalk, G., and T.M. Hout (1990). *Competing Against Time*. New York: Free Press.

Stopford, J.M. (1989). *Edwards High Vacuum International*. London: London Business School.

Stopford, J.M., and C.W.F. Baden-Fuller (1982). *Note on the European Man-Made Fibre Industry*. London: London Business School, mimeo.

———(1990a). "Corporate Rejuvenation." *Journal of Management Studies*, 27, 4: 399–415.

———(1990b). "Flexible Strategies—The Key to Success in Knitwear." *Long Range Planning*, December, 23, 6: 56–62.

———(1993). "Organizational Strategies for Building Corporate Entrepreneurship". In P. Lorange, B. Chakravarthy, J. Roos, and A. van de Ven (eds.), *Implementing Strategic Processes*. Oxford: Basil Blackwell, chapter 2.

———(forthcoming). "Creating Corporate Entrepreneurship." *Strategic Management Journal.*

Stopford, J.M., and S. Strange (1991). *Rival States, Rival Firms.* Cambridge, England: Cambridge University Press.

Strebel, P. (1993). *Breakpoints: How Managers Exploit Radical Business Change.* Boston: Harvard Business School Press.

Sugiura, H. (1990). "How Honda Localizes Its Global Strategy." *Sloan Management Review*, 32, 1: 77–82.

Taylor, W. (1993). "Message and Muscle." *Harvard Business Review*, March–April: 99–110.

Teece, D., G. Pisano, and A. Schuen (1992). "Dynamic Capabilities and Strategic Management." Working Paper, University of California, Berkeley.

Teitelman, R. (1991). "The Magnificent McCoys." *Institutional Investor*, July.

Tichy, N.M. (1983). *Managing Strategic Change.* New York: Wiley.

Tichy, N.M., and R. Charan (1989). "Speed, Simplicity, Self-Confidence: An Interview with Jack Welch." *Harvard Business Review*, September–October: 112–120.

Tyson, L. (1992). *Who's Bashing Whom?: Trade Conflict in High-Technology Industries.* Washington D.C.: Institute for International Economics (IIE).

Uyterhoeven, H. (1972). "General Managers in the Middle." *Harvard Business Review*, March–April: 75–85.

Walton, R.E. (1985). "From Commitment to Control in the Workplace." *Harvard Business Review*, March-April: 76-84.

Weick, K. (1979). *The Social Psychology of Organizing*, 2d ed. Reading, Mass.: Addison-Wesley.

Wickens, P.D. (1993). "Lean, People Centred, Mass Production." In *Lean Production and Beyond: Labour Aspects of a New Production Concept.* Geneva: International Institute for Labour Studies, Occasional Paper No. 2, Chapter 3.

Williamson, P. (1991). "Supplier Strategy and Customer Responsiveness: Managing the Links." *Business Strategy Review*, summer: 75–90.

Williamson, P., and M. Hay (1991). "Strategic Staircases." *Long Range Planning*, 24, 4: 36–43.

Wilms, W.W., and Zell, D.M. (1993). "Reinventing Organizational Culture across Boundaries." California Worksite Research Committee working paper, presented at the Carnegie Bosch Institute Symposium, Stuttgart, Germany, May.

Womak, J.P., D.T. Jones, and D. Roos (1990). *The Machine That Changed the World.* New York: Rawson Associates.

Yip, G. (1992). *Total Global Strategy.* Englewood Cliffs, N.J.: Prentice Hall.

Index

273